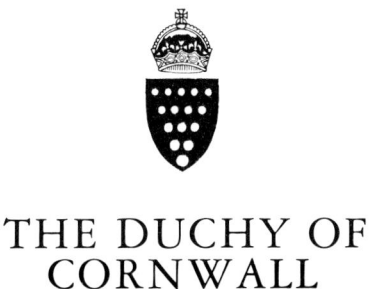

THE DUCHY OF CORNWALL

THE DUCHY OF CORNWALL

Edited by Crispin Gill
Foreword by HRH The Prince of Wales,
Duke of Cornwall

CONTRIBUTORS
Martin Argles · Michael Atkinson · Roger Burt
Tony Carne · Oliver Franks · Helen Harris · Graham Haslam
Michael Havinden · Nicholas Long · James Mildren
Clive Tregarthen Mumford · Robin Page · Peter Rose

David & Charles
Newton Abbot   London   North Pomfret (Vt)

Publisher's Note

Acres	Hectares
1	0.4047
10	4.047
100	40.469
200	80.937
300	121.406
400	161.874
500	202.343
1000	404.686

British Library Cataloguing in Publication Data

The Duchy of Cornwall.
  1. Duchy of Cornwall – History
  I. Gill, Crispin   II. Argles, Martin
  942.3   DA670.D7/

  ISBN 0-7153-8891-6

Phototypeset by Typesetters (Birmingham) Ltd
Smethwick, West Midlands
Printed in Great Britain
by Butler and Tanner, Frome and London
for David & Charles Publishers plc
Brunel House   Newton Abbot   Devon

Published in the United States of America
by David & Charles Inc
North Pomfret   Vermont 05053   USA

CONTENTS

THE CONTRIBUTORS

Martin Argles MA, Chartered Surveyor, aged 61. Qualified 1951 with Smith-Woolley, remained in firm, managing and advising on agricultural estates in private and institutional ownership. Land Steward eastern district of Duchy 1977, appointed Acting Secretary on the death of Sir John Higgs in 1986. President of Royal Institution of Chartered Surveyors 1972–3, member of Northfield Committee of Enquiry into landownership.

Michael Atkinson MA, PhD, WEA tutor-organiser for west Dorset and south Somerset, author of *The Rise and Decline of the South Wales Iron Industry, Dartmoor Mines*, etc.

Roger Burt BSc(Econ), PhD, senior lecturer in economic history, Exeter University; author of *The British Lead Mining Industry, Cornish Mining, Cornwall's Mines & Miners*, two volumes on the *History of Mining Technology*.

Tony Carne BA, born of old Cawsand Bay family, joined Royal Navy as instructor officer 1962, schoolteacher since 1973, chairman of Torpoint Old Cornwall Society, author of *Cornwall's Forgotten Corner*.

Oliver Franks OM, GCMG, KCB, CBE, PC, FBA, life peer, sometime Provost of Worcester College Oxford, Chancellor of East Anglia University, some-time Professor of Philosophy Glasgow and Oxford, British Ambassador in Washington 1948–52, chairman of Lloyds Bank 1954–62, member Prince's Council, Duchy of Cornwall 1966, Lord Warden of the Stannaries 1983–5.

Crispin Gill OBE, FSA, born Plymouth, journalist *The Western Morning News* 1934–71 (assistant editor 1950–71), editor *The Countryman* 1971–81, Dartmoor National Park Committee 1955–65, editor *Dartmoor: A New Study, Countryman's Britain*, author *Dartmoor, The Isles of Scilly, Plymouth: A New History*, etc.

Helen Harris, born Devon, trained in agriculture and dairying, sometime member of Ministry of Agriculture's Advisory Service, author of *Industrial Archaeology of Dartmoor*, etc.

Graham Haslam, born in Lancashire, grew up in United States. BA in history Washington University, MA Western Washington University, PhD Louisiana State University. Librarian and archivist Duchy of Cornwall since 1976. Married to an American, two Anglo-American sons.

Michael Havinden MA, BLitt, FRHistS, senior lecturer in economic history, Dean of Faculty of Social Sciences, University of Exeter, author of *The Somerset Landscape*, co-editor of *Rural Change and Urban Growth*, farming chapter in *Dartmoor: A New Study* (ed Crispin Gill).

Nicholas Long, surveyor with Duchy's Kennington agents. Family has lived in Lambeth for over a century; he lives at Clapham and is chairman of the Clapham Society. Educated Munich, spell in Merchant Navy, has written many articles on local history and co-author of *The Buildings of Clapham*.

James Mildren, West Country-born, journalist with *The Western Morning News* for twenty years as environmental correspondent, latterly as literary editor. Author of *Dartmoor in the Old Days*.

Clive Tregarthen Mumford BA, born Scilly of old island family, for twenty-five years a mainland journalist, now back on islands running family newsagency. Editor *The Scillonian*, author of *Portrait of the Isles of Scilly*.

Robin Page, born small family farm in Cambridgeshire where he still lives, various jobs before settling to farming and writing. Board of Governors of Wilderness Foundation, member of Duchy of Cornwall Wildlife and Land-scape Advisory Group. Author of *The Decline of an English Village, Journal of a Country Parish, Wildlife of the Royal Estates, A Fox's Tale*, etc.

Peter Rose, senior field officer with the Cornwall Archaeological unit, has a degree in archaeology from Reading University. Field surveys for Berkshire Archaeological Unit before taking up present post in 1978.

FOREWORD BY
HIS ROYAL HIGHNESS
THE PRINCE OF WALES
DUKE OF CORNWALL

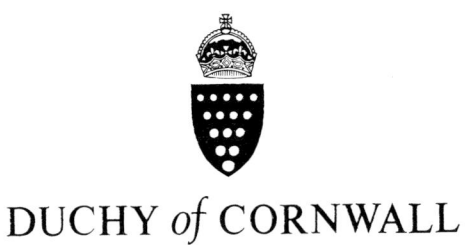

DUCHY *of* CORNWALL

10 BUCKINGHAM GATE   LONDON SW1E 6LA

This book is being produced in the 650th year of the Duchy of Cornwall and will, I hope, give some insight into the way the Duchy has evolved.

This is a period of rapid change in which we live now. The Duchy is not immune from this and it has to take a business-like approach to the management of its estates and assets. But I am concerned that at the same time it should provide an example of the best kind of stewardship of the land. This means acting responsibly and sympathetically towards all those directly and indirectly concerned with the Duchy and towards the environment; and it means taking initiatives to help solve problems in housing, farming and employment which are intensified in this time of change.

The Duchy is above all else a landed estate and will continue to be so. Its relationship with the people who work on the land is of paramount importance and it is the farmer who is the backbone of the whole operation.

DUKES OF CORNWALL[*]

Edward, the Black Prince, 1337–1376 – the first Duke of Cornwall.

Richard of Bordeaux became Duke in 1376 at the death of his father, the Black Prince, then as King Richard II.

Henry of Monmouth, 1399–1413, assumed title when his father, Henry IV, became king, later King Henry V.

Henry, 1422, then as King Henry VI.

Edward, son of Henry VI, 1453, killed 1471.

Edward, son of Edward IV, 1470–1483, then as King Edward V. One of 'the princes murdered in the Tower'.

Arthur, 1486–1502, eldest son of Henry VII.

Henry, younger son of Henry VII 1502–1509, then as King Henry VIII.

Edward, 1537–1547, then as Edward VI.

Henry Frederick, eldest son of James I, 1603–1612.

Charles, younger son of James I, 1613–1625, then as King Charles I.

Charles, son of Charles I, 1630–1649, then as King Charles II.

James Francis Edward, the Old Pretender, 1688–1689.

George Augustus, son of George I, 1714–1727, then as George II.

Frederick Lewis, son of George II, 1727–1751.

George Augustus Frederick, son of George III, 1762–1820, then as King George IV.

*The title is through the male line only. There were many princes who survived only very briefly and are not included in this list.

Albert Edward, eldest son of Queen Victoria, 1841–1901, then as King Edward VII.

George Frederick Ernest Albert, second son of Albert Edward, 1901–1910, then as King George V.

Edward Albert Christian George Andrew Patrick David, son of George V, 1910–1936, then as King Edward VIII and later the Duke of Windsor.

Charles Philip Arthur George, eldest son of Queen Elizabeth II, 1952.

INTRODUCTION

Crispin Gill

In the English peerage there is no higher rank than that of a duke. A Russian grand duchess, daughter of the Tsar, who married the second son of Queen Victoria, was always a little displeased that her husband was only a duke, not a grand duke. Yet the senior English duke, the very first creation of a dukedom in this country, hardly ever uses his title, and is never addressed as 'your Grace'. He is of course Charles Prince of Wales, and though he was Duke of Cornwall before he was Prince of Wales – a Duke of Cornwall is duke from the second he is born, or his parent ascends the throne – it is still only his second title.

To confuse matters even more, the Duke owns more land outside Cornwall than he owns in the county. His Duchy is not the county and the county is not the Duchy. It was Quiller-Couch who called one of his books *The Delectable Duchy*, and it became a phrase to entice the infant tourist trade of his day, but the largest part of the Duchy that the visitor is ever likely to see is the beach on which he disports himself. The Duchy owns less than three per cent of Cornish land, only twelve per cent of its total land holding.

The Cornish historian, A. L. Rowse, who also has the vision of a poet, sees the Duchy as going back further than its creation 650 years ago by King Edward III for his son, the Black Prince. It grew out of the Norman earldom of Cornwall, and that in turn grew from the conquests of the Saxon house of Wessex in Cornwall. It is still significant that the bulk of the Duchy's holding in the county is in east Cornwall, the rump of the land which the Saxons first overran west of Tamar and which was always held either by the king (Saxon and Norman) or his close family. Even today the Duchy owns very little land east of a line from Gloucester to Poole. It is almost all west of the great forest of Selwood which in the eighth century was the western limit of effective Wessex settlement.

It is thus the rump of the largest English estate outside the crown lands, and the oldest. At the same time it is the very model of a modern landholding, efficiently run on good commercial lines with due and proper concern for the well-being of its tenants and the health of the countryside, its wildlife and its antiquities.

The Duke of Cornwall receiving feudal dues from his Cornish estates at Launceston Castle in November 1973 (right). The manors of Swannacott and Week St Mary were held by knight service and their representative (Mr L. K. Hutchings) has to appear clad in goatskin before the Duchy Court at Launceston. (below) Representatives with their presentations: Stoke Climsland rendered 'a salmon spear and a carriage of firewood daily when our lord the Duke should come to Launceston'; Lt Col (now Sir John) Molesworth-St Aubyn with a brace of greyhounds from the manor of Elerky in Veryan; the Mayor of Truro with a bow of alder; the Mayor of Launceston with a hundred silver shillings and one pound of peppercorn; the manor of Trevelga (near Boscastle) a pair of white gloves. (Photographs from Launceston Town Council through its honorary archivist, Mr Arthur Bate Venning)

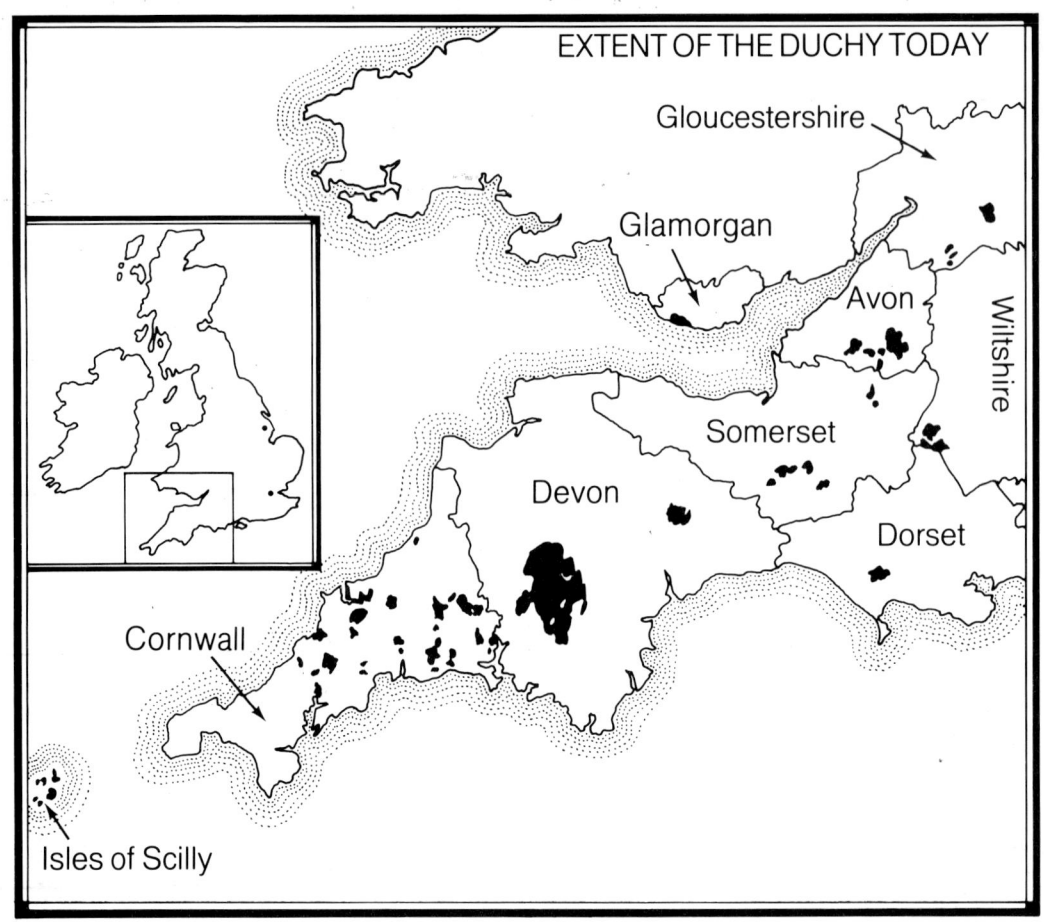

EXTENT OF THE DUCHY TODAY

Gloucestershire

Glamorgan

Avon

Wiltshire

Somerset

Devon

Dorset

Cornwall

Isles of Scilly

Modern Duchy land holdings

This has not always been the case. Twenty-five years ago a land steward could be more concerned with preventing adverse publicity falling upon his master than in efficiency. In those days, when the land stewards in charge of various districts of the estate were largely left to run things their own way (the steward in mind resented 'those chaps in blue suits coming down from London and telling us what to do'), the Dartmoor National Park Committee was much plagued by an itinerant ice-cream vendor. The only legal way to remove him seemed to be to get the Duchy to prosecute, and the land steward would not have this. 'Can you see the headlines,' he protested, '"Prince prosecutes ex-serviceman".' But the man was a pest.

Dartmoor has always been a problem for the Duchy, like the off-islands of Scilly. Both have been unprofitable parts of the estate and for a long time were neglected, their farms left unimproved and the farmhouses unfit for a woman, a farmer's wife, to live in. In those days a great many tenants resented their royal landlord. They grumbled. Another difficult part of the

16

Duchy holding for a century or two past has been the inner London area of Kennington, around the Oval cricket ground. After new bridges were built over the Thames and new roads driven through the old market gardens, London houses rapidly spread. Then came the railways to carve into the houses, the better-class moved further out into newer suburbs and by mid-nineteenth century the Duchy holdings were slums, which copyhold tenure and low rents made near impossible to improve. The Duchy was a pioneer of inner-city rehousing; it brought in good architects to rebuild, but memories die hard over the generations. The children and grandchildren of those slums became the left-wing members (and the wilder extremes) of London County Council and its heir, the Greater London Council, and the Lambeth Council. They resented the Duchy as landlord, with an undefined republican senti-ment, not because in their eyes it was a rich and grasping grinder of the poor, but just because it was rich. There has always been a tendency to expect the Duchy to be a wealthy benevolent institution, instead of its rightful role as provider of income for the heir to the throne. Today it not only does this, but the Duke gives voluntarily a quarter of his income to the state.

Yet there were and are many tenants on this Kennington estate who are

The Prince's Council Chamber at 10 Buckingham Gate, the Duchy's London headquarters, photographed in 1950 after reconstruction following wartime bombing. (Planet News)

proud of having a royal landlord, just as there are many up and down the farming estate who take pride in being Duchy tenants. They might prefer to be their own masters, but if they have to be tenants then having a royal landlord is better than any other kind. They are very proud of their invitations to Buckingham Palace garden parties. Modern transport, making it easier for the royal family to visit outlying places, has also done much to improve relations, and the modern, more relaxed style of princes helps even more. Queen Victoria made her state visits in great pomp, as did her son Edward VII and grandson George V. It was Edward VIII as a less formal Prince of Wales who began to break the ice: in fact soon after he ascended the throne (but still possessed of the Duchy, as he had no son) he caused great indignation by going across the road from Buckingham Palace to the Duchy office at 10 Buckingham Gate, on foot. A king walking, even carrying an umbrella! Not that he was always tolerant; once when riding on Dartmoor a photographer from *The Western Morning News* was driven off by the royal entourage. When the man popped up from behind a gorse bush to get his picture, the Prince reined in his horse with the exclamation 'There's that bloody photographer again'.

Not that the Queen Victoria was so stiff. On an early visit to Scilly she was being driven down the steep hill from Star Castle in a pony and trap. The pony began slipping and the young Queen, alarmed, climbed out of the trap followed by Prince Albert and the pair walked down to the Quay. It is rumoured that the Prince of Wales escaped the formalities of that visit and went bird-nesting on Samson, but as he was only six it may be an apocryphal tale.

The Duke of Edinburgh, who largely directed the affairs of the Duchy in his eldest son's young days, set the precedent both for keen interest in the countryside and for an informal and friendly approach. He set the pattern for Prince Charles who has improved upon it. The present Duke takes tea in farm kitchens with the family. He is interested in farming, and his nearly secret visits to spend a few days working on farms on Dartmoor and in Somerset and Cornwall have been noticed and appreciated. His private visits to some corner of his estate to study a particular problem, his obvious concern and his grasp of problems, have all endeared him. And of course when he makes a formal visit with Princess Diana and they make their friendly walk-abouts then he makes the Duchy come alive, and becomes a reality in people's minds instead of some distant unknown landlord.

It is with the Duchy that this book is concerned. A group of writers has applied itself to various of its aspects, its history, administration, wildlife, mining, archaeology, the various estates. It means the Duchy is seen through differing eyes. Michael Havinden as an agricultural historian sees farms,

Hugh Town pier, St Mary's, Isles of Scilly, one of the public utilities in the islands which the Duchy is negotiating to pass into public ownership. The mailship Scillonian *lies astern of a pleasure craft and two of the inter-islands launches.* (Molly Gill)

James Mildren as a journalist sees people, Clive Tregarthen Mumford as a native sees Scilly through the eyes of a tenant (although nowadays he is nót) and as one imbued with the vague mistrust of past generations. Nicholas Long sees London as buildings; Robin Page sees only the birds and the bees. It makes for a wide-ranging approach.

10 Buckingham Gate, the London headquarters of the Duchy, in some ways epitomises the whole. No name on its pillared portico announces its purpose. Inside its octagonal hall a central lantern from Prinny's Carlton House, the old prints around the wall and the eighteenth-century Parliament clock behind the reception desk, declare its antiquity. The Prince's Council Chamber on the floor above looks across the top of Buckingham Palace Road to the Palace itself, proclaiming its closeness to the seat of royal power. The long table, the faded carpet with the Prince of Wales' feathers at each corner reflecting the plastered ceiling above, the gold bezants of the Duchy embroidered into the sides of the carpet, all give the place an air of time-worn, tired elegance. Yet above the Prince's chair hangs a colour photograph of a seated Princess of Wales with her husband behind; both smiling, informal, young.

Next door is the Secretary's room – 'Secretary and Keeper of the Records' – again elegant in its furnishing, opulent in its size. But the papers, the documents strewn about, the contents of bookcases, all reflect that this is the powerhouse of an institution that in spite of its six hundred and fifty years of history is still vibrant, active and concerned.

CHAPTER ONE

EVOLUTION

Graham Haslam

On a spring day in 1337 Edward III created the first English duchy. It was accomplished with all the solemnity and dignity which could be mustered; the King proclaimed the charter before the nobility and commonality assembled in open Parliament making his son and heir, Edward of Wood-stock, Duke of Cornwall. The origins of the Duchy are not, as are so many other important English institutions, obscured by the mists of time. It did not grow, develop or evolve from modest, arcane features. On 16 March 1337 it did not exist; on 17 March it did. A contemporary copy of the charter of creation still exists. It provides, in the style of the times, exact details concerning the lands and hereditaments, the castles, the jurisdictions and powers which the first Duke acquired, but it is vague in the extreme about why the King decided this economic, political and social departure.

It was usual, of course, that the heir to the throne be vested with lands and honours which could properly support him. But the King seemed to be reaching for something more. He was twenty-five years old, his heir not yet seven. The long wars and famous victories were still years ahead of them. The great estates in western and southern France which the English monarchy had inherited from William the Conqueror or through the fortuitous marriage of Henry II to that most famous beauty of the age, Eleanor of Aquitane, had been re-possessed by successive French kings. An empire which had rivalled any of Europe served only as a mocking echo of grandeur and an excuse for the English nobility to grumble.

Edward's own journey to the throne had been horrendous. He was forced to support a rebellion against his father, sanction the execution of those around the King and finally even be party to the murder of the King. Even after he had been proclaimed sovereign, Edward III continued to live in the shadow of his mother and her lover, afraid that the fate of his father might overtake him. Once he became independent of them he may have sought to ensure that these circumstances could never be repeated. Personally way-ward, capable of an expedient lie, he had a gift for improvisation which allowed him to shape royal government so that it served his policies with a success unmatched before the end of the Middle Ages.

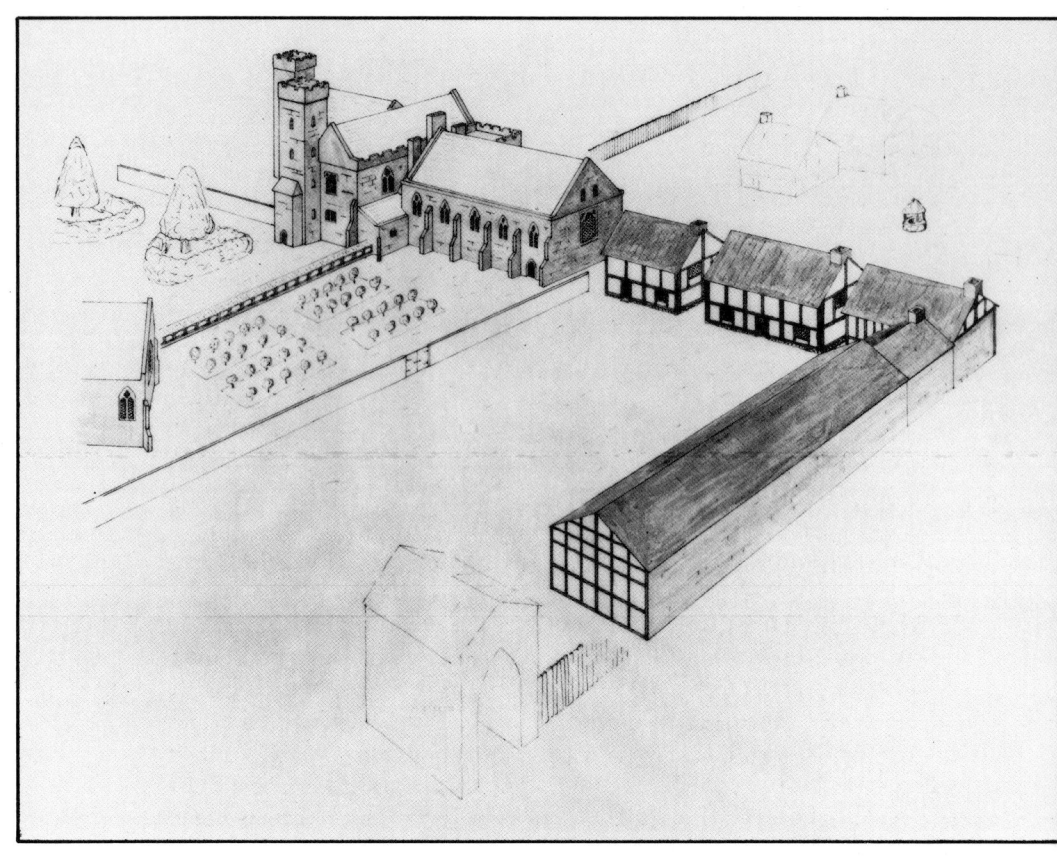

A reconstruction of the Black Prince's palace at Kennington. The stables and kitchen are in the foreground and the great hall, chamber and tower were in stone. (Duchy)

The King probably intended to order more perfectly the peerage and the succession to the throne. He was in pursuit of definition. The heir to the throne was placed above all other English peers from the moment of his birth by the charter. His title of duke made him as pre-eminent in England as his title of prince did in Wales. By rank he became the premier English peer. The traumas and crises Edward III experienced dealing with his own father resonate in the words of the charter. It was and is a remarkable constitutional ploy; he who holds the Duchy by definition succeeds to the throne. The charter stipulates that only the first-born son of the monarch may be Duke of Cornwall. It put the lie to all the quarrelsome, contentious barons who thought an opportune foreign alliance could enhance a tenuous dynastic claim to the throne. English monarchy was most ineffective when the succession was open to question. To Edward III this weakness had been only too apparent; it was this constitutional and personal wound he wished to staunch once and for all.

He established the Duchy in a novel form. The charter states that when no duke exists the Duchy reverts to the crown. This is not exceptional, the crown is the fount of all honours and they revert automatically if legal succession fails. The unique difference in the Duchy charter is that Edward constrained all future monarchs to surrender the Duchy when a male heir exists.

The form and circumstances of the creation of the Duchy of Cornwall may have been exceptional but the King fashioned the first English duchy from what he happened to have at hand. It was created from the earldom of Cornwall which had passed to the crown in 1336 when John of Eltham died without heirs. One of the largest, most important landed estates in England, it had long existed, though the details of its fate before and for a time after the Norman Conquest are uncertain. The earldom was joined to the English monarchy from the time of the conquest of Cornwall in the tenth century. It first emerged into good light in 1227 when Richard, second son of King John, received the title and lands.

This younger brother of Henry III received the grant just before leading a major expedition to France. As one of the largest and most lucrative estates in England, the earldom's resources served to finance his army. Richard, in fact, went on to enjoy a varied career as soldier, diplomat and crusader; it culminated in 1231 when he was elected king of the Romans. No treasury could cope with that most difficult of all medieval royal assignments.

The first well known influence on what was to become the dukedom, Earl Richard's escutcheon – quite literally – is embodied in it. The shield of contemporary dukes consists of a black field upon which are emblazoned fifteen golden 'byzants'. These represent gold coins brought home by knights who had been to the crusades via Byzantium. Silver was the usual coinage in the west, gold a precious novelty. Richard, a pious man, and proud that he had been on crusade, adorned the edges of his shield with them. Other crusaders would have recognized this symbol immediately. Though differing patterns were subsequently devised, bezants are the abiding symbol of the Duke of Cornwall.

Richard's son, Edmund, succeeded to the earldom in 1272, but he died eight years later and the estates according to law reverted to the crown. The only other investitures of the earldom were in 1307 to Piers Gaveston, hated favourite of Edward II, and then on his death to Richard and John of Eltham, younger sons of the King. The earldom's status, then, was like that of the later Duchy of York; an honour normally reserved for second sons of the monarch. It may be that, because Edward III had no French lands to confer on his eldest son, he decided the wealth of one of the most important English earldoms would be worthy.

It may be that the creation of the Duchy was inspired in part by French models. However, the Duchy quickly became a peculiarly English institution, but also something greater, more significant, perhaps, than had appeared on the political horizon before. Whether Edward III created the Duchy to spite the French or to ape them, to ensure the succession by a defensive constitutional ploy or to expand the role of the heir apparent and give him the means to take a lead when it suited, remains an enigma. Perhaps he intended to accomplish all of them. No matter for what reasons it was created, the Duchy was moulded and shaped ultimately by the successive princes who inherited its mantle.

The modern Duchy, about 128,000 acres, is really only the rump of the original. Many estates have been sold. The Duchy has retained primarily what was 'demesne' land, that is, the part of each manor reserved for the personal use of the lord. Though the twentieth-century estate, imposing even by comparison with Texas ranches or Australian sheep stations, is large, it was originally much more extensive. At its creation, and subsequently, it has continued as one of the largest private landed estates in England. The Crown Estates, Church Commissioners and British Rail are much larger, but they are institutions rather than individuals.

The new Duchy conformed to the existing patterns of most other large English estates. The lands, or manors as they were called, were scattered over more than a dozen counties from Lincolnshire in the north to Sussex in the south, from Suffolk in the east to Cornwall and the Isles of Scilly in the west. Many people confuse the Duchy with county, but the two had, and have, different identities: only about seventeen per cent of the land surface of the county has ever belonged to the Duchy. Though much of its character is rightly subscribed to the ways of the western peninsula, it is wrong to think of it as only a regional institution. All in all, it represented a fair sampling of local landscapes and customs which existed in abundance across the face of England.

In Lincolnshire the new Duke was granted the Soke of Kirton in Lindsey comprising over eighteen thousand acres, the Honour of Berkhamsted in Hertfordshire, the manors of Isleworth in Middlesex, Byfleet in Surrey, the Honour of Knaresborough in Yorkshire, the only land owned by a duke north of the Trent, and the key Honour of Wallingford in the Thames valley. By a subsequent charter, dated 4 September 1337, the King also granted to the Prince as Duke of Cornwall the manor of Kennington in Surrey. The manor of Rysing, with its imposing Norman fortress and a fourth of the tolls from the Tollbooth at Kings Lynn were added by charter on 1 December 1337.

In Cornwall Edward received the seventeen assessionable manors. These included Launceston, Trematon, Restormel and Tintagel, each with a fortress, a focal point of ducal power. Located in the Tamar valley were the manors of Calstock and Stoke Climsland and in or near important Cornish towns were situated the manors of Moresk and Lostwithiel. Rillaton and

Launceston Castle, in the original grant of 1337 to the Black Prince and a focal point of ducal power. (Western Morning News)

24

Helstone in Trigg were near Bodmin moor. The others, Tybesta (in Creed), Tywarnhaile (in St Agnes), Tewington (St Austell), Penlyne (Lanlivery), Penkneth (Lanlivery) and Talskeddy (St Columb Major) lie in the eastern and central areas. Helston-in-Kerrier was the only land in the west of Cornwall.

In Devon the Duke received the town and manor of Bradninch, which included Rougemont Castle in Exeter. Also annexed to the Duchy was the manor of Lydford and the former royal forest and chase of Dartmoor extending to over sixty thousand acres. The manor and liberty of Mere in Wiltshire and other lands in Somerset were also included in the original charter. By grant under the King's privy seal Prince Edward received on 9 July 1342 the manors of Fordington in Dorset, Parva Weldon and the town of Rockingham in Northamptonshire, the hamlet of Southtenge (in the Teign valley) in Devon and a tenement in Shoreham, Sussex.

The first Duke, as with all his successors until the end of the Middle Ages, enjoyed other titles and incomes. Prince Edward held extensive estates in both north and south Wales. As Earl of Chester he controlled the palatine county and later, when his father had re-conquered the extensive Plantagenet lands in France, he was granted lucrative French titles and honours. He was suzerain, the lord, of a vast collection of lands and peoples whose only real tie was through the prince. The Duchy of Cornwall was only one important element in this medieval structure.

Edward of Woodstock, called by later generations the Black Prince, was a man of enormous prestige in his own time. The personal emblem of a Prince of Wales, three ostrich plumes, was a device taken by Prince Edward when he defeated in combat the King of Bohemia at the battle of Crecy. Love of war and energy characterised his youth. Personal bravery capped by military success in France founded his lasting reputation. He was conscientious and attentive to the affairs of his tenants and a vigorous landlord.

Prince Edward's personal prestige helped to enshrine the way he governed the Duchy. Subsequent dukes looked to his principate as a model for their own activities. The founding statute limited all future dukes in only one major way. They were constrained not to alienate the lands granted so that they were obliged to pass on the Duchy intact to their heirs. A duke can spend the proceeds from the estate, the rents, dues and incidental income, as he wishes. Edward III limited the action of all future sovereigns: they must maintain the Duchy until such time as a male heir 'of the body lawfully begotten' is born. He would then automatically be duke. Dukes of Cornwall are born, not made.

This arrangement appears very much like a trust. However, such a form of tenure was unknown to the law of fourteenth-century England and almost three hundred years later, Sir Edward Coke, Chief Justice of Common Pleas, marvelled at its unique place in English law. This limitation has saved more than one duke from himself and helped the Duchy survive the occasional predatory attack by a sovereign.

Prince Edward was also left entirely free to organize the administration of the Duchy. Naturally he adopted the procedures then current. He employed 'receivers' to act as bankers, collecting money and holding it until needed by the household cofferers or treasurer. Auditors annually determined the accounts of rents and incidents owed by tenants. The Duke also had certain powers usually reserved to the crown alone. He possessed the right to nominate the high sheriff of Cornwall. This gave him effective control of county government and its courts. Much more important in daily life than today, it extended the practical influence of the Duke into virtually every hamlet in Cornwall. All royal writs were returned by the Duke's officials, including election writs to Parliament. Also, in his lands the Duke had the right to escheat, which was the right to the goods and chattels of outlaws and those who died without heirs. Petty customs in Cornwall belonged to the Duke and his successors also. The Prince's attorney-general need not have been called to the bar, his solicitor is not required to have a practising certificate; and his auditor until 1982 did not have to be a chartered accountant. In fact, they invariably have been members of their professions.

The most important of these regalities, as the royal powers were called, was responsibility for the stannaries. These were the districts in Cornwall and Devon where tin was mined and smelted. Cornwall and Devon produced tin for the world, more than a million lbs a year. It provided a lucrative source of income. First, the Duke received mineral dues when the metal was mined from his soil. More importantly, he enjoyed annual revenues from the

The 1734 Buck engraving of the ruins of the ducal palace at Lostwithiel which the Black Prince made his headquarters in Cornwall, including within its walls palace, exchequer and prison. (Royal Institution of Cornwall)

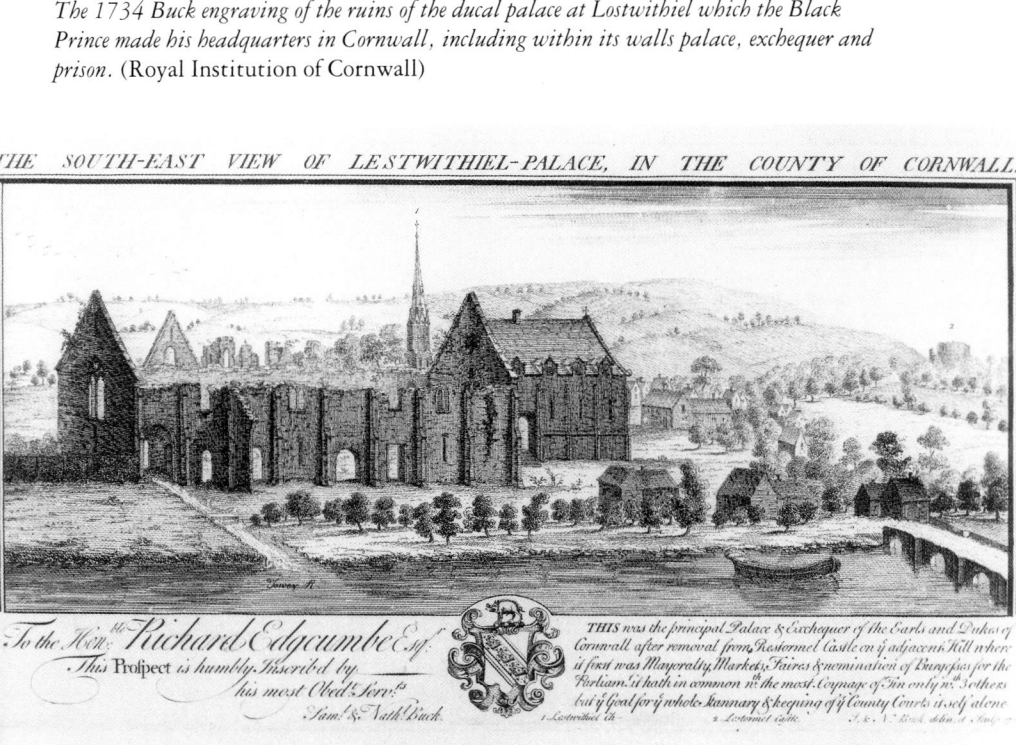

coinage of tin. Each year miners brought ingots to the Duke's coinage halls where their purity was assayed and weighed. A tax was levied based on weight and once this was paid, the ingots were struck with the Duke's emblem or 'coined' to indicate that the standards had been met and the dues paid. This tax was extremely lucrative, and often equalled and sometimes surpassed revenues from rents and incidents. This wealth gave the Duchy a vital second income; it was less vulnerable than other landed estates because it had two quite distinct sources of wealth. To administer these stannaries, four in Cornwall and four in Devon, Prince Edward appointed an officer known as the Warden of the Stannaries. The first known recipient was Lord Bartholomew Burghersh, Warden in Devon, who died in 1355.

Prince Edward also created a council to advise him. All subsequent dukes who have governed the estate have also appointed a council. It has no power other than that vested in it by him. Edward of Woodstock may have appointed a council only because he needed support for his planned campaign in France. When in England, he seems to have ruled his lands directly without reference to it.

Edward spent much of his time in his Duchy. He frequently stayed at Wallingford and Berkhamsted and maintained a hunting stable at Byfleet. He twice made the long, arduous journey to Cornwall. In 1362 he kept Christmas at Restormel, receiving many of his tenants, offering his blessing to a couple who wished to wed and receiving homage from others. At Kennington he commenced work on his palace in 1353. This was an extensive complex of buildings which included a great hall, church, kitchens and stables. A vineyard was incorporated in a century when the climate was more supportive. The hall was over eighty-five feet long, the supporting columns were of Purbeck marble, probably brought to London in a ship the Prince purchased in order to carry materials for the project. A lead roof, much like those on the great medieval cathedrals, covered the hall. It was at Kennington that the Prince stayed through his long, debilitating illness. After his death his widow received a third of the revenues of the Duchy, a precedent set for all subsequent widowed duchesses.

The dead Prince was succeeded by his son, Richard of Bordeaux. The boy was only nine years old when his father died. He and his mother continued to live at Kennington Palace and it remained a favourite residence for the whole of his life. In July 1389 Geoffrey Chaucer was appointed clerk of works for the manor. The Prince's grandfather, old and in disrepute, saw the spectre of danger again threaten the succession. The charter of 1337, ratified by Parliament, limited the title of Duke of Cornwall to the eldest son of the king. This seemed to exclude Prince Richard. However, Edward III was not deterred by what he perceived as legal niceties and created his grandson Duke of Cornwall. This charter was an act of desperation. It was blatantly illegal both because the King did not seek the consent of Parliament and also because the specific terms of the charter excluded a surviving grandchild.

Nevertheless, Prince Richard was styled Duke until he eventually succeeded King Edward III in 1377.

The course chosen by the new Duke nearly destroyed the institution his father had carefully nurtured. From the time he became king, he began to bestow Duchy estates upon members of his own family. After the coronation of his wife Anne in 1382, he ceded to her the Cornish Duchy manors. He granted Duchy lands to servants such as Sir Richard Abberbury and John of Cornwall. When his mother died in 1385 he recovered the third of the Duchy assigned to her, but this too he quickly dissipated amongst his followers and family. He kept in his own hands only the castles and deer parks; in effect the Duchy existed in name only.

Five years after Henry IV seized the throne in 1399, the Commons petitioned the King to grant his own son the honour of his rightful title and lands. The King obliged and the new Duke, Henry of Monmouth, quickly initiated a suit in Chancery to recover the Duchy lands granted by the profligate Richard II. The effort remained only partially successful. A suit was effectively prosecuted in Chancery against Dame Margaret Sarnefield to recover the manor and borough of Helston in Kerrier. Following the precedent of the Black Prince, he established a council and appointed a household and officers, including Thomas Chaucer as constable of Wallingford.

The interest of the Prince in the Duchy was overtaken by events. The rebellion of Owen Glendower in Wales, troubles along the Scottish border and the political needs of his father forced him to adopt an active political life which left the Duchy behind. In 1421 by act of Parliament the now King Henry V severed the manor of Isleworth, Middlesex, from the Duchy so that he could endow Sion Abbey. To compensate, he granted Curry Mallet, Stoke under Hamdon, Milton Falconbridge, Stratton-on-the-Fosse, Inglescombe, Midsomer Norton, Welton, Widcombe, Farrington Gurney, Laverton, a half of West Harptree and Shepton Mallet, as well as other lands in Dorset, Berkshire, Wales and Kent, to the Duchy. The collective receipts of these lands exceeded the revenues of Isleworth, but administration was more costly. This action also gave the Duchy a much greater presence in the South West.

The history of the Duchy in most of the fifteenth century was much like it had been in the reign of Richard II. Duchy lands not already alienated, were granted to favourites and followers. All the Somerset lands exchanged by Henry V were bestowed on William, Earl of Huntingdon, in 1481. Many of these grants were really executed to secure short-term political advantages. The dynastic struggle between Lancaster and York only served to accentuate the situation. In 1442 rival stewards actually engaged in a pitched battle. Prince Edward of Westminster, eldest son of Henry VI, was granted a Prince's Council in 1457, but he was killed at the battle of Tewkesbury in 1471 at the age of eighteen.

More subtle changes had been at work in the fifteenth century. The effects of the Black Death, which visited England in 1348, changed the relationship between successive Dukes and their tenants. In 1337 each manor preserved an area known as 'demesne' land and the lord's tenants were obliged to provide a certain amount of work on this land as a condition of their own tenure. After the Black Death labour became a scarce commodity. Dukes were forced simply to 'farm' or lease their demesne land to individuals rather than try to become involved in direct farming. This allowed tenants to escape from onerous work which produced nothing for their own farms, but it did mean that a direct source of involvement by the Duke disappeared and it made an already absentee landlord even more remote and disinterested.

Henry VII, blessed with heirs, set about reconstructing the medieval Duchy. His eldest son, Arthur of Winchester, became the last truly autonomous medieval heir. The King and his son busied themselves recovering lands and creating a western empire which Prince Arthur could govern. In 1495 an act repealed the gift of the Somerset lands to Huntingdon and united them again to the Duchy. In 1499 Henry granted seisin, which actually bestowed the estate, to Prince Arthur. The centre of the young Duke's apanage was the fortress of Ludlow in Shropshire where the Prince would be close to the Marcher counties, Wales, Chester and the Duchy. Household officers were appointed. There is no doubt that the King expected his son to govern his lands and wished to establish him as rightful head of his tenants. It was a grand design which fell to nothing when Arthur died in 1502.

Henry VII found himself immersed in a constitutional crisis. His remaining heir, Henry of Greenwich, had been made Duke of York. He could not in theory succeed his dead elder brother in title. However, the King was anxious to secure a peaceful, unopposed succession. The title of Duke of Cornwall had propaganda value because it implied legal succession. The King arranged a unique and perhaps characteristic compromise. He secured from Parliament in 1504 an act which bestowed upon Henry the title of Duke of Cornwall. The King, perhaps because he did not wish to surrender the enormous revenues of the Duchy a second time, or because he did not wish his only remaining heir to venture westward, did not actually grant seisin. For the five remaining years of the reign, Henry of Greenwich was Duke in name only. He had no household officers of his own and he did not appoint his own administrators. He was thirteen when his brother died, and it would have been usual to grant control of his lands to him when he was fifteen or sixteen. The prudent King kept his heir near at hand for the remainder of his days. When he in turn succeeded to the throne, he was not kindly disposed towards the estate he had never quite possessed.

When Henry VII died in 1509, the King took the revenues of the Duchy into his personal possession. The net receipts were not paid into the Exchequer, but directly into the coffers of the King's chamber. The resources were at last at Henry's immediate disposal. They were considerable. In 1500

An old photograph of all that remains of the Duchy palace at Lostwithiel, now used as a masonic hall. The structures to the left of the surviving hall, shown in the Buck engraving, are incorporated into latter buildings. (Duchy)

Duchy receipts represented almost five per cent of the whole of crown receipts. It was thus a vital source of income for the King. Nevertheless, Henry's attitude remained ambivalent. The inability of the King and Queen to produce children who survived and the somewhat humiliating experiences Henry had suffered at the hands of his father left the institution and eventually some of its servants in a tenuous position.

In the changed political climate of England in the 1530s, Henry VIII undertook to modify the Duchy also. His kinsman, Henry Courtenay, Marquess of Exeter, had been made Warden of the Stannaries in 1523. He was the greatest of West Country peers; beyond members of the King's immediate family Courtenay also possessed a real claim to the throne.

31

However, he did not bend easily with all the abrupt changes during the Reformation. He withdrew from court hoping perhaps for a swing of the pendulum. But his office of Warden made him a powerful warlord, who could raise an army in the west by his own order. The King did not allow even Exeter the luxury of private opposition. The Marquess was tried and executed for treason and his land forfeited to the crown.

The King desired the manor of Wallingford. In 1540 he passed a private act of Parliament severing the great estate from the Duchy and incorporating it into the newly erected Honour of New Elm. This action was constitutional. Henry V's exchange had provided a precedent, but it did for the first time give the Duchy an unequivocal western bias. Further, the King through the Duchy replaced the Courtenay family as the most important landlord in the South West. For the rest of the sixteenth century Cornwall had no member of the House of Lords other than the Bishop of Exeter. In exchange for Wallingford the King annexed to it twenty-eight small Cornish manors. From the dissolved Priory of Launceston the manors of Bradford, Carnedon Prior, Climsland Prior, Treworgie, Eastway, Bradridge, Bucklawren and Bonyalva were granted. Additionally, the Duchy received St Austell, Fentrigan, Trevennen, Fowey, Grediowe, and Porthea Prior from the former Priory of Tywardreath. The third group, which included West Antony, East and West Looe, Northill, Landreyne, Trelowia, Tregamere, Trelugan, Crafthole, Treverbyn Courtenay, Landulph, Leigh Durant and Tinten, had been the property of the Duchy's former Warden, the Marquess of Exeter. As had been the case at Isleworth, the revenues from these small annexed estates were greater than the net annual sum derived from Wallingford, but the costs of administering twenty-eight small estates were far greater than those associated with the single, large estate of Wallingford.

The King's ambivalence for the Duchy did not cease even after he had legitimate male issue. Prince Edward, eventually Edward VI, was proclaimed Duke at his birth in 1538. Only nine when he succeeded his father, he did not receive seisin of his lands or the opportunity to manage them. King Henry attached the Duchy to the Court of Augmentations which he had created to dissolve the monasteries. This removed it from the immediate control of the King's chamber and out of his orbit. In 1542 the sovereign granted to Thomas Howard, Duke of Norfolk, a royal charter ceding to him the manor of Castle Rysing in Norfolk. For the second time the King deprived the Duchy of an important property. The crown did not provide any kind of compensation. More importantly, this grant did not receive parliamentary consent and contravened the original statute of 1337. This time the King ignored even the legal formalities.

The restored façade of Prince Henry's Council Chamber at No 17 Fleet Street and (below) *the Prince's Council Chamber on the first floor in use as a barber's shop, circa 1890.* (National Monuments Record)

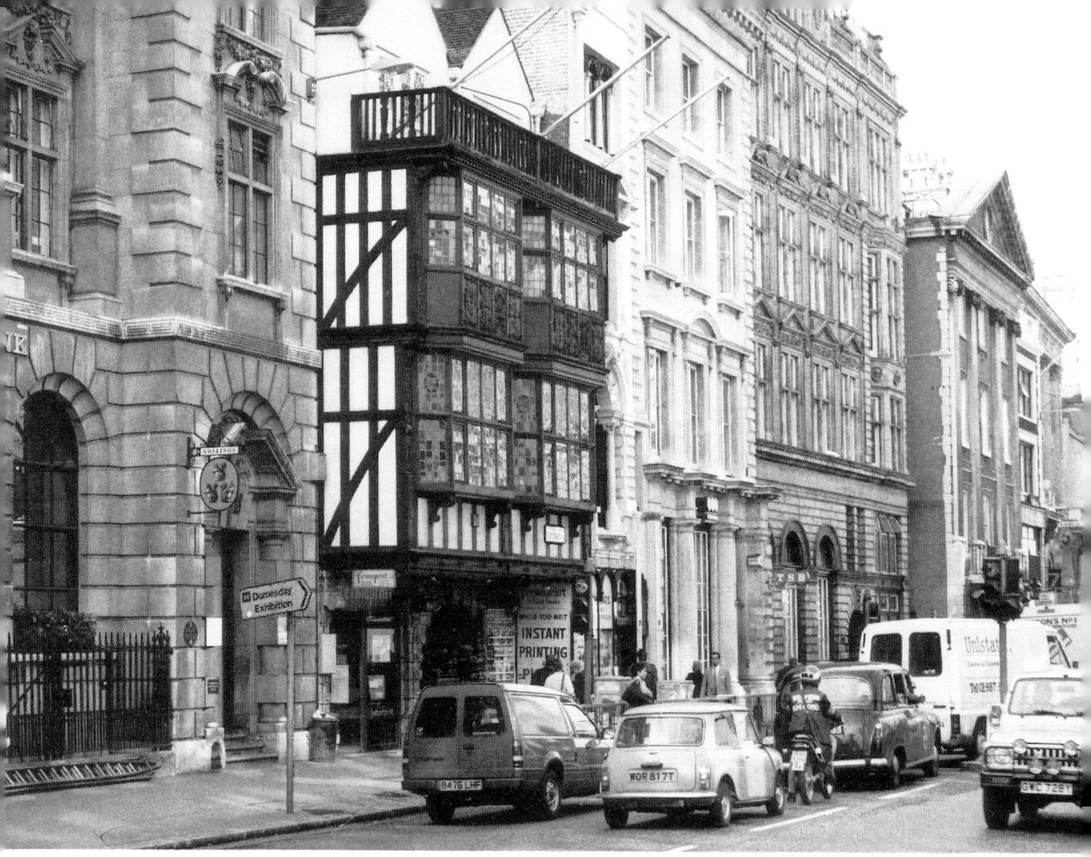
Domesday
Exhibition
INSTANT
PRINTING
TSB
WOR 817T

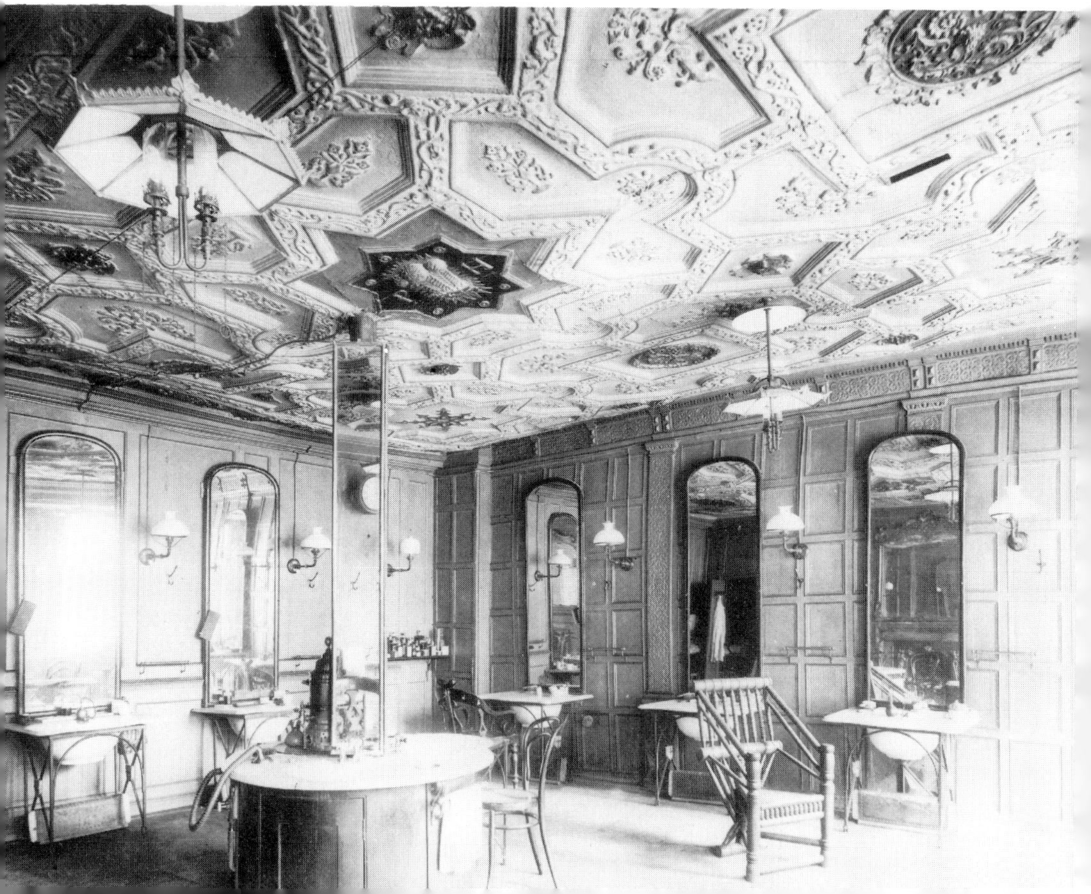

The accession of Edward to the throne in 1549 brought no real relief. When the Cornish rebelled against the new prayer book that year, the King's Council, led by the Duke of Somerset, ordered the Lord Warden of the Stannaries, the Earl of Bedford, to use the receipts of the Duchy of Cornwall to pay troops to march into Cornwall and subdue the rebels. Rents paid by Cornishmen were thus used to pay the army sent against them. The Duchy became a treasure chest for those who served the emerging new order. A man who enjoyed meteoric rise and became Chancellor of the Court of Augmentations, Sir Richard Riche, received also the office of Attorney-General to the Duchy. A skilled administrator completely devoted to his royal master, Riche was the man who testified against Sir Thomas More. Eventually created baron Leighs, he was widely known as baron "Lies". Sir Henry Gate, who succeeded Riche in the Augmentations, took the office of Receiver-General of the Duchy in 1552.

Under Queen Mary a brief, savage reform was instituted. Gate, attainted of high treason, was executed and in his place the Queen appointed her trusted servant, Sir Edward Waldegrave, in 1553. As master of the Wardrobe, he once again brought the Duchy within the orbit of the royal household. In place of the zealously protestant Earl of Bedford, she appointed in 1556 Sir Edmund Hastings, another Roman Catholic.

When Elizabeth I came to the throne in 1558, Waldegrave, an unswerving Catholic, was committed to the Tower. Hastings, by then Lord Loughborough, retired to live under voluntary house arrest. Both had been given office by letters patent *pro vita*, for life, and they continued in office although without any practical power. Sir Edmund died in the Tower in 1561. The Waldegraves, who translated from East Anglia to Somerset, remained recusants until the middle of the eighteenth century. By then the family had been reduced to a precarious poverty only saved by the sudden conversion of James, Earl Waldegrave, to the Anglican faith. This allowed him to take government office and on 7 May 1741 he was created Lord Warden of the Stannaries. In order to relieve the considerable distress to his family, the King granted an extraordinary £1,000 annually, the only time a Warden of the Stannaries has ever received a salary.

The Elizabethan regime adopted a policy of benign neglect towards the Duchy. Attached to a far more subdued office of Augmentations, the Duchy was governed through the Exchequer. The receipts, however, were once again paid directly into the Queen's chamber which guaranteed a personal contact not enjoyed by other crown lands. The office of Warden continued to be occupied by an important figure at court. Many other Duchy positions were taken by Cornish families. In the early sixteenth century the Arundells had been active in Duchy administration, but their Roman Catholic faith caused them difficulties. In the early reign of Elizabeth, the Cosoworth family of St Colan parish entered Duchy service. John Cosoworth, who made money as a London silk merchant, served as deputy and fellow officer with Sir Edward Waldegrave. A Protestant, he continued in office alone, until his death in 1575. He, in turn, was succeeded by Thomas Cosoworth, his son until 1586. In St Colan church there is a truly splendid large brass of John Cosoworth indicating his important Duchy position.

The office of Receiver-General was then taken by Sir Francis Godolphin in 1586. The Godolphins, probably the richest family in sixteenth-century Cornwall, had married into the Glynns nearly a century earlier. They then concentrated their entrepreneurial skills in the tin mining industry. They served in several minor offices until in 1520 Sir William Godolphin was made controller of the coinage of tin for life. In 1555 Queen Mary granted a patent of the office to William Isam who arrived in Truro ready to receive the hammers and seals used to certify that the blocks of tin had been weighed, assayed and taxed. Godolphin, with ten of his relatives, attacked Isam and several were wounded in the ensuing fight. Isam withdrew in order to secure royal protection. However, Godolphin pointed out that his patent was for life; he remained in office.

Sir Francis, who built Godolphin House in the Italian style, took a lease of the Isles of Scilly in 1571. This commenced a relationship between the

Star Castle above St Mary's, Isles of Scilly, built by Sir Francis Godolphin in 1593: an 1821 engraving based on a 1669 drawing. (Gill Collection)

35

Godolphins and the islands which endured for more than two centuries. The conversion to leasehold provided security for the tenant and he constructed a fortress, Star Castle, in 1593. The Godolphins organized its government much as a plantation in the New World would later be run. The lessee became the governor, a proprietor in absentia, and he ruled through a steward and council of twelve. The council had absolute jurisdiction over the civil population. If they found an individual guilty of a capital crime, the prisoner was transported to the mainland for execution of sentence. For lesser offences they possessed a ducking stool, stocks and the whip.

The influence of West Country families over Duchy affairs grew in 1585 when Elizabeth I appointed Sir Walter Raleigh as Chief Steward and Warden of the Stannaries. The Queen continued to administer the estates without a council so that the officers enjoyed greater freedom of action since they were not subjected to close scrutiny. Actually, the Elizabethan Duchy was a triumvirate of power. The Receiver-General represented the West Country, the auditors were Exchequer men and acted for the Lord High Treasurer, while Raleigh, as a courtier, had direct access to the monarch. The division worked well when Bedford was Lord Warden because he enjoyed great landed wealth and could operate independently. This was not the case with Raleigh. His interests depended entirely upon the goodwill of the Queen and those nearest to her. He could not afford to alienate Lord Burghley, the Lord High Treasurer, or his son, Robert Cecil. Raleigh was effectively their captive.

Raleigh's subservient role became all too evident in the late 1590s. It is hardly surprising that the Virgin Queen, the last of her dynasty, too old to bear offspring, showed no interest in the Duchy of Cornwall or its purpose. When England became involved in an Irish war, and sought to defend itself against the resurgence of a belligerent Spain, needs were desperate and immediate. The government began to sell crown land. Included in these hurried auctions were eighteen manors belonging to the Duchy. These sales were certified as lands which were 'no part' of the ancient possessions, but the manors were all property which had been annexed to the Duchy by act of Parliament in exchange for the surrender of ancient possessions. At least some of the ministers involved recognised a bargain when they saw one; Robert Cecil acquired five manors, while Essex bought three.

Probably the only thing which saved the Duchy from piecemeal destruction was the death of the Queen. The new monarch, endowed with sons, was far more careful of the institution. Raleigh's fall from power was swift and ignominious. In 1603 he was evicted from his London townhouse into the streets on the advice of Cecil. His imprisonment in the Tower followed and he was forced to give up the seals of office. Those who had exploited him refused to protect him.

The great advantage which James I possessed over his Tudor predecessor was his children. Legitimate succession was secured; the threat of civil war

Sir Walter Raleigh, Queen Elizabeth's Lord Warden of the Stannaries. A copy of the Marc Geerhardt portrait, c.1588. (Western Morning News)

receded. Naturally, the King sought to honour his heir, Prince Henry Frederick, with the title of Duke of Cornwall. Despite Henry's relative youth, only nine at his father's accession, the cost of maintaining him quickly increased. In 1608 his diets cost £10,000, his wardrobe £3,000. He spent £1,400 through his privy purse and £8,000 on his household. These were colossal sums. Partly to offset this expenditure, the King had Duchy revenues still in his possession, but net revenues were running at less than £5,000 annually. The financial situation was uncomfortably bleak, but the King was forced to look beyond mere money considerations. Above all, he needed to secure the position of his dynasty. This meant that his heir, his Queen, the Duke of York and Princess Elizabeth all must be supported in a way which would place their dignity beyond dispute. He could not be frugal at the expense of his family.

Despite the misgivings of the Marquess of Salisbury, the King's Lord High Treasurer, on 1 September 1610 Prince Henry Frederick received seisin of the Duchy. The nation rejoiced. Some £1,300 went up in the smoke of fireworks and a like amount went on the cost of the Prince's robes. The Prince, now sixteen, began to establish his own household, and his costs continued to increase. He now spent £51,000 annually, which was nearly ten per cent of all crown revenues. The necessity of achieving a larger income from his estate was rapidly becoming manifest. The years of Tudor neglect led to considerable confusion. One hapless individual applying for the post of clerk to the Prince's Council, probably in 1612, found the existing officers 'remembered so little of it at that time' that he was forced to look out old patents. The lack of immediate precedents, no matter how disconcerting to contemporaries, was not without advantage.

Moves had been made as early as 1606 to restore the Duchy. Chief Justice Coke delivered a judgement that lands annexed to the Duchy by parliamentary act could only be severed by subsequent acts. This cleared the way for the recovery of lands sold in the 1590s. The politically adroit, such as Cecil, surrendered Duchy manors they had acquired as a free gift, while others waited for a writ of *scire facias*, which demanded that a supposed freeholder prove his title, to be served. The lands ceded by Henry V in 1421 had disappeared from the rent roll in the 1540s while Lord Russell was Lord Warden. By 1615 seven had been restored and by the 1630s all were recovered.

In 1611 Prince Henry established a council which extended control. Unfortunately, the Prince died suddenly the next year. This curtailed the independence of the Duchy, the council was dissolved and revenues again flowed to the Exchequer. His death also affected Sir Walter Raleigh's fate. The Prince had continued an admirer; at one point he even annexed Raleigh's confiscated property, Sherborne in Dorset, to the Duchy, perhaps with the idea of eventually returning it. When Prince Henry died Raleigh was without support amongst members of the royal family.

The death of Prince Henry Frederick meant that the Duke of York, Prince Charles, was heir to the throne. Gossip within and without the court reported that he could not succeed his brother because he was not the eldest son of the monarch. The precedent of Prince Henry of Greenwich was not satisfactory because, though he had received the title, he had not been granted the revenues. Early in 1613 the crown published a legal opinion affirming Prince Charles's right to the title and revenues as eldest surviving son. This precedent has endured. For two years King James hesitated, but on 21 June 1615 he formally granted livery of the Duchy. Eight months later he also added the other titles which Henry had held. He bestowed these honours by charter; he did not refer the matter to Parliament.

The new Duke acted swiftly to create an independent household and administration. For a brief period Sir Francis Bacon was made Chancellor of the Prince's Council. The principate of Charles was pivotal to the history of the Duchy. He not only preserved, but extended its independence and ensured its continued survival. Some of his measures continued into the twentieth century. Sixteen years of age when given control of the Duchy in 1615, he shaped policy for the next ten years. Charles adopted the policies initiated by his elder brother. A small, effective council, composed of Duchy servants, household officers and lawyers, directed affairs. Though his second chancellor, Sir Henry Hobart, was a national figure at the end rather than the beginning of his career, many of the Prince's council members were relatively young. John Walter, the Prince's Attorney-General, was typical of the new men. When Charles became king in 1625, Walter moved on to national office as chief baron of the Exchequer. Thomas Trevor, Solicitor-General to the Duchy, only thirty years old, eventually was numbered amongst the twelve judges who answered a favourable verdict for the crown in the ship money issue in 1637. James Ley, an active councillor from 1619, became Chancellor of the Exchequer under King Charles.

Not all Council members prospered: Thomas Murray, the Prince's tutor, became his Secretary. Honest, with a puritan disposition, he opposed the proposed marriage of the Prince to the Infanta. He lost his appointment and was placed under house arrest. The most notable of the Prince's Council whose fortunes suffered was Sir Oliver Cromwell. Uncle and benefactor of the future Lord Protector, he held the office of master of the Prince's game. Favoured by both King and Prince, neither was willing to help him out of difficulty. In 1627 Sir Oliver sold his estate at Hinchinbrook to pay his debts.

The Prince's Council remained a London-based group intent upon managing the whole of the estate. John Norden, the cartographer, was hired to survey Duchy land. Initially engaged by Prince Henry Frederick, he worked extensively for the Duchy between 1616 and 1622, reporting and sometimes mapping Duchy estates, noting rents and indicating the real values of land. Because the Duke now possessed the Duchy, all former leases and copyholds were declared invalid. This allowed the Prince's Council to review all rents before new leases were issued. Again, this was a process commenced by Prince Henry Frederick. Hugh Paulet, who had received a lease of the demesne land at Curry Mallet in the reign of Elizabeth, lost his title. After protracted negotiation, Paulet agreed to pay the Prince's Council £500 for a lease of three lives. Any who balked at the authority of the Council were threatened with the dreaded writ of *scire facias*. Those who submitted were usually left in peace provided they paid a fine. An officer related that a Cornish gentleman complained that a visit from the Duchy rent collector, 'was like that of the gospel that when one devil was cast out seven worst came instead of him'.

The aggressive pursuit of the Duke's prerogatives was balanced by a measured paternalism for the poor. The Council protected tenants from the predatory acts of other landlords and defended their interests. In 1618 a letter was dispatched to an individual at Stratton Sanctuary in Cornwall to cease calling poor Duchy tenants before church courts because they could not afford a defence. The Prince's Council offered to consider the case and act on behalf of the tenants. Local disputes were settled by the Council also.

Between 1608 and 1618 net revenues of the Duchy increased by well over three hundred per cent. In an era unused to drastic change, this was spectacular. The aggressive policies of the Prince's Council also extended to the mining industry. The Duke had the right to the pre-emption, that is, a monopoly right to buy all tin offered for sale. After a number of failed attempts, this right he leased to various groups, including merchants involved in the Levant Company, the East India Company and the Pewterers Company. It represented one of the most important exports for the emerging trading companies. This proved a lucrative source of wealth for the Duke, but he also attempted to ensure that Cornish miners received a price which would allow them a reasonable return. This was more difficult, but genuine efforts were made on their behalf.

Many of the initiatives fostered by Prince Charles led to complaint. The method used by his Council to void all leases and tenancies was positively controversial. In 1623 an act was passed by Parliament which guaranteed leases and tenancies granted by the Prince even if he were succeeded by another Duke. There is no record of any opposition by the Prince to this measure, but it clearly implied criticism. The law was re-enacted no less than twenty-three times in the ensuing two centuries especially to protect the interests of subsequent Duchy tenants.

After he came to the throne in 1625, even though he was without heir, King Charles decided to maintain the Council. This was a great departure from medieval precedent; it preserved continuity and provided detailed management of Duchy affairs. Through his principate, and slightly less frequently when he became king, the Council continued to meet an average of seven times a month.

West Looe seen across the river with East Looe in the foreground. Both these small towns were granted two Members of Parliament in Tudor times. Cornwall returned forty-two members, giving the Duchy considerable political power. (Western Morning News)

The policies pursued, the 'fiscal feudalism', the methods used to manage the Duchy by Prince Charles, resemble the policies and the methods the King and his ministers later employed in the 1630s to govern the whole realm. Just as he was always able to spend more than his lands yielded when Prince, the fragile polity of the 1630s collapsed as the King was drawn into war and its expense. Effective royal and council control of the Duchy broke down rapidly after 1643. By 1646 Parliament had assumed full control of the administrative machinery. After the execution of the King in 1649, it rapidly accomplished the surveying of most of the lands of 'Charles Stuart, late Prince of Wales, Duke of Cornwall'. Piecemeal sales continued through the interregnum.

The King's son, Prince Charles, born in 1630, was granted livery of his dukedom on 13 January 1645. However, the Duchy provided the young Prince with something more important than a title: an escape route. When, during the Civil War, in 1646 the King wished his wife and son to escape to France, it was through Cornwall and the Isles of Scilly they travelled.

After the Restoration, Charles II vigorously pursued the reconstruction of the Duchy. Much of the land had been sold by Parliament to pay the army. The purchasers were forced to take leases in exchange for the absolute title to the land. The King did not grant the Duchy the same degree of autonomy which his father had extended to it. He did not create a council. Its affairs were managed by its traditional officers and the King's Exchequer. This remained the practice until the advent of the Hanoverian princes.

The real date of reconstitution was 1715 when George, Prince of Wales, commissioned a council which included the Duke of Argyll, Samuel Molyneux and Lord Lumley. From this date forward, with only the exception of the brief period from the death of Prince Frederick Louis in 1749 until the first council of Prince George Augustus in 1783, the council became a permanent body. Local jurisdictions, such as the manor court, gradually became moribund; tenants addressed their petitions directly to the Prince's Council in London. Each prince, of course, determined how many and who would serve this Council. Prince Frederick Louis, father of George III, issued thirteen separate commissions in his twenty years as Duke. Like the Jacobeans, the Hanoverians favoured a mixture of lawyers, courtiers and Duchy officers. The politician, James Pelham, the avuncular Lt-Gen Gerrard Lake, the improver, Thomas Tyrwhitt, son of a clergyman and eventually Black Rod of the House of Commons, and the naval hero, Admiral Lord St

A 1741 engraving of Vauxhall Gardens with the Prince of Wales, 'Poor Fred', son of George II, seated at the table, centre, wearing a sword. The Gardens, a popular if slightly shady London rendezvous, was on Duchy land at Kennington. (Duchy)

Vincent, were each influential. One of the more unusual appointments was in 1804 when Prince George Augustus created Richard Brinsley Sheridan Receiver-General and Councillor. His last appointment came in 1812. In fact, the playwright held several government appointments, and he was on intimate terms with the Duke.

At a time when the Council centralised power and completely usurped the role of the Duchy's local officials, successive Dukes of Cornwall took little direct interest in their tenants. Both Prince Frederick and Prince George Augustus spent much of their time absorbed in their building projects. Prince Frederick built Cliveden and Kew; Prince George, Carlton House and Brighton Pavilion. Travel in the eighteenth century was difficult, but Prince George Augustus visited Europe and the Highlands. Prince Frederick made a celebrated journey to Bath, but there is no evidence that he bothered to meet any of his tenants who lived near. He became involved in the Duchy through Vauxhall Gardens, or Spring Gardens as it was first known. Located in Kennington, it was the most famous of English eighteenth-century pleasure gardens. A public rehearsal by Handel for the first London performance of the *Messiah* was held there.

Duchy headquarters, as under Prince Charles, continued in Somerset House. An elegant series of rooms included a Council Chamber, an auditor's and a surveyor's office. There was a wine cellar. Duchy servants ate their lunch in the record room, perhaps to encourage the rats to eat something besides the parchment. The Duchy has always had a London headquarters. In the time of the Black Prince the Duchy had offices in the City, and by the river at Prince's Wardrobe, and also an establishment in Old Jewry. By the beginning of the sixteenth century it had acquired a room known as the 'Prince's Council Room' in Westminster Palace. This had ceased to be used by the Jacobean period. The councillors of Prince Charles rented a room above an inn located in Fleet Street. After the death of his mother, Anne of Denmark, the Prince moved into Denmark House, which became Somerset House.

The Duchy and its Duke had a political role. A duke was a member of the landed aristocracy which played a crucial role in parliamentary elections. The origins of Duchy political patronage were tangential. In the sixteenth century Cornwall was one of the least populated counties in England, but by the end of the reign of Elizabeth it was the most represented county in Parliament. It returned forty-two members. Of course, the sixteenth century was innocent of popular representation. The many new seats in Cornwall were acquired in the reign of Edward VI and Mary as well as the early years of Elizabeth I. These were years of relative weakness when the monarchy was most in danger. Cornwall had no peers of its own and this gave the Duchy and its dukes great influence. The sheriff returned electoral writs and in Cornwall he was appointed by the Duchy. Of the many new seats created, the Duchy controlled about fourteen directly. In these constituencies, the

Duke nominated one candidate and the burgesses or another patron found the other.

Towns such as Grampound, Saltash, Camelford, Bossiney and Tregony were far too small to be able to afford the expenses of sending members all the way to London. Looe, divided into East and West by the river, returned not two, but four members. This did not mean that the crown or a duke could ignore the wishes of the local gentry, but it created for any future duke a considerable reservoir of political patronage. Charles I, a dutiful son, wielded his Duchy political influence to serve the interests of the King. Virtually all those listed by the Duke were elected. This patronage reservoir did not remain wholly intact. Great aristocratic families such as the Russells and Cecils were able to secure the odd seat from time to time. But at the advent of the Hanoverians a significant influence could still be utilised by a duke.

The Hanoverians quarrelled. George I fell out with Prince George. George II and Prince Frederick Louis grew apart and then argued. It supplied a deep well for gossips and lasting embarrassment for nonplussed courtiers not knowing which way to turn. The most scandalous and spectacular of all the rifts was between George III and Prince George Augustus. Their relationship soured early, became bitter and then a virtually permanent characteristic of the reign.

The arguments manifested themselves in disputes about money. The crown depended upon supplies voted by Parliament. Revenues derived from crown lands, the Duchy included, had declined drastically as England acquired wealth through commerce, empire and industry. Dukes became dependent upon an allowance from the sovereign. They never considered it enough to support their position. Prince George as Duke possessed political patronage and gathered around him a coterie of politicians to harass and embarrass the King's ministers. The notion of political opposition, which emerged in the eighteenth century, was in part established because a Duke of Cornwall could resist the policies of the king and his ministers without being accused of treason. Those linked with a duke obviously supported the legitimate heir, and their opposition to policies could not be branded treason. Charles James Fox and Richard Brinsley Sheridan both associated with the Prince. In those years successive Dukes of Cornwall helped to create constitutional principles of opposition now basic to all democracies. To the jaundiced eye of nineteenth-century political reformers, Duchy boroughs represented everything wicked in the system, and virtually all were swept away by the Reform Bill of 1832. Entirely forgotten in the welter of reform fever was the crucial incidental constitutional development, which antagonism between monarch and duke fostered.

By the end of the eighteenth century, Prince George Augustus assembled a council and administration of beavering whigs. Amongst them was Benjamin Tucker. Not unlike Samuel Pepys, more than a century earlier,

Tucker was a naval administrator. He had been clerk at Chatham dockyard, marshalled materials, scheduled ships for repair, victualled them and maintained the accounts. Eventually, he became private secretary to Admiral John Jervis, Lord St Vincent, which gave him an entree to the most important and powerful. His interests served his career; he advocated a large and powerful navy with the shore facilities to maintain it.

Tucker's introduction to the Duke's affairs was rather oblique, but hardly untypical of the unreformed Duchy. Sir John Morshead became Warden of the Stannaries in 1798. The Prince was acutely embarrassed a few years later when Morshead proposed to sell the patent of his office to an unknown, but obviously ambitious apothecary. Tucker interceded and secured the patent which he gallantly returned to a grateful Duke. The Prince appointed him Surveyor-General and Councillor in 1808. He continued in both appointments until 1827. The year after he joined the Prince's Council his former patron, Lord St Vincent, was also appointed and served seven years.

With the support from Lord St Vincent and the Duke, Tucker embarked upon an ambitious career of speculation and controversy. He secured a very long lease of the whole of the Waters of Tamar, which was a part of the Honour of Trematon. He built the elegant house standing in Trematon Castle precincts. His son Jedidiah he appointed deputy surveyor and John Jervis Tucker became gamekeeper of Boyton in 1848. Benjamin Tucker, junior, was a Duchy clerk in the 1820s and eventually became Deputy-Receiver.

His lease of the Tamar had been granted in order to stop the many encroachments he had catalogued. The rent was minimal and the lease granted him a virtual carte blanche. Plymouth breakwater was built in those years; it is likely that Tucker was instrumental in suggesting that prisoners move from the unhealthy hulks in the Hamoaze to Dartmoor. He may have been anxious to establish the stone quarries to provide material for the harbour improvements. In about 1820 a horse-drawn railway line from Princetown to Plymouth was constructed to carry stone for the new breakwater. Tucker lost favour latterly in the reign of George IV, and under King William IV in the 1830s the Duchy Council proposed legal proceedings against him. The conclusion of the Napoleonic Wars had made his politics unfashionable. His proposed development of the Scilly Islands into a naval dockyard was never implemented. But there is no doubt that he did exercise a lasting influence on the development of the Tamar basin.

In 1797 the Duke appointed Thomas Tyrwhitt Secretary and Keeper of the Privy Seal. By 1803 he had been made Warden of the Stannaries. He continued to serve on the Prince's Council until 1819. A driving intellect coupled with an innate paternalism made him an 'improver' by nature. Just as Tucker turned to the Tamar, Tyrwhitt concentrated upon Dartmoor. In the 1790s the major local families, including the Bullers, persuaded the Duchy to enclose the whole moor, but the bill failed in Parliament as many small farmers protested. Tyrwhitt determined to introduce new agricultural methods and change the moor. The latter he definitely accomplished: he founded the village of Princetown, eventually the site of the prison, but initially a French prisoner of war camp. The village and the prison remain as witness to his initiative. Tyrwhitt wanted also to bring the benefits of the new agriculture to Dartmoor. He acquired Tor Royal newtake on lease and built the house. He has been blamed for the creation of this and other large newtakes. In fact, they already existed. Most were created in the middle of the eighteenth century by tenants through the Lydford manorial court. The Prince's Council knew nothing of them until local complaints were received, but by then it was too late to reverse the action. Instead, the Council decided at last to make them accountable by granting a series of leases in the first decade of the nineteenth century.

The efforts of Tyrwhitt and Tucker have a common theme: dynamic change. This the Duke was ill-equipped to accomplish. Land law was archaic and cumbersome, designed to cope with an unchanging agricultural and urban scene. In 1750 Westminster Bridge was opened. At a stroke this made possible the transformation of Kennington from an area of market gardens into a suburb of London. Most of the land was let by copyhold for three lives. This meant the Prince had no control over most of the estate and the copy-holders were free to do as they wished with their estates.

The archaic nature of the land law in fact created a class of kulaks who took advantage of the system to acquire land without actually living on it. In Cornwall the traditional farmstead had been divided and subdivided until some individuals held legal title to minute fractions of farms which only extended to a few acres. At Stoke Climsland Richard Hele held 1/1000th of an eighteen acres tenement. This is a meaningless figure, except that it suggests that the land was probably worked by a farmer paying a rack rent to a group of copyholders who expected to make a profit.

As the ether of ancien regime began to dissipate in the face of rapid urban and agricultural change, the Duchy was shackled by archaic laws and by two indifferent kings, George IV and William IV, who had no heirs. The Duchy was again threatened by continued neglect.

The original gates to Dartmoor Prison, Princetown, built at the instigation of Thomas Tyrwhitt, Lord Warden of the Stannaries, in 1809 to house French prisoners of war, hence the inscription which means 'spare the subjected'. (Western Morning News)

47

CHAPTER TWO

MODERNISATION

Graham Haslam

By the third decade of the nineteenth century the Duchy was again at a low point. In retreat on virtually every front, its political influence in disrepute, the Duchy's income had long been stagnant. The reputation of Prince George Augustus and his inability to live within his means starkly highlighted the shortcomings of the unreformed Duchy. In several ways he had fostered original, sometimes noteworthy policies within his dukedom. His initiative on Dartmoor illustrates this, but it was high-minded thinking; none of his policies really confronted general economic realities represented by the accelerating changes taking place on the Duchy agricultural scene.

In the 1780s William Simpson was commissioned by the Council to survey most Duchy property. A part of his brief included establishing realistic land values. Also, he interested himself in the quality of soil, suggested the need for marl at Farrington Gurney, noted the proximity of Shepton Mallet and West Harptree to Bath and pointed out that improved roads would allow tenants to market their produce more readily. Despite his recommendations, nothing was done by the Prince's Council. Other than the attempt by Tyrwhitt to transform Dartmoor and the personal initiative of Benjamin Tucker in the Tamar basin, the Prince and his Council had little interest in direct management of the estate.

This lack of direction may be explained on the one hand in the character of the Prince, and on the other hand in constitutional vagaries. A leader of society, a man of fashion and a patron of the arts, Prince George Augustus had no real interest in farming. In this, as in so much, he was not his father's son. It is true, too, that after 1788 the Prince, as Regent, had really much wider responsibilities. It is equally true that none of his advisers actually proposed a plan of reform which was capable of yielding much greater sums.

The Duchy was left in an isolated constitutional niche after 1760 when the King surrendered his crown land to Parliament in exchange for an annual income, the Civil List. An even more damaging measure was the Land Tax in 1798, fixed at 4s, which was applied in the Duchy. This Act specifically gave the Duke of Cornwall the power to sell land and apply the proceeds to the purchase of government stock for the redemption of the tax.

48

Tor Royal near Princetown on Dartmoor, built by Thomas Tyrwhitt in the early nineteenth century and remodelled by Albert Richardson in 1919. (Helen Harris)

Robert Graham, the Prince's Attorney-General and Vicary Gibbs, the Solicitor-General, considered the clauses affecting the Duchy before they were inserted in the bill. On 1 August the Council noted the passage of the Act and only seventeen days later Maidencote, Berkshire, was sold to John Butler for £790 and part of Kirton in Lindsey purchased by John Bowman for £330. Portions of Tewington and Tybesta in Cornwall were sold to Thomas Carlyon for £500, and the remainder of the manor of Tewington successfully offered to Charles Rashleigh for £2,630. Reginald Pole-Carew acquired West Antony and Portwrinkle for the large sum of £10,930.

The sales continued one after another: Tywarnhaile, Fowey, more land at Tybesta, Helston-in-Kerrier, Calstock and Lostwithiel in Cornwall. Early in 1799, Porthia Prior in Cornwall and yet more of Kirton in Lindsey were sold in fee simple. Lewis, Lord Sandes bought Grimethorpe, Leicestershire, for £930 and Henry Andrews purchased Moresk, Cornwall, paying £1,140. Charles Rashleigh returned to this extraordinary market to buy Austell Prior for the price of £1,600. The Duke of Norfolk successfully bid for Old Shoreham, Sussex.

Although a retreat, it was nevertheless a sensible move to dispose of these estates in order to redeem the remainder. Thomas Coutts, the royal banker, may have been instrumental in framing this policy. However, after 1800 the Prince was forced to play an increasing role in the politics of the country; in 1816 he became Regent and ruled thus until his succession in 1820. Childless, there is no doubt that Duchy affairs were put aside. His successor, William IV, was equally uninterested in Duchy affairs.

In the public mind, too, the Duchy was associated with the excesses of the ancien regime. Many of the pocket boroughs under Duchy patronage were swept away in the reform of 1832; it was forgotten that their political influence had at times been used to advance the constitution. Perhaps the Duchy had become rather too close to the Whig administrators, Lord St Vincent and Tucker, and their advocacy of a strong defence. This policy, too, after the defeat of Napoleon, was in disrepute. Both Prince George Augustus and King William allowed Duchy income to stagnate. They preferred to rely upon occasional fines from renewal of copyholds or leases. Between 1783 and 1830 George IV realised £370,000 from these sources. King William IV between his accession and his death in 1837 derived £171,343 from fines. In both cases, the money was paid directly into their privy purse. It provided a valuable source of personal income. However, fines were occasional and entirely unpredictable. It was impossible to plan the future of the estate from a source of income which could not be anticipated.

In 1838 the Duchy had been placed in the hands of a special commission under the direction of the Lord Warden of the Stannaries for the purpose of investigating expenditure and planning ways of retrenching. There can be no doubt that the Duchy was near to the precipice of oblivion. In an era of economic expansion, static income was in reality a shrinking income. The report of the committee was published in July 1839. It noted the neglect of local courts, the fact that property boundaries had been allowed to become doubtful, and that timber had been cut illegally throughout the estate. Annual income between 1829 and 1835 averaged £42,262, but expenditure in these years averaged £14,884 a year. Additionally, Duchy officers took fees as requisites of office which cost £9,661 each year. This left only £17,717 as a net surplus, a sum not nearly enough to maintain a future prince. He would not only have to pay his personal staff, but also his household and find money for any building he would care to undertake.

The committee made six fundamental recommendations in their report. First, it suggested changes to the management structure; second, appointment of local agents; third, abolition of copyhold estates; fourth, leases should only be granted for a definite term of years; fifth, most fines for leases and copyholds should be abolished; and sixth, fees and requisites of office should be curtailed. These were sweeping proposals. Alternatively, it would have been possible to integrate Duchy estates with crown lands and settle for an annual income from the Civil List for the Prince of Wales. Changes to the organisation and prerogatives of office were daunting tasks. In the later stages of the deliberations of the committee the new monarch, Queen Victoria, appointed an additional commissioner, her husband Albert, the Prince Consort.

It was his stature and his determination which accomplished the difficult tasks set by the commission. He was appointed Lord Warden of the Stannaries on 16 April 1842. The Queen extended to him a virtually free hand in Duchy management. Energetic, interested in agriculture, seemingly anxious from the first day to introduce radical reforms, over the next nineteen years the Prince Consort accomplished a root and branch reform of the Duchy. No area of management escaped his scrutiny. He tackled each issue with energy and enterprise. Of course, he did not work alone. A Council continued to act as a corporate body and sanction all decisions collectively, but there is no doubt that his views were usually sought and usually followed. For the whole of his term of office, until his death in 1861, he never allowed the Duke of Cornwall, Prince Albert Edward, to participate in any of the Duchy's business. The heir remained a stranger to his inheritance until the death of his father.

The Prince Consort attended Council first in 1840. By that time the coinage duties had been abolished, by statute in 1838. Widely seen as a retrograde tax on trade, the duties were surrendered in exchange for a fixed annuity of £16,216. In an age innocent of inflation, no provision was made to index this payment. It remained immutable until it was finally redeemed in the new Management Act of 1983. Another act, also in 1838, established that an annual account of receipts and disbursements should be presented to Parliament. This ensured that in future Dukes and their servants would be publicly scrutinized and held accountable for the measures they adopted.

The Oval, famous cricket ground of the Surrey County Cricket Club, on the Kennington estate of the Duchy. The celebrated gasholders look down on the 1880 match against the Australians. (Illustrated London News)

Not exactly a private company, nor a government department, the Duchy became a publicly accountable private estate, a paradoxical solution not untypical of the British constitution.

These early reforms, effective in their way, were really aimed at placing the Duchy on an acceptable footing. They were essentially legalistic. The Accounts Act may have been passed by Parliament as a means of ensuring that no future Duke could again become enmeshed in the kinds of difficulties which plagued Prince George Augustus.

In 1844 Prince Albert secured powers from Parliament to allow the Duchy to buy and sell land and enfranchise copyholds. This was extended to the Duchy's ancient possessions in the same year by different legislation. Fundamental to his reform programme, this legislation allowed the Prince Consort to take advantage of the new dynamism in English agriculture. For a few years before the Act, the Duchy had not renewed copyhold estates when they fell into hand, but the legislation sped the process by allowing the purchase of existing rights. From the eighteenth century enclosures became an important phenomenon within the Duchy. Though this allowed tenants to take advantage of the new agriculture, it did not provide fundamental advantages for the landlord. This was not possible until the Prince's Council moved from copyhold to annual tenancy as the prevalent form of agricultural tenure. This crucial change meant that rents could be renegotiated as circumstances dictated. The Prince's Council would in future deal directly with the people actually farming the land. Copyholders had often been absentee tenants, rack-renting in turn to under-tenants, of whom the Duchy knew nothing. This group of intermediaries disappeared from the scene as the new form of tenure was introduced.

The bold changes in the forms of tenure introduced by the Prince's Council meant that the Duchy could venture capital for the technical changes taking place in agriculture. Improvements were made across the whole estate. Broadly, they were of three kinds: repairs or replacement of farm-houses and out-buildings; building and repairing cottages; and draining, fencing, levelling and introducing other improvements to the land. In the period from 1842 until 1861, at Mere in Wiltshire, more than £13,000 was spent on repairs and new farm buildings and over £5,500 on improvements to the land. On Dartmoor in the same period £783 was expended on repairs and new farm buildings and over £1,400 on improvements to the land. In total for these nineteen years the Prince's Council sanctioned £21,000 on new and repaired farm buildings and £16,400 on field improvements.

The effect on Duchy tenants varied. In a very real sense the extremes of rural poverty were banished. This process required a steady emigration from the land. In the nineteenth century the newly expansive industries of the cities could absorb many; equally the Americas and British colonies also received many emigrants. Dislocation was not an easy fate, but the hard-won prosperity achieved by these settlers was testimony to their spirit.

Those left on the land faced many problems throughout the century. However, as a landlord willing to invest in improvements, the Duchy was often able to help tenants adapt in response to changing conditions. In 1861 over £1,168 was spent on repairs and improvements. By contrast, in 1838 exactly £8 was expended for the same purpose. Changes in the form of tenure also meant that for the first time since the middle of the fourteenth century the Prince's Council took a direct interest in the day-to-day activities of farms. Once capital had been deployed, the skill of the tenant, his health, the happiness and welfare of his family all became important factors in his ability to utilize fully the resources available to him. The nineteenth century witnessed not only the rise of intensive farming, but also intensive paternalism. Tenants could no longer remain anonymous.

These changes called for far more local knowledge than a London-based Council could reasonably hope to possess. In February 1845 Robert Watt, probably a Scot, certainly with Border connections, was engaged as the first directly employed, full-time land agent. He was known, as his successors in office still are, as Land Steward. He was originally based at Lostwithiel. Watt's instructions included the collection of rents, to become familiar with the cares and concerns of tenants, to scrutinize the methods of cultivation used by them, and to make specific recommendations to the Council concerning these matters. His appointment – later other stewards were also employed – represents a departure in management. Surveying emerged in the nineteenth century as one of the new technical professions. There had always been local individuals nominated to report to the Prince's Council, but they were normally unskilled and only possessed knowledge of a particular area. Of course, the Duchy had employed surveyors in the past: John Norden by Prince Charles, and William Simpson by George Augustus: but their terms of employment were for a limited period and for specific purposes. The Prince's Council ceded no formal power to the new surveyors; every single proposal made was considered and approved by it as before. For the first time, the Council received consistent, objective, first-hand reports, and could structure its business so that the interests of tenants were fully reflected.

The Council decided to sell estates. Though the advent of railways made an agent's job easier in the 1850s, a trip from Newton Abbot to Brimpts Farm on Dartmoor still took two days. These limitations encouraged consolidation. Berkhamsted in Hertfordshire was sold to Earl Brownlow in 1862 and Langton Herring in Dorset was successfully offered seven years earlier. The capital accumulated by those sales could be deployed to purchase other properties.

The substantial changes wrought in the composition of the estates and on the land were accompanied by sweeping administrative reforms. The Prince Consort began to employ salaried personnel in place of office holders dependent upon fees and emoluments. This system, which had existed without substantive changes since the Middle Ages, encouraged individuals to acquire as many offices as they could in order to enhance their fees. It also led to an extremely complicated system of charges for virtually every task. Salaried employees were far more willing to adapt and change their routine because they were not dependent upon a particular procedure.

A new senior officer was created. The Prince Consort appointed James Robert Gardiner as the first Secretary of the Duchy. A barrister, Gardiner began as secretary to the Lord Warden of the Stannaries, but the advantages of maintaining an individual to deal with day-to-day correspondence, organise the Council's agenda and marshal the paper work became immediately apparent. Ancient titles were merged with the new appointment. He became auditor in 1841, clerk to the Council in 1843 and surveyor-general in 1849, vice-warden of the Stannaries in 1852 and steward of most of the manorial courts. He often toured estates with Robert Watt. He was not a member of the Prince's Council. The Prince Consort continued to direct the whole of the Duchy's business personally. In a typical year, 1852, the Council met on nine occasions, including two meetings in June and two in November. Agendas included relations with government, pending legislation, notes concerning Duchy personnel, all proposed sales and purchases of property, all suggested improvements and proposals from prospective new tenants.

The Victorian Council, and all since, have remained small, no more than a dozen members. Duchy personnel and legal advisors were appointed as before. Later in the nineteenth century and after, the Council included individuals from the West Country who were in touch with the local point of view. No woman has ever been appointed to the Council or any senior Duchy office.

In 1857 the staff moved from Somerset House to new offices at Buckingham Gate. For some time there had been pressure on the limited space available at Somerset House by expanding government departments. In 1854 the Duchy of Cornwall Office Act stipulated that the government would bear the costs of a new office equal in value to the old. A new site in Pimlico, across from Buckingham Palace, was found. The government employed James Pennythorne, architect of the Public Record Office in Chancery Lane, and the Duchy retained Decimus Burton, designer of the Marble Arch. Planned in the neo-classical tradition which reflected the ministries in Whitehall, the building has remained headquarters for the Prince's Council and the secretariat.

The financial results of the reform introduced by the Prince Consort were spectacular. In 1838 receipts amounted to £24,885, disbursements equalled £13,349, leaving only £11,536. In 1861 gross income was £60,753, dis-

10 Buckingham Gate after being struck by a German bomb on 10/11 May 1941: Buckingham Palace is in the background. (Duchy)

bursements came to only £14,119 and net revenue equalled £46,676. This truly was an impressive gain. It was not entirely due to inspired management. Mineral income from metals other than tin was a negligible £174 in 1838, but in 1861 this source produced £7,083. Improvements in management played an important part. In 1838 costs were £11,111. Fifty-three years later, they were only £6,865. In agricultural, in administrative and in financial terms the changes initiated by the Prince Consort were an outstanding success. His work was an expression of his interest in agriculture. In a wider sense, it was the response of a man alive to the romantic age which glorified the natural landscape and saw in it a reflection of the ancient roots of British life.

These impressive advances were not reflected in areas where the Duchy held urban property. The sale of Berkhamsted, which eventually came into the orbit of suburban London, is indicative of the lack of interest in the problems posed by London's expansion. The most notable failure was Kennington. Here market gardening had rapidly given way to working-class housing after the opening of the Thames bridges from the middle of the eighteenth century onwards. The Duchy's lack of control of development there, which was almost entirely in the hands of copyholders, was not substantially altered by the legislation allowing purchase of copyholds. In Kennington the compensation necessary was probably beyond the Duchy's means.

Inability to influence direction was compounded by the decision to sell rights of way to the railways. While Prince Albert was Lord Warden of the Stannaries the Duchy realised about £40,000 from such sales. Some £28,000 of this total came from Kennington alone. A flat, relatively featureless area, the topography reflects development almost immediately. Through the crowded streets came the elevated, arched railway lines cutting the community into isolated sections. No attempt was made to moderate the changes. A model housing scheme developed at Kennington in 1854 for working-class families was quickly recognised as a failure.

It was often most difficult to bring about change in urban areas. Copyholds were more valuable and a landlord could do little until they had been recovered. Nevertheless, the problems were not insurmountable and the Duchy did not compare well with other estates. Evidence that the Prince's Council saw urban problems as secondary is evident also from its manor of Fordington in Dorset. The market town of Dorchester extended into the manor where some of the worst slums were located. There were occasional outbreaks of cholera and Thomas Hardy's *Mayor of Casterbridge* is set in this area. The Prince's Council was only occasionally responsive, but not innovative.

The surpluses produced year after year by the Victorian management of necessity had to be banked until redeployed for the purchase of new estates. This gave the Duchy a connection with the City which later changed the nature of its assets. A portfolio of shares and government bonds would eventually provide a substitute income as receipts derived from mining declined.

The coping stone of the Prince Consort's reforms was the Duchy of Cornwall Management Act of 1863. Though enacted after his death, the act enshrined in law the many reforms already implemented by him. This act extended to the Duchy an almost corporate structure, providing it with a seal which is used even when no Duke exists, describing how capital may be deployed and indicating how records should be maintained. The changes which had proved profitable for twenty years were given full parliamentary sanction. The Prince Consort had brought the Duchy back from the precipice, reinvigorated it by establishing a new management structure, and provided it with a sense of purpose. However, the Management Act of 1863 tended to offer legal prescriptions and formulae in a rigid form which came to limit the ability of future Dukes to implement necessary changes in their turn.

A grim drawing by Gustave Doré showing the high-arched railways that bestrode Kennington in mid-nineteenth century, and the slum conditions that resulted in the houses below.

Prince Albert Edward took his first Council meeting on 6 February 1863. The estate over which he assumed control was in a very strong financial position. The accumulated surplus revenues provided the money with which he purchased Sandringham. This Norfolk estate, characteristically, had been chosen as his country residence by the Queen and the Prince Consort. Nevertheless, he seems to have enjoyed life there and took a genuine interest in stock-breeding. His town residence, Lancaster House, was located on the opposite side of St James' Park from the Duchy office.

Important purchases were made in 1862. Gillingham, Dorset, which extended to 795 acres was purchased from the Crown Estate Commissioners. In the Somerset levels the 800 acre estate of Isle Brewers was sold to the Duchy by Sir John Michel. Rialton, in the area of Newquay, Cornwall, was also bought by the Duchy from the Church Commissioners. It extended to over 1,500 acres.

These purchases of over three thousand acres helped further concentrate the Duchy in the West Country. In 1880 the Prince also added the Whiteford estate near the existing Duchy property of Stoke Climsland. This estate had been founded by Sir John Call in the 1760s. From an obscure Cornish family, Call made a fortune in India and returned to live the life of a nabob. He built a large country seat and purchased copyhold estates from the Duchy. However, the family circumstances declined until Call was forced to sell the house and estate. It was the old story of the Duchy eventually gaining what it appeared to have lost. The house, which was partly run down, was stripped of its fine furnishings and some of its ornaments were used in rebuilding Duchy farm-houses in Cornwall. Its Adam fireplace now graces the Duke's Council Chamber at Buckingham Gate.

Prince Albert Edward married Princess Alexandra in 1863. They spent a part of their honeymoon in the West Country, staying in the Tamar valley. While not exactly an estate visit it does indicate that modern forms of travel made the various estates much more accessible to a Duke interested in his tenants.

As the future sovereign of a world-wide empire, it was desirable for him to travel the world. This meant that for long periods, the Prince's Council had to function without his direct involvement. In 1886 he appointed Maurice Holtzmann as Secretary and also made him a member of the Council. All subsequent Secretaries have been members of the Prince's Council. Holtzmann was an archetypal Victorian. A European, rather than an Englishman, he had studied under the German chemist Bunsen. He was brought to England by the Prince Consort to work as the Prince's German secretary and librarian at Marlborough House. He pursued that most Victorian of pastimes, mountain climbing, returning to the Alps each year. He was the only Duchy Secretary prior to World War II who did not possess a legal background.

Holtzmann's practical leadership guided the Duchy through a very

Stoke Climsland village, with Duchy-built cottages to the left. (Western Morning News)

difficult economic era. The mining industry, that great Duchy pillar for nearly 600 years, collapsed after 1880. Also, the grassland farming systems of the South West began to suffer as the advent of refrigerated shipping after 1880 meant that cheap imports of dairy products began to compete in the domestic market. By 1900 tenants sought relief either in the form of rent reductions or by decreasing the size of their farms. However, Prince Edward and Holtzmann remained committed to renewal and rebuilding of the estate. The stock of buildings continued to be repaired and improved throughout the principate.

The programme was extended in 1912 when Walter Peacock, the then Duchy Secretary, appointed Albert Richardson and Lovett Gill, two young London architects, to design new farmhouses for £600 each and cottages for £300. They were an unlikely choice, virtually unknown and without background in rural architecture, but they had a significant impact on the estate. Between 1912 and 1930 they regularly designed new houses, including terraces in Princetown. In 1919 they completed the remodelling of Tor Royal, the Dartmoor residence used by Prince Edward. Richardson adapted his work and gradually incorporated traditional West Country slate and stone in his designs. He also designed terraces on the outskirts of Dorchester. These, completed in 1924, represented a belated response to the Rev Henry Moule, who until his death in 1880 had pressed the Duchy for change to counter the appalling housing conditions there. Richardson called upon Thomas Hardy, who had also been active in the campaign to eliminate poor housing conditions, in his case those at Max Gate.

For some time the Prince's Council had been seeking to resolve outstanding boundary disputes. Accommodation was eventually reached with the government concerning title to undersea minerals, and Duchy rights to the fundus of Cornish estuaries were confirmed. The Duchy also sought to assert its ancient rights to regulate the common land of Dartmoor. On this issue its fortunes were rather mixed. A new pressure was recognised for the first time. Writing in the 1850s a clerk in the London office, W. E. Brooshooft, pointed out that railways were opening up what before had been a remote wilderness. Trains could carry people so rapidly that they seemed almost to 'annihilate time'. Dartmoor, he predicted, would become a place where masses of people would tour and spend their holidays. It was a remarkably

Visitors enjoying the Dartmoor wilderness, an idea foreshadowed by a Duchy clerk in the 1850s. (Western Morning News)

prescient observation. In 1880 the Attorney-General did marshal much of the available evidence for the Duchy's ancient title to Dartmoor. In the end little of lasting authority was done to challenge encroachments or regulate grazing, because he could see only expense without return. Instead, the Council fought a rear-guard action, asserting its rights without actually initiating large-scale legal proceedings.

The advent of Prince George in 1901 represented a continuation of policy and not a departure. Holtzmann retired in 1908. In his place the Prince appointed Sir Walter Peacock, a barrister. He was an energetic man, but not always a success. When Prince Edward visited Kennington in 1919, a local government official pointed out that curtains had been hung in empty houses to give the appearance of being occupied. The Prince defended Peacock by saying publicly that he did realise they were empty, and explained that the Duchy was only trying to avoid the appearance of dereliction. Privately, he may have been far less sanguine.

Prince George, just as his father, spent much of his time travelling the Empire. Imbued with the traditions of the navy, he never quite came to terms with the Duchy as an institution. Writing to his son, he commented that he had something 'called the Duchy of Cornwall' to provide for him. It betrays a diffident attitude towards the management of the estate; he developed the policies of his father rather than attempted any new departure. He did, however, have a lasting impact in terms of personnel.

A fundamentally important appointment was that of John Lord Revelstoke to the Prince's Council in 1907. Dominant partner in his family's merchant bank, Baring Brothers & Co Ltd, and architect of its startling recovery from the crisis of 1890, he was a figure of national and international importance. He served the British government and the world financial community, achieving a significant influence in the sphere in which he operated. By 1910 he had succeeded to the office of Receiver-General of the Duchy. From the bastion of this ancient office, he controlled the financial affairs of the Duchy. This provided the Duke and the Duchy with expert financial advice. There was no immediate change of investment strategy; the Duchy continued to be almost exclusively a landed estate, but the expertise needed to diversify assets became available through this appointment. In 1929 Edward Peacock, a Canadian partner in Baring Brothers Bank, succeeded Lord Revelstoke. A friend and confidant of Prince Edward, knighted in 1934, he continued to serve the Duchy long after he left Barings, and did not retire until 1960, at the age of 89. The Baring family has resumed direct contact with the Duchy since that date. Alexander Lord Ashburton became Receiver-General in 1961 and in 1973 was succeeded by the Hon Sir John Baring, his son.

Though he was technically Duke of Cornwall from the accession of his father, Prince Edward did not actually become active in Duchy affairs until 1918 when he was twenty-four years old. In many ways Prince Edward represents a turning point in the history of the Duchy and a transition from the nineteenth to the twentieth centuries. Agriculture, which had recovered in the war, slumped in the 1930s. The Prince, more than any previous Duke, took a direct interest in the welfare of Duchy farming tenants and the activities of the estate. He visited Kennington in 1919, 1933 and 1935, Stoke sub Hamdon in 1934, and stayed at Tor Royal, visited Stoke Climsland, Cornwall in 1936 and also visited Star Castle Hotel in the Isles of Scilly, flying there in a seaplane. Measured against the expectations of the post-war era, this may seem a modest schedule, but it helped to secure a new outlook which eventually became much more systematic and frequent. When he was invested as Prince of Wales at Caernarvon in 1911, Duchy tenants were invited to attend the ceremony.

Since the appointment of the first Land Steward, the system had become more elaborate. In 1889 it was decided by the Prince's Council to establish an additional office in Shepton Mallet and a separate Land Steward was appointed for it in 1899. A third 'district', as they are called by the Duchy, was created in 1920 when William Proudfoot, Steward in the eastern district, took over the Dartmoor estate. This network was further extended in the 1920s when the Dorrien Smith family surrendered their lease of the Isles of Scilly, maintaining only Tresco. The Duchy established an office on St Mary's and appointed an agent. A further elaboration of this system came in 1930 when Holroyd Chambers was appointed Land Steward for the manor of Kennington. Until then a number of rent collectors had worked from the Buckingham Gate office, but this had proved unsatisfactory because it was impossible to exercise sufficient control over the cash collected from the hundreds of tenants. Chambers successfully overhauled the system and introduced proper accounting procedures.

The era between the wars was dominated by the Land Stewards. Their recommendations for 'expenditure' and farm improvements were approved by the Prince's Council with almost no comment. Victorian and Edwardian councils had examined every matter in detail, and ensured all purchases and sales conformed to its strategy. These forms of management, still maintained in theory, were largely conceded in practice to the Land Stewards. The Prince's Council met far less frequently than its Victorian predecessor and typically in the 1930s would meet only three times annually. In part, the nuts and bolts decisions previously taken by it could be delegated to the cadre of professional agents running the districts. However, the Council failed to evolve or impose any coherent management plan which would unify the work of the land agents.

The Duchy, especially in the decade after World War I, did buy a number of estates and farms around the periphery of Dartmoor. This is an investment

Edward Prince of Wales, later Duke of Windsor, showed much interest in the reviving agriculture of the late twenties; seen here at a cattle show. (Keystone)

decision not easy to understand. However, Prince Edward had a special interest in the area and he was anxious to strengthen the Duchy's management position there. He set another modern precedent in 1927 by purchasing Grove Farm, Lenton, in Nottinghamshire. It broke the pattern of acquisitions for the previous century. However, the purchase was an isolated event. On the whole the Prince's agriculture initiatives led him away from the Duchy rather than towards it. He purchased a cattle ranch in western Canada, EP Ranch, and chose to live in Fort Belvedere, Surrey, relatively removed from the Duchy.

It is a remarkable feature of the Duchy of Cornwall that it possesses no great house as a focal point. Since the time of the Black Prince each Duke has been able to impose his own style on the Duchy by choosing where and how he wishes to live. This has given them a freedom many other estate owners must have occasionally longed to enjoy.

The Prince's Council did extend the network of managed farms which were created as models for Duchy tenants and as a place to provide training in the best agricultural techniques. At Landulph, Lower Marsh Farm became a poultry enterprise in 1920. A young South African, Arthur du Plessis, who fought in the war, married a Cornish girl, and found employment and training on the farm. In 1923 on St Mary's, Isles of Scilly, Holy Vale became an experimental station to demonstrate the best methods of bulb cultivation. This was a joint effort by the Duchy and the Ministry of Agriculture; it later provided information about dairy farming. At Tor Royal on Dartmoor the Prince maintained a stud.

The most extensive of the home farms was built at Stoke Climsland. Opened in 1912, its imposing range of buildings designed by Richardson remains an impressive tribute to this episode of Duchy history. Costs, increased government involvement and the work of the agricultural colleges eventually made these farms unnecessary, and one by one they were given over to tenants or assigned other uses.

The hardships of the 1930s were understood by Prince Edward. At Kennington he visited clubs for the unemployed. Canon Andrews, rector of Stoke Climsland, appealed to the Duke for help to create market gardens for the unemployed. His success with this project was admired by the Prince and a genuine friendship developed between them.

Within the Duchy the Prince was especially dependent upon the advice of Sir Edward Peacock and the man he appointed Attorney-General to the Duchy in 1932, Sir Walter Monckton. Eventually Viscount Monckton, he was especially close to the Prince. Roland Clive Wallace Burn, eventually Sir Clive Burn, a solicitor, became Secretary in 1936. When the abdication crisis arose, the King turned to the Attorney-General to the Duchy: it was Sir Walter Monckton who acted as liaison between the King and the Prime Minister. He helped the King draft the Instrument of Abdication. In the last three days he and Sir Edward Peacock were constantly with the King. Sir

The Prince's council of the Duchy of Cornwall, November 1985. Seated left to right, Sir Nicholas Henderson, the incoming Lord Warden of the Stannaries; Lord Franks, the retiring Lord Warden; His Royal Highness; the Hon Sir John Baring, Receiver-General; Andrew Morritt QC; Attorney-General. Standing, John Pugsley; Michael Galsworthy; the late Sir John Higgs, Secretary and Keeper of the Records; John James; Sir Peter Miles, Keeper of the Queen's Privy Purse; Sir John Riddell, the Prince's Private Secretary.

Prince Edward shows his concern for the unemployed; a visit to Trenance Gardens, Newquay in 1933 to see the unemployed voluntarily constructing a lake rather than be idle. (Western Morning News)

Walter attended the Duke of Windsor's wedding and was in regular contact for several years. When the Duke and Duchess of Windsor visited England in 1956, they dined at his home.

King George VI and Queen Elizabeth introduced an active management. The King personally attended Council meetings. After the abdication in December, 1936, the new King and Queen toured the Duchy estates in Devon and Cornwall the following year. World War II enveloped the Duchy and on the night of 10/11 May 1941 bombs fell in Buckingham Gate and one side of the building collapsed. There were no casualties, and Duchy archives had been sent to Dartmoor Prison for the duration. The building was not finally restored until 1950. Another floor was added in the post-war rebuilding work.

The first Duke of Cornwall; effigy of the Black Prince on his tomb in Canterbury Cathedral. (Butlers, Chartham)

An early Prince of Wales: Charles, later King Charles I.

Under the management of the King the Duchy purchased an impressive amount of new acreage. Newton Park Estate, located just west of Bath, was bought in 1941. This estate included 4,797 acres. In the last year of the war Pawton estate in Cornwall, extending to 2,127 acres, was added to the Duchy's Cornish holdings. In the same year, the smaller St Kew estate, also in Cornwall, only 600 acres, was also purchased. In 1951 the Duchy bought from the Church Commissioners the manor of Duloe, over 2,900 acres. There were two further purchases in Cornwall, both in 1952, the Pencalenick estate of 918 acres and the 2,500 Arrallas estate. Within seven years the Duchy had increased by about 14,000 acres. Of this, just over 9,125 acres were concentrated in Cornwall. As never before, the Duchy's resources were concentrated in West Country grassland farming without any other productive investment. Much of the money for these later purchases came from the sale of Prince's Meadows, a part of Kennington just east of Waterloo Bridge, to the London County Council. This was not a sale which the Prince's Council wished to make, but they felt compelled by the pressure brought to bear.

The accession in 1953 of Queen Elizabeth brought a continued interest in Duchy affairs, and in its management. The post-war Duchy Secretary, Sir Patrick Kingsley, appointed in 1959, like Holtzmann, did not have a legal background. He was a farmer and spent his working life in the Duchy. Queen Elizabeth and Prince Philip visited all areas of the Duchy. Prince Philip had a special interest in the welfare of Scilly. They added to the Duchy's acreage in 1959 by purchasing the Daglingworth estate in Gloucestershire. Running to 1,247 acres, the estate lies further afield than any of the previous purchases by King George VI.

The post-war Duchy demonstrated an interest in the changing needs of dairy farmers. Increasingly, landlord and tenant formed a de facto partnership as the former made capital available for fixed improvements in return for higher rents. The Duchy, especially under the leadership of Prince Philip, was made aware of wider social responsibilities: effort and money were expended in the modernisation of dwellings.

The Duchy of 1960 was much like the Duchy of 1860. It had evolved into a south-western-based farming estate with assets concentrated in dairy farms. It possessed a large stock of cottages built in the nineteenth century for farm labourers, and had a small, but potentially important portfolio in the City. Its capital position had been eroded by years of inflation. Since the end of World War II governments have insisted that while no Duke existed or he was in minority, the net profits had to be paid to the Treasury. This hardly encouraged efficient management. Even more seriously, it meant that the Duchy had been unable to plough its profits back into the 'business' in those years when they were not needed to support an heir. When a trust fund is augmented with new capital then its real value gradually decreases as inflation erodes its base.

His Royal Highness, Charles Philip Arthur George is Prince of Wales, Duke of Cornwall and Rothesay, Earl of Chester and Carrick, Baron of Renfrew, Lord of the Isles, Knight of the Most Noble Order of the Garter, Knight of the Most Ancient and Noble Order of the Thistle, First Knight Grand Cross of the Most Honourable Order of the Bath and Aide de Camp to The Queen. Each of these titles is evocative of British history. Of them all, however, only one provides an income.

At the age of 21, on 15 April 1969, at what was an interesting moment in Duchy history, Prince Charles assumed his ancient inheritance and presided at his first Council meeting.

Edward Prince of Wales enjoyed horse riding; seen here riding on Dartmoor, from Holne waterworks to the Warren House Inn. With him is Major H. McCormick, Secretary to the Duchy. (Western Morning News)

CHAPTER 3

THE DUCHY TODAY

Martin Argles

Since 1969, changes have taken place in the Duchy which have had effects as far-reaching as those instigated by Prince Albert. To appreciate the reasons for this, one has to look at what has happened to landownership in this century. From the 1880s to the late 1930s there had been agricultural depression, relieved only during and just after World War I. The basic cause was the ability to import grain, meat and dairy products from the Americas, Canada, Australia and New Zealand. No longer did land in Britain have to support a growing population. Land values and rents declined and though many owners went on improving and repairing (as did the Duchy) up to World War I, the worst of the depression in the 1920s and 1930s brought expenditure by owners to a virtual halt, with many farmers going out of business and land in many cases commanding very low or even nil rents.

The tide started to turn with the formation of the Milk Marketing Board and other measures in the thirties but it was not until World War II that the government became committed to supporting agriculture, a commitment buttressed by the Agriculture Act of 1947. Farming became profitable, rents started to rise, particularly after 1958, and at that time grants were introduced for the improvement of buildings, dwellings and land. At the same time, the second agricultural revolution was starting; bigger and better machines replaced some expensive labour; tractors and combine harvesters, milking machines and parlours became universal; crop sprays were invented, fertiliser use extended, new varieties of cereals and grasses increased production.

All this meant that a huge new investment in farm equipment, and better housing for fewer but skilled men, was needed. Landowners and their tenants had to find money for this. For the owner, faced with very high taxation on income and an increasing spread of capital taxation, landowning had to become a business. Farms were amalgamated into larger units to take better advantage of new farming methods and money was often raised by the sale of surplus dwellings, of some farms to tenants and of farms with vacant possession. Few estates managed to modernise without selling land and without a complete re-appraisal of management policy.

A view of Cornish farmland looking towards Stoke Climsland, a typical stretch of a Duchy Cornish holding. (Western Morning News)

The Duchy, true to historical form, lagged behind. Active 'asset management' did not take place and central policy dictated that rents should remain low while tenants should be encouraged to repair and improve their farms, the Duchy being involved only in a limited way; the districts were managed by Land Stewards whose dealings with people were sensitive and benevolent but who exercised autonomous control with little reference to the Duchy as a whole. Significant purchases of land were made but these eroded the fund capital which might otherwise have been used for improvement.

While the foregoing relates to the country estates, Kennington was also absorbing capital while rent control ensured a low return on the housing stock.

Francis Anthony Gray succeeded Sir Patrick Kingsley as Secretary in 1972. As Treasurer of Christ Church, Oxford, for twenty years he had been involved in the rationalisation and management of its endowment estate. He

71

could see that the Duchy needed to be two things – first an investment fund to provide an income for the Duke and a secure capital base to provide that income in the future; second it must inevitably remain primarily a landowner, accepting that it must be a good owner with its property well maintained and improved. In essence the Duchy needed to treat itself and its landownership as a business and yet act fairly and reasonably with its tenants and others with whom it had dealings. This was never going to be an easy task.

Income was the first consideration. Gross income had to be increased to provide both for proper repair and management and for a larger net income for the Duke. Regular rent reviews on farms were instituted, though increases were not, to begin with, substantial. Other property was also examined to ensure that rents should be properly set – houses, playing fields, golf courses, garages, shops; and an appraisal of the value of moorings in the bed of tidal rivers in Devon and Cornwall (the fundus) was instituted. All this action was taken only just in time, since the rate of inflation was rising and in 1974 reached seventeen per cent, so that costs were rising fast.

On the capital side, the Duchy was invested almost entirely, Kennington apart, in farmland in the South West. The Secretary used to say that two-thirds of the Duke's income came out of the udder of a cow. No investment fund would base its investment solely on farms. Even the Oxford and Cambridge colleges, which had been endowed largely with land, had since 1945 diversified their investments. It was seen that the Duchy must, in a more limited way, also do so, in order that a spread of investment might better protect the income. There was also an urgent need for capital to be spent on farm and house improvement. Some cottages were without any modern conveniences, and a policy of encouraging farm tenants to spend their own money on improvements ran counter to normal landlord/tenant practice and would have been increasingly difficult to follow when tenants needed more and more capital for actual farming.

A few farms had been sold in the previous twenty years but this had been more than counter-balanced by purchases. Under the new regime the first farm was sold in 1975 when a tenant retired and the extra value with vacant possession could be realised. But the Duchy had large numbers of cottages on farms and in villages; farms carried less labour and needed fewer cottages and, even with rent control, cottages let direct to tenants became empty and could be sold at good prices without affecting the total investment or income to any degree.

One of the problems which the Secretary faced was that in London there was little information about the farms and assets in the districts. The Isles of Scilly, Dartmoor and Kennington were problem areas which needed separate consideration, but it was obvious that the greatest potential for easy realisation of assets (and indeed for increased income) lay in Cornwall and the counties east of Dartmoor, from Dorset up to Gloucestershire, forming the eastern district. So reports were commissioned in 1974 from two firms of chartered surveyors, one on Cornwall and one on the eastern district. Both reports identified assets which could or should be sold, suggested rent levels and indicated what expenditure was needed on the estates. They proved useful tools in formulating general policy.

Another thing which made easier the change of attitude from passive to positive management of assets, was that in 1976 and 1977 the Land Stewards in the country districts were due to retire. Positive management required much more work and it is not surprising that management had tended to be passive when, in the eastern district as an instance, the Land Steward with one assistant and a building surveyor was responsible for 27,000 acres of land in a hundred farms and numerous small lettings; Dartmoor, upward of three hundred let houses and cottages; much leasehold property; woodlands; and the waters of the Dart and Tamar.

New Land Stewards were appointed in Cornwall and the Isles of Scilly. Two innovations were made in the eastern district: Dartmoor, 3,000 acres in Devon and three manors in west Somerset were taken from it and formed again into a central district, thereby recognising the amount of work necessary, particularly on Dartmoor; the second innovation was to bring in a firm of land agents to manage the reduced eastern district, with the senior partner appointed as Land Steward. A firm had been used on the same basis in Kennington for many years.

New, younger Land Stewards, somewhat larger staffs and more definite policy control from London increased the impetus of management. Farming was in a boom period following Britain's accession to the European Community, rents and all property values had been rising fast and the Duchy was able to take advantage by sharp increases in rent (though levels still remained lower than on many estates), and profitable sales of surplus property and of land for development. At the same time, increasing amounts of those higher rents were spent on repairs to achieve a higher standard and large amounts of capital realised from sales were returned in new farm buildings and other improvements; also, when the Duke decided that he needed to have a house of his own, Duchy capital was available to buy it.

A base at Highgrove in Gloucestershire intensified the increasing interest the Duke was taking in the Duchy. While in the Royal Navy he had little time to spare, and visits took the form of whistle-stop tours to meet as many tenants as possible, in a rather formal way. By 1980, visits to farms had become relaxed and informal. A typical day would embrace lunch on one farm, tea on another, looking at buildings on a third and crops on a fourth, with a quick unplanned dart into the village shop. Farm men, stone-wallers, people in the road or their gardens got a wave or a quip in passing.

Three other changes were made in Gray's time as Secretary. The first concerned *Bona Vacantia* – the estates of those dying intestate and without next of kin. In Cornwall these revert to the Duke rather than to the crown as

The western region of British Rail named a Paddington-Penzance express of the late 1950s
The Royal Duchy – *seen here steaming out of Paddington.* (Sport & General)

is the case elsewhere. Most of such estates are small but can sometimes include a house or other property. It seemed wrong to the Duke that his personal income should benefit from such windfalls and the idea was conceived of setting up a Benevolent Fund into which the proceeds would be put and from which donations could be made to charitable organisations primarily in the South West and to a large extent in Cornwall.

The second change concerned the Prince's Council, an advisory body of eminent men consulted by the Duke and the Secretary on matters of weight and policy. With a young and interested Duke, younger men replaced some of those who had served for a long time and John Higgs was appointed a member for his wide knowledge of farming and rural affairs. The third change was the setting up of a pension fund for Duchy staff. Hitherto pensions had been paid, as needed, from income.

In 1981 Gray retired as Secretary and his place was taken by John Higgs.

Outside the Duchy this might have seemed an odd choice. He was in his late fifties and had spent most of a varied career in universities and the Food and Agriculture Organisation of the United Nations. But he had proved himself an able administrator (he and Gray had been on the Estates Committee of Oxford University together and he had been Estates Bursar of Exeter College); his main interests lay in the sphere of rural development; he had been concerned with estate management, and he was a practical farmer. Further, he had a very wide acquaintance of experts in all these fields. A strong rapport was quickly established, with a Duke interested particularly in conservation and rural employment and concerned that the Duchy should be in the forefront of landowners facing these problems.

Between 1981 and his death in June 1986, Higgs master-minded the evolution of the Duchy started by his predecessor. He received a knighthood in March 1986 in recognition of his service. The commercial approach to the management of all Duchy assets was intensified, investment policy clarified and the administration of the Duchy overhauled. This approach aimed not only further to strengthen the financial base but to allow the Duchy to face its responsibilities to Dartmoor and the Isles of Scilly and on all the estates to take various initiatives in conservation and employment.

A formal investment strategy was adopted by the Council in 1984. The policy of increased sales was by then bearing considerable fruit. It had already

Middle Town, St Martin's, Isles of Scilly, showing the narrow fields on the far hillside. The off-islands of Scilly have given the Duchy particular concern in recent years. (Molly Gill)

been decided to reduce the acreage owned in the South West, particularly in Cornwall, and a presumption was adopted that farms and land which became vacant would be sold or, if of reasonable quality or part of a block of farms, would if possible be relet by moving a tenant from a poorer farm which could be sold. It had always been Duchy practice to relet farms to sons and the act of 1976 which gave a statutory right of succession reinforced this, so that opportunities for sale were recognised not to be large and the switch of investment was gradual.

Kennington was a different problem. The letting of houses and flats had become unattractive to private landlords, rents showing a very low return on capital value, but values with possession being high. A decision to sell property in Kennington was taken in 1977. Again it was recognised that this would be a gradual process, that problems would arise where vacancies occurred in part only of blocks, that existing tenants must not be disturbed by selling over their heads and that meanwhile improvement of sub-standard property must continue.

Nevertheless, both in Kennington and the country districts, the number of properties and their diversity ensured that a steady stream of sales took place and a large fund was being accumulated on the Stock Exchange for re-investment. The 1984 strategy decided that while it would be prudent always to keep a portfolio of stocks and shares to buttress the land holding, capital receipts in excess should be re-invested in commercial urban property and in arable farmland. By the summer of 1986, surplus capital had been re-invested in urban property in London and various towns in southern England; and in over two thousand acres of farmland in the vale of Glamorgan and Lincolnshire.

The purchase in Wales was made at the instigation of the Duke who felt that, as Prince of Wales, he should own some land in the principality. Boverton comprises 700 acres, half of which was let. The other half was bought with possession and, a departure from normal practice, is occupied in partnership with a young Welsh farmer, rather than let to a tenant.

The organisation of the Duchy can be compared, though far from exactly, with that of a company. At the head is the Duke (the chairman). He is advised by the Prince's Council (non-executive directors) headed by the Lord Warden of the Stannaries (vice-chairman). The Secretary is appointed by the Duke, is normally a member of the Council and is in the position of managing director. He in turn delegates management powers to Land Stewards in five districts (divisions of the company) and has a staff at head office in Buckingham Gate. The Duchy is governed in what it can and cannot do by the Management Acts of Parliament.

The Council meets formally three times a year but its members are called on for advice by the Duke and the Secretary at any time. Particularly is this true of the office holders who, apart from the Lord Warden, are the Receiver General (overseeing investment and the use of money) and the Attorney

76

General dealing with the legal problems inherent in the Duchy's peculiar position. The day-to-day legal work is done by the Solicitor to the Duchy; formerly he was an employee but with the increasing complexity of the law and the much larger workload of conveyancing, he is now a partner in a London firm of solicitors which carries out the work. He is in constant touch with the Attorney General. A recent innovation has been the appointment of specialist members to the Council. While there has always been a member from Cornwall, aware of feeling and happenings in the Duchy, two recent appointments have been a farmer from Exmoor and an expert in urban property.

Head office includes an assistant secretary and supporting secretarial staff and three departments of Accounts, Property Services and Records. Because most Duchy property was granted by charter, title deeds in the modern sense are non-existent and ownership is evidenced by accurate estate maps kept by the Clerk Surveyor who is accountable for all information on property transactions. All conveyances and other legal documents are enrolled in the Duchy records which are the responsibility of the Record Clerk and are themselves a fascinating and valuable archive.

The district offices are in Kennington, Bath (eastern), Bradninch near Exeter (central), Liskeard, Cornwall (western) and St Mary's (Isles of Scilly). Except in the Isles of Scilly, the Land Stewards are chartered surveyors with qualified assistants and building surveyors making up teams of land and property managers. This structure had evolved from Prince Albert's reforms. The Management Acts dated from the 1860s and many of the accounting, recording and reporting procedures were rooted in the same era. Much duplication of work was taking place in the districts and at head office and one of John Higgs' first actions was to set up an internal working party to review all the office procedures. Gradually these are being modernised; computerised accounting and estate record keeping are being introduced and budgets and forecasts, both for revenue and capital, are improving the management of money.

The idea of a new Management Act had been mooted in the seventies; one was finally achieved in 1982. Under the 1863 Act, each Duke controlled the revenue and had power to buy and sell land but the capital arising from sales or returned to the estates in improvement was, effectively, in trust and could not be spent personally by the Duke. While that remained the position, the use of capital was severely restricted by the Acts. What the new Act has done is to give the Duchy greater flexibility in the use of its capital.

There have also been some other legal changes. The Duchy, as part of the crown, is only subject to an act of Parliament if that act specifically so provides. It is subject, for instance, to the Agricultural Holdings Acts but not to compulsory purchase. It may sound attractive to be outside the law, but in management terms it causes difficulties. The Duchy has to abide by the spirit of the law but cannot benefit from the formal appeal procedures

available to the private citizen against decisions made under that law. Recent changes have made the Duchy subject to the Rent Acts and to parts of the Town and Country Planning Acts. Until the latter change was made, the Duchy could not obtain a formal planning permission for development of land before it sold; that made sales difficult to organise.

It is on the estates in particular that John Higgs's influence and the partnership of thinking with the Duke has wrought change. A central policy for the Duchy as a whole, concentrating more decision-taking in the hands of the Secretary rather than in those of individual Land Stewards, the broadening of the capital base, better control of capital expenditure on improvements, increasing revenue and more accurate forecasting of what revenue would be available – the whole approach to the Duchy and landowning as a business enabled initiatives to be taken and problems to be tackled reflecting the other side of the Duchy, that of trying to be a responsible landowner.

Like most estates, the Duchy has property which will show a return, either in income or capital appreciation or both, as an investment and also property which will not do so but which cannot just be forgotten or disposed of. Responsible ownership must include carrying the burdens of such property and trying to make the best of them for the people who live there and for whatever other purpose is appropriate.

The two areas in the Duchy which were tackled with skill and energy by Higgs, with the Duke's encouragement and participation, were Dartmoor and the Isles of Scilly. Dartmoor is a National Park but also provides the livelihood of farm tenants. After an initial report by the Land Steward and a great deal of consultation with every interested party, a management report was produced in 1983, setting out the guidelines of how the Duchy intended to manage the estate, balancing the interests of the farms with the aims of the National Park. Such a report cannot solve all the inevitable conflicts of interest but it provides a framework for consultation and compromise.

The Isles of Scilly are entirely owned by the Duchy, though Tresco is let on a long lease to the Dorrien Smith family and Hugh Town on St Mary's was largely sold in 1950. Ownership had included involvement in local services – the harbour, the airport and so on. Here a report was commissioned on the future of the islands, and a great deal of time and effort was spent on discussing with the Island Council their acceptance of some of the public responsibilities, in producing a scheme for taking mains electricity to the off-islands and in involving agencies from the EEC Commission to the Countryside Commission and the Nature Conservancy Council in the future of the islands.

Perhaps the most interesting results of the partnership between Duke and Secretary were the various initiatives on the estates. If something sparked an

The restored 10 Buckingham Gate in 1950. Duchy Secretaries now have a flat on the top floor. (Planet News)

interest in the Duke's mind, the Secretary knew the people to talk to and involve and was able to help convert the idea to reality. Until this time, the Duchy had adopted what is known as a low profile; publicity was shunned and though there were the inevitable bits of bad news which were seized on by the press, there had been no attempt either to invite interest by press releases of good news or to encourage press or television coverage of Duchy affairs. That was consciously changed, recognising and accepting the risk that increased awareness of the Duchy could also bring bad publicity, and more articles and television or radio coverage of the Duchy have appeared than ever before, including a 50 minute television programme prepared with full co-operation, and (of course) this book.

There was more purpose in this than being open about the Duchy. What the Duke did was news and if he instigated ideas to be carried into practice on Duchy estates, then they would get publicity which would help promote them among others who owned land and to the public. One of the Duke's early interests was the wide subject of conservation; and then came concern about unemployment generally and in the countryside, and about architecture and the need to involve local communities in what was designed, built or improved. These strands have been woven together with great success in the Duchy to its own benefit and that of a wider audience.

Conservation has always been practised consciously or unconsciously by landowners and farmers. Where damage has been done by modern farming methods in the dash for better production it has often been through ignorance of effects. The Duchy effort has been consciously to encourage tenants to practise conservation on farms – for the improvement of landscape and wildlife habitat – and to plant trees and do other work of improvement itself. Help and advice has come from the Farming and Wildlife Advisory Groups in all counties; surveys by the Nature Conservancy Council; multi-discipline surveys of a few individual farms and of the important historical features on the manor of Inglescombe outside Bath; from the Game Conservancy. A definite allocation from gross income goes into conservation work of all kinds, including stone walling and the use of good materials in repair and new buildings. Two advisory groups for the Duchy have been set up – on archaeology and on wildlife and the landscape, consisting of experts who as a whole or as individuals can advise on general or specific problems.

Contractors are used in many cases for conservation work but, particularly where the work is inappropriate for them or would not normally be done at all, volunteers of the British Trust for Conservation Volunteers and Manpower Services Commission teams are called in.

The most significant contribution to employment has been the workshop scheme under which, and in conjunction with the Council for Small Industries in Rural Areas, redundant buildings on farms or in villages are converted (or in some cases new buildings erected) and let to self-employed people starting or extending businesses which range from traditional crafts to

The informal style of Prince Charles's visits: Tavistock, a former Stannary town, in 1983.
(Western Morning News)

computers. By the summer of 1986, 40 workshops had been created supplying 80 jobs, and a further 50 workshops were in the pipeline.

The interest in architecture and the community has resulted not only in the employment of architects for new farmhouses and for some special buildings but also in a village study at Curry Mallet involving the whole community, and in Kennington. Here, Newquay House, built in 1932, contains seventy-six flats. The policy of gradual sale in Kennington poses particular difficulties in a case like that. The Duchy wanted to sell the flats but since the building needed refurbishment it was difficult to sell them piecemeal as they became vacant and there is an existing community of tenants to be considered as well as twenty-three vacant flats. The Duchy commissioned a community architects' study and the solution accepted was to sell the whole block to a housing trust which borrows the purchase money from a building society, leases the block to a co-operative of the tenants and refurbishes the whole block with aid from the housing corporation. The Duchy realises its investment but the community is preserved and manages its own block of flats.

The Duchy had in the past several home farms in hand to offer example and advice to tenants. By the seventies only one remained, at Stoke Climsland in Cornwall. This was not, like most Duchy farms, a dairy farm and advice was available to tenants from the Ministry of Agriculture and elsewhere. The original purpose of the farm had disappeared and, as a home farm in the traditional sense, it was a long way from the Duke's home. When Cornwall County Council wanted a teaching farm, the home farm was closed and let to the Council. At the same time, in 1984, a search was started for a new home farm near Highgrove.

In early 1985, Broadfield Farm, 420 acres just the other side of Tetbury came onto the market and was bought. The 300 farming acres at Highgrove had until then been farmed under contract by nearby farmers. After the harvest of 1985, all the 720 acres were combined into one farm with a manager. The aim is to run the farm as a commercial farm with due regard to conservation – planting of trees, clearance of ponds, restoration of a meadow have all started and one eighty acre block has been set aside as an experiment in organic crop production.

While all these initiatives are important, it should not be forgotten that the Duchy is and remains primarily a landowner which lets its property to tenants. Ownership now comprises over 70,000 acres of farmland in nine counties; 50,000 acres in the Forest of Dartmoor; 3,000 acres of woodland; 1,500 dwellings in London and in the country; office and shop investments; a large number of small leased properties – garages, school sites, golf courses and so on; 230 miles of foreshore and 14,000 acres of fundus.

The Duchy also had the right of presentation (that is the right to appoint the incumbent) to twenty-five livings. Due to schemes of unification, the number is currently twenty-one and in most cases the right is taken in turn with other patrons.

There are 240 farms ranging from 10 acre holdings on the Isles of Scilly to 900 acres in Dorset and 1,600 acres on Dartmoor. The farm tenants are still the backbone of the Duchy and relations with these and other tenants are of vital importance. Amalgamation of farm units has virtually ceased and farms, both large and small, have recently been relet, normally by advertisement only within the Duchy. Tenant relations are fostered by biennial lunches or dinners in each district, by getting groups of tenants together to discuss problems, by encouraging tenants' shoots on the large blocks of land, by normal visits by Land Stewards to farms and by interest in families and the training of children likely to succeed to tenancies.

It would be wrong, however, to imply that the Duchy is perfect. No organisation could be changed in outlook and approach as radically and as quickly as the Duchy has been without causing disquiet among its tenants

The company of Princess Diana on Prince Charles's tours has even more enhanced his popularity; again Tavistock in 1983. (Western Morning News)

Modern investment in Kennington; the riverfront development by Southbank Estates Ltd on land leased from the Duchy; right to left, Camelford, Tintagel and Alembic Houses. (Duchy)

and others who rely on it or see what it is doing. Nor is it always easy for them (or indeed for those working for the Duchy) to reconcile the twin approaches of commercial reality and responsible stewardship. The past was comfortable, farming was generally prosperous and tenants very much their own masters. For farming nationally, the sudden change in 1984 from a policy of forty years' expansion to one of constriction, quotas and falling profits was traumatic. In the Duchy that has coincided with the last stages of bringing rents up to national levels and a more commercial approach to general management.

The Duchy may be seen by some tenants as mainly responsible for the difficulties they face, whereas national policies are primarily to blame. Apprehension exists that at such a time the new commercial policy of the

Duchy will mean continuing rent increases against the trend and little help for those in financial difficulties. Such feelings do not give sufficient weight to the other side of the Duchy – responsibility in ownership. That means much time and trouble being given to those under financial strain and very careful appraisal of what rents are appropriate in the varying circumstances of different farms. Good relations with tenants are one of the agricultural landlord's best assets – a view strongly held by the Duke. Samuel Johnson said 'A man, Sir, should keep his friendship in constant repair'. That is a continuing aim of Duchy management.

The Duchy is stronger today than twenty years ago. Its investment is better spread, its farms better equipped and repaired, its other property no longer poor. It is not so dependent on farm rents, which may be static or fall, for its income. But all concerned with it, whether as tenants, managers or outsiders, still have to come completely to terms with its present form.

CHAPTER FOUR

CORNWALL

James Mildren

If the association with the Duchy has been one of the most permanent features in the history of Cornwall, then it must be balanced with the long periods during which the Duchy has been not in a single duke's possession, but in that of the parent crown. The twentieth century has been a notable exception and not merely for the personal interest taken by the Dukes in their Cornish domain.

The Dukes inherited an estate largely settled for them by the activities of Richard, king of the Romans, brother of King Henry III, and Earl of Cornwall. It was to Lostwithiel, where stood both the Duchy Palace, created by the earls, and Restormel Castle, also their creation, that the charismatic war hero the Black Prince repaired, to establish himself as ruler of his Duchy. If there is any tendency to believe that medieval administration could not compare with modern methodology, then the Black Prince should have put such thought to shame. Simple it might have seemed, effective it most certainly was. The Black Prince inherited a Custos Portum, or Havener, as 'Keeper of the waters of the King's ports in Cornwall'.

The Prince's man, appointed, in fact, a month before Edward III conferred the Duchy upon his son, was Thomas Fitz Henry Le Botiller. A true and loyal servant he proved himself. Thomas combined his job with that of weigher of tin at the Duchy coinages as well as being keeper of the dread tinners' gaol in the Palace at Lostwithiel. That Duchy Palace, the late Cornish historian Charles Henderson informs us, was a small-scale model of the great palace at Westminster, and it comprised a hall, exchequer, prison and government offices. The Palace existed until the eighteenth century, adorning the little quayside at Lostwithiel, but only a few fragments of its former glory now remain to excite the imagination.

Thomas Fitz Henry's appointment set the pattern for the long tradition of the Duchy association with south-east Cornwall in particular. The Havener was rewarded with ten marks a year plus a robe at Christmas, or another mark in lieu: there were also gifts of venison from the royal chase.

Many distinguished men occupied the post of Havener after Fitz Henry's death in 1373: they included Thomas Asshenden of Dartmouth, Richard

Fowey, early base for the Haveners of the Duchy who collected the harbour dues. The harbour is now controlled by a harbour board but the picture illustrates the modern problem with yacht moorings. (Western Morning News)

Hampton who combined the role with that of keeper of the Duchy castle at Tintagel, Thomas Chaucer, the king's chief butler, and Thomas Treffry, a Fowey merchant whose family home survives in that town to this day. Quite the most sinister and notorious of Haveners was the last, Sir James Tirrell, MP for Cornwall in 1477, a Duchy Steward, and a man whom many historians implicate in the murder of the young princes in the Tower.

Income from tin-rich Cornwall alone in the middle of the fourteenth century accounted for about one-sixth of the Duchy's total estimated revenue. The Havener was responsible for the collection of rents from the fishing ports, fines from merchants, wreck of the sea and royal fish. Cornish ports paying dues included Fowey and Polruan, Marazion and Mousehole, Penzance and Newlyn, St Just, Porthminster, Porthgwarra and Penberth (called Londysend), the ports of Kerrier, Trigg and Porthia – the latter, it is thought, situated between Godrevy and St Ives Island. Porthia, of course, means the port or harbour of St Ia, whose name has been changed over the years into St Ives. These, with Sutton Water, later to become Plymouth, reveal the extensive interests of the Duchy – though the dues do not imply possession by the Duchy of the ports themselves.

It was Fowey which took pride of place as headquarters of the Havener, conveniently close to the Duchy Palace at Lostwithiel, where the wine cellars were often stocked with vintages from Spain or Portugal, Crete or Gascony – 'the prise of wines and the royal customs in the ports of Cornwall'. The Duke was entitled to a tun of wine from ships of less than twenty tons, and two from the larger vessels. Business was brisk. Spain sent fruit and iron, and its ships returned laden with Cornish tin; the Gascons came for cheese and fish, tin and hides; the Bretons brought in linen cloth and canvas, salt and onions, and departed with Cornish woollen 'straits', narrow strips of cloth.

Inland, the pastoral activities of the Duchy's possessions in this outpost, further from London than the ports of Brittany, were enshrined in seventeen manors – the antiqua maneria whose names still sound melodious in the modern ear. Rillaton, Stoke Climsland, Helstone in Trigg, Liskeard, Tybesta, Tywarnhaile, Talskiddy (or Talskedy), Penmayne, Calstock, Trematon, Restormel, Penkneth, Penlyne, Tewington, Helston in Kerrier, Tintagel and Moresk, in whose glades Tristan and Isolde may have roamed.

The Dukes, few of whom followed the Black Prince's example, continued to be absentee landlords, although the estate was largely administered on the lines he had established. Dr A. L. Rowse sums up the situation with exquisite clarity in his *Westcountry Stories*.

> Politicians and royal favourites came and went at Westminster, dynasties changed: there was civil war and battles raged upon English soil. Still the administration of the Duchy went on, the most permanent feature in the landscape of society in Cornwall, the diurnal routine of its tenants living close to the soil, undisturbed, unchanging, or changing slowly only with the slow tides of the ages.
>
> One derives the impression of an institution tenacious and conservative, one that neither relaxed its right nor vexed its tenantry with new and unexpected impositions; the fines it took upon leases remained stable over long periods. At bottom, it was the age-long reverence for custom and tradition, the bed-rock of human history, that prevailed and ruled in and through the Duchy.

The Duchy of Cornwall was, it seemed, custom-made for the shrewd and reforming zeal of the workaholic Prince Albert. It was an age marked by the opening, performed by the Prince himself, of Brunel's great rail bridge across the divide – the River Tamar – in 1859. Effectively, it marked the beginning of the end of Cornish isolation from the remainder of the kingdom: it is not without significance that Albert gave his name to this towering structure.

It also coincided with an awakening interest by the Dukes themselves, beginning with King Edward VII (born in 1841) and continuing through King George V (who visited Cornwall as Duke in 1909) to King Edward VIII, upon whose succession the Duchy reverted back to the crown until the accession of Queen Elizabeth II and the natural emergence of her heir, Prince Charles, as the rightful Duke of Cornwall. He, quite spontaneously, offered a quarter of the income from the Duchy to the nation.

The huge advances in communication have made Cornwall increasingly accessible, and not merely to dukes. That, allied to the desire of successive members of the royal family to mingle more closely with their subjects, has created changes undreamed of by Queen Victoria. By yacht and train Edward VII and his Queen and Duchess, Alexandra, visited Cornwall.

Upon becoming heir apparent in 1901, the then Duke of York, later to

A distant view of Kit Hill in east Cornwall which has been given by the Duke to Cornwall County Council for development as a country park. (Western Morning News)

become King George V, also became Duke of Cornwall. Could it have been, as one of Queen Mary's biographers expressed her belief, that the title was still, even then, an irrelevancy: 'What mattered more were its vast estates which produced substantial income.'

When the young and handsome David, heir-apparent, later to become King Edward VIII, succeeded to the Duchy title in May 1910 on the death of his grandfather, his sole income was said to have been a weekly shilling of pocket money doled out at the Naval College: at a stroke he had become one of the richest men in England – though his father's advisors administered the funds.

In May 1921 the young Prince appeared at Launceston Castle to receive his dues, the origins of which are lost in the mist of time. From the manor of Cabillia – one grey cloak: from the Mayor and Commonalty of the borough of Launceston – one hundred shillings and a pound of pepper: from the manor of Elerky in Veryan – a brace of greyhounds: from the manor or barton of Penrose in the parish of St Tudy – a pair of gilt spurs: from the manor of Clymselond, otherwise Stoke Climsland – a salmon spear and a carriage of wood daily. And so it continues. From Battons, or Battens in the parish of North Hill – one pound of cummin (for spiced hare, perhaps); from the manors of Swannacott and Week St Mary – a goatskin mantle: from the manor of Trevalga – one pair of white gloves.

It was the Duke's place to acknowledge the fees by presenting each donor with a white rod and stating: 'I confirm you, and those you represent, tenants, and give you and them peacable and quiet seizen and possession of the manors, lands and tenements which you hold or represent according to custom.'

In December 1937 King George VI received his dues, and in November 1973 his grandson, Prince Charles, was accorded the time-honoured custom. The objects presented now stand in the Lawrence House Museum at Launceston. Prince Charles retained one shilling (pre-decimalisation) and the spurs. The greyhounds, which rejoiced in the names of Whisky and Soda, were especially loaned for the occasion, and were presented by Lt Col (now Sir Arscott) Molesworth-St Aubyn, whose father, the late Sir John, had made a similar presentation to King George VI in 1937.

Readers will, however, seek in vain for more than a passing reference to the Duchy of Cornwall from Prince Charles's uncle, the late Duke of Windsor. His memoirs, A King's Story, contain but a fleeting glimpse of what, by all accounts, were happy visits to Cornwall.

The recollection of those days are contained in greater outline in the auto-biography of Canon L. Martin Andrews entitled Canon's Folly.

Martin Andrews was appointed as rector of Stoke Climsland, one of the livings in the gift of the Duke of Cornwall, by the Duke in 1922, after a chance meeting between the two men at Buckingham Gate. He moved into a large and sparsely furnished, rambling old rectory and, with his boundless

Canon Martin Andrews, sometime rector of Stoke Climsland and a personal friend of Edward Prince of Wales, photographed in 1968. (Western Morning News)

energy and endless good humour, transformed a quiet backwater into a thriving and lively centre, where the Duke became a frequent visitor. For a period during the 1920s and 1930s the old rectory became a focus for Duchy activity in Cornwall, a place where the future King Edward VIII felt at ease, and free to share his troubled thoughts on the unemployment situation – thoughts which were, in fact, to be transmuted into action by Martin Andrews and his lifelong devoted companion, Vincent Curtis.

Encouraged by the Prince, they began a horticultural scheme at the rectory farm which mopped up fifty-two men and women from the unemployment register. It became a byword for caring action, and the Duchy

Secretaries of the time, Walter Peacock and Hilgie McCormack, played an important advisory role. The scheme attracted widescale interest and the author S. C. Williamson was to describe it thus: 'Of the many schemes to settle unemployed men on the land this has been one of the most successful.'

The young and popular Prince had set a new style in relationships between the Duchy and its tenants. Martin Andrews, born in 1886, continues to endear himself to royalty and commoners alike, though now long retired from active fray. He celebrated his 100th birthday on 24 September 1986.

Stoke Climsland rectory, no longer owned by the Duke, is far from being a typical example of the Duchy buildings, which are more sensibly geared to functional rather than aesthetic taste.

One architect who found employ in the Duchy's service in the early years of this century was Sir Albert Richardson, a journalist's son, who later became President of the Royal Academy from 1954 until 1956 (in which year he was knighted). Richardson, a leading figure on the Georgian group, lived in the manner of a Georgian gentleman surrounded by period furniture at his lovely home in Ampthill. Apart from restoration work at Tor Royal and the reconstruction of the Duchy Hotel at Princetown in 1912, Richardson remodelled what remained of the sumptuous and historic mansion of Whiteford, Stoke Climsland, incorporating what was possible into the Prince of Wales' home farm. Whiteford, built in 1775 for Sir William Call, son of a nabob returned from India, with the help of local craftsmen and an Italian or two drafted in for the stucco decoration, was pulled down in 1913. Much of the worked granite was used in the new Duchy Manor Farm house. The spirit of the often controversial and delight-fully eccentric Richardson lingers on in the Manor Farm at Stoke Climsland.

In 1984, the home farm itself was leased to Cornwall County Council as an agricultural training establishment.

Without doubt the most interesting of the castles of the Duke of Cornwall is at Trematon for there, within the ruins, Benjamin Tucker, a Duchy Surveyor-General, had erected in the early nineteenth century a splendid castellated mansion. Not, perhaps, as picturesque as Restormel Castle or as proud and bold as Launceston, Trematon is their equal in strategic place-ment. Its recent tenants have included Lord Caradon, a member of the famous West Country Foot family, who distinguished himself as a post-war British diplomat. Sir Francis Drake also used Trematon as a store for the treasure looted from the Spanish on his voyage around the world.

The Duchy owns much – a golf course, old barns now being converted to useful enterprise in association with the Council for Small Industries in Rural Areas. It possesses around seventy-five farms in Cornwall, with an average size of 230 acres. Most of the holdings are on Grade 3 land, with some grade 2 – a generally typical Cornish farming category. Dairy farming predomi-nates, with the remainder of farms producing beef, sheep and corn with fairly limited cash crops, principally potatoes.

However, there is some specialisation, notably in the fertile region of the Tamar valley, famed for its early strawberry crops and especially for its spring flowers. The river Tamar, the natural boundary between Cornwall and Devon, curls a path through a highly mineralised zone including, at Devon Great Consols, the area which produced in the 1850s around two-thirds of the world's entire copper production. It combines mineral wealth with sylvan beauty. Nature has restored the steep hillsides once blanched from the blast of noxious fumes from the stubby mine chimneys and covered with mundic, the rock from which arsenic was obtained – to treat the boll weevil pest in the cotton fields of America. Today, one of the valley enter-prises owned by the Duchy exports not miners, but golden daffodils to all corners of the earth.

Dan and Peter du Plessis, brothers, specialise in bulbs at Marsh Farm, Landulph. They grow the crop on about sixteen acres of land. 'We have the largest number of varieties of any commercial grower in the country', said Dan du Plessis. 'We grow just over seven hundred different varieties.'

The bulbs sell all over the south-west of England, but a retail catalogue ensures that du Plessis bulbs go all over the world. 'USA, Canada, Australia, New Zealand, Tasmania . . . ' the countries, of course, to which the miners of Victorian times emigrated, 'Russia – we've had an order this year –

The river Tamar which separates Devon from Cornwall, showing the twisted chimney of Gawton arsenic mine and works. (Western Morning News)

Germany, Czechoslovakia, Italy, Portugal. Basically, it is worldwide.' Commercially, the yellow daffodil is the most popular, the yellow large cup and the yellow trumpet are favourites. The retail market is more varied, with many types in demand, from daffodils with short, five-inch stems to the tall pseudo-narcissi type.

The farm does not breed its own varieties, but the brothers buy seedling stocks which are registered internationally with the Royal Horticultural Society, if they prove satisfactory. The Russians seek the named varieties, names which reflect the character of the area in which they are grown. Kingsand and Cawsand daffodils will cross Europe to grace many a Russian table.

Dan du Plessis was born at Marsh Farm. 'My father came here in 1920, as manager to the Duke of Windsor when it was a poultry unit, and took the tenancy in 1928.' Dan became a joint tenant shortly before his father's death in 1944, and now runs the business with his brother, Peter. 'We do open our gardens to the public. Usually, the flowers start blooming around the seventh and eighth of January each year – the pre-cooled daffodils which have been in a cold store at 9°C.' The bulbs flower through until the middle of May, sometimes longer, culminating with the Tamar Valley double white variety. Whites, yellows, pinks, reds, orange-petalled varieties flaunt their beauty down to the banks of the river Tamar at Neal Point – an amazing spectacle, especially in April.

There is beauty of another kind to be found on the Duchy farm at Kingston, Stoke Climsland, where Kevin Uglow is a fourth-generation tenant. He has been involved with the county Farming and Wildlife Advisory Group, in which Prince Charles is taking a keen and personal interest.

'FWAG is there to promote a joint venture of farming and wildlife as an advisory group. It is fair to say its aim is to promote conservation without confrontation,' said Kevin Uglow, 'between the farming community and the conservationists. Very much in support of farmers and to give them help, and free advice, because we now have our own county adviser.' Mr Uglow said he found that conservation and farming went hand in hand: 'They work very well together, not just at Stoke Climsland. The same principles can be applied no matter where you are.'

'With the Prince being a very busy man, we don't see him taking a personal interest in each and every farm, but when my wife and I were winners last year of the FWAG competition in Cornwall, Jack Hickish (the Cornwall land agent) was very keen to send a report to London for the Prince's attention, and we did receive a communication of congratulation from him. So he does take a very great interest in what is going on.'

The Uglow family have been tenants through four generations and Kevin hopes that his seven-year-old son, Paul, will one day want to carry on with the tradition. 'Farming is, in a lot of ways, easier than it was in my grandfather, or great-grandfather's day, because of the mechanisation we've got, but on top of that we do have our problems especially with the economic problems. We live under much more pressure. Our pace of life has quickened considerably, from the days of the horses. We need to be rather more technical. But the traditional farming is still there – very much so, and I think that, in the future, is going to keep these places together.'

Kingston's 247 acres is slightly larger than the average for a Duchy farm in Cornwall. 'Being a Duchy tenant doesn't bring immediate privileges. It's rather nice, though, to be, shall we say, associated with a member of the royal family, just through the connection of being a tenant to His Royal Highness. We've found that he is definitely concerned about his tenants, and shows a genuine concern, which we find rather pleasing – and occasionally he does make private visits to his tenants, so we do see him from time to time.

'One of the great qualities of Prince Charles, in line with other members of the royal family, is that he immediately puts you at ease – an absolutely marvellous quality. He knows an awful lot about farming, and I think that if he had the time, he would like to spend much more of it with his tenants and his farming business. I think other duties prevent him from doing a little more of what he would like to do. I'm certain he enjoys himself when he comes down.'

Mr Venning Davey has been farming the Duchy properties at Bodriggan and Hendra, near Bodmin, since 1953. Farming, he believes, is getting a lot more difficult. The pressures? 'Financial, because for the first time in my life everything we produce nobody seems to want. Ecological, because we are worried about nitrates, slurry – the whole picture has changed, from being the good boys who feed the country to being the bad boys who are polluting everything and growing stuff nobody wants. That is the image. I'm not saying that's fact.'

It is an image which instant media attention, focussed upon the farmer, has produced not merely in Cornwall, but nationally as well as from a European consumer standpoint.

'I could take a camera and show that things haven't changed or, equally, I could take a camera and show that farmers are raping the countryside. It's so easy, whichever you want to do. At the moment, some sections of the media want to portray the bad part, but what we are doing practically is being very conscious of conservation on farms, and taking conservation advice through the Farming and Wildlife Group. Good news, sadly, doesn't make headlines: if the farmer's effluent goes into the river that's headlines, but if he plants a thousand trees, that's not printed.'

Venning Davey would, he says, prefer to be an owner-occupier of a farm: 'But I feel rather proud of the fact – and I think we all are – that we farm under the Duchy, and that Prince Charles takes such an interest in the whole industry and in his tenants individually. Genuinely interested. A lot of tenant-landlords have a good relationship but ours is a little bit different, because every two years we have a dinner and Prince Charles is there. And what wife doesn't like being taken out to dinner!

'It is always a relaxed, informal evening. My wife was sitting next to him and we were chatting to him at this year's dinner. He had just come back from Japan, and had a terrific programme. He said that one of the hardest things was to get people to relax. If you start to think about it, everyone is so het up because they are being presented for the first time and his job is to relax them. That's hard work.'

Mr Davey originally farmed only Hendra until, in 1968, the 150 acres of Bodriggan were 'tacked on' to Hendra's 110 acres. It is said that there is a Hendra, the old homestead, in almost every Cornish parish. Most of the land is grade 3, and he runs a hundred Friesian cattle and a beef unit.

The Duchy of Cornwall also owns over two thousand acres of woodlands in Cornwall, which are primarily stocked with conifers. Most of them have been planted in the past quarter-century, principally Douglas fir and larch, although conifers are not novelties in Cornwall. The Prince himself has taken a lead in the planting of more trees, with an emphasis on producing a greater variety of trees in these plantations. The coniferisation of much of Britain's woodlands has led to protests, especially from the conservationist lobby, of an over-indulgence in commercial forestry at the expense of scenic value and

Prince Charles inspected timber on a visit to the Duchy woodlands' sawmills at Restormel, near Lostwithiel, in 1970. (Western Morning News)

wildlife populations whose habitat may have been adversely affected by a lack of real variety.

The Prince, visiting the Restormel area with Princess Diana in 1984, expressed himself firmly on the subject, and promised more hardwoods in Duchy forests. Change cannot occur overnight, but the new policy for more hardwood planting is being implemented by head forester Brian Wilson and his staff at the Duchy Woodlands Estate headquarters at Lostwithiel. More hardwood trees were planted on the Duchy estate in 1986 than ever before. Ladock Woods, the Seaton valley (near Looe), Stoke Climsland have all benefitted from the policy change as a mixture of cherry, sweet chestnut, lime and beech trees have been introduced.

The conifers, however, do produce a relatively quick return, and the soft-woods have provided employment at the Duchy sawmill at Lostwithiel for upwards of twenty men. The conifer woodlands also provide some splendid walks for residents and visitors to Cornwall, especially at Restormel, Stoke Climsland and Ladock. At Luckett the Duchy has modified its management of one wood to maintain an environment designed to support the survival of a rare species of butterfly.

A wide variety of items are produced at the sawmill, from agricultural requirements to garden furniture. There is a retail outlet at Lostwithiel, Penlyne Nursery, which also has a large area devoted to roses, shrubs and flowering trees which is proving increasingly popular with enthusiastic Cornish gardeners. The quality of the work ensures a wide demand for the finished timber products, especially throughout Devon and Cornwall.

The Duchy still owns one farm, on the eastern edge of Bodmin Moor, where time itself seems to have stood still. Michael Hooper and his wife Margaret, with their three youngsters Kevin, Elaine and Timothy, live on this marvellous upland. Michael runs some hundred hardy cattle and 500 sheep on this lonely rock-strewn pastureland of around a thousand acres in extent. The farm, Wardbrook, Henwood, is perched on a moorland plateau not far from Sharptor, a fantastic outcrop of granite which resembles the Matterhorn in miniature.

On a warm July evening, the scent of new-mown hay lingers in the valley at St Cleer: the narrow roads wind their serpent-like way through a fantastic and continuous ribbon of wild flowers: campion and cow parsley, honey-suckle and dog roses. Around Minions, the hillsides are brown where nature has yet to reclothe the waste from the mine tips. An engine house here, a chimney there – thumbprints of past industrial activity. In the distance looms the great backcloth of Kilmar, its sombre silhouette rising above the moorland like a stairway to heaven itself. This land, so immeasurably old, is not part of any tourist trap, except to those who seek out the mystical Hurlers, the majesty of Kilmar Tor, or the magical curiosity of the Cheesewring, a vast block of granite which wind and weather have shaped to their own design.

Daniel Gumb's cave, home of the eccentric stonemason who cut geometrical problems into rocks around. The Cheesewring, a fantastic natural pile of flat rocks, is on the skyline. (Western Morning News)

There once lived here a stonecutter, Daniel Gumb. A true eccentric, Gumb made himself a home up here of rough moorstone, selecting granite slabs for chairs and beds. He mastered Euclid, but he was no dried-up academic, no scholar gipsy, nor indeed was he a grammarian. Gumb lived a full life: married thrice between 1732 and 1743, and reared a large family whom, it is said, he christened himself on the ancient stone altars of this extraordinary environment. At night, he studied the stars; by day, he incised the hard granite with theoretical algebraic problems, carving his way to immortality. Gumb died in 1776.

At Rillaton Barrow, just sixty-one years after his death, workmen stumbled upon a prehistoric treasure trove, which included a famous gold

Residences of Dukes of Cornwall (above), Restormel Castle near Lostwithiel in Cornwall, base of the Black Prince, and (below), the home of the present Prince of Wales, Highgrove House, Gloucestershire.

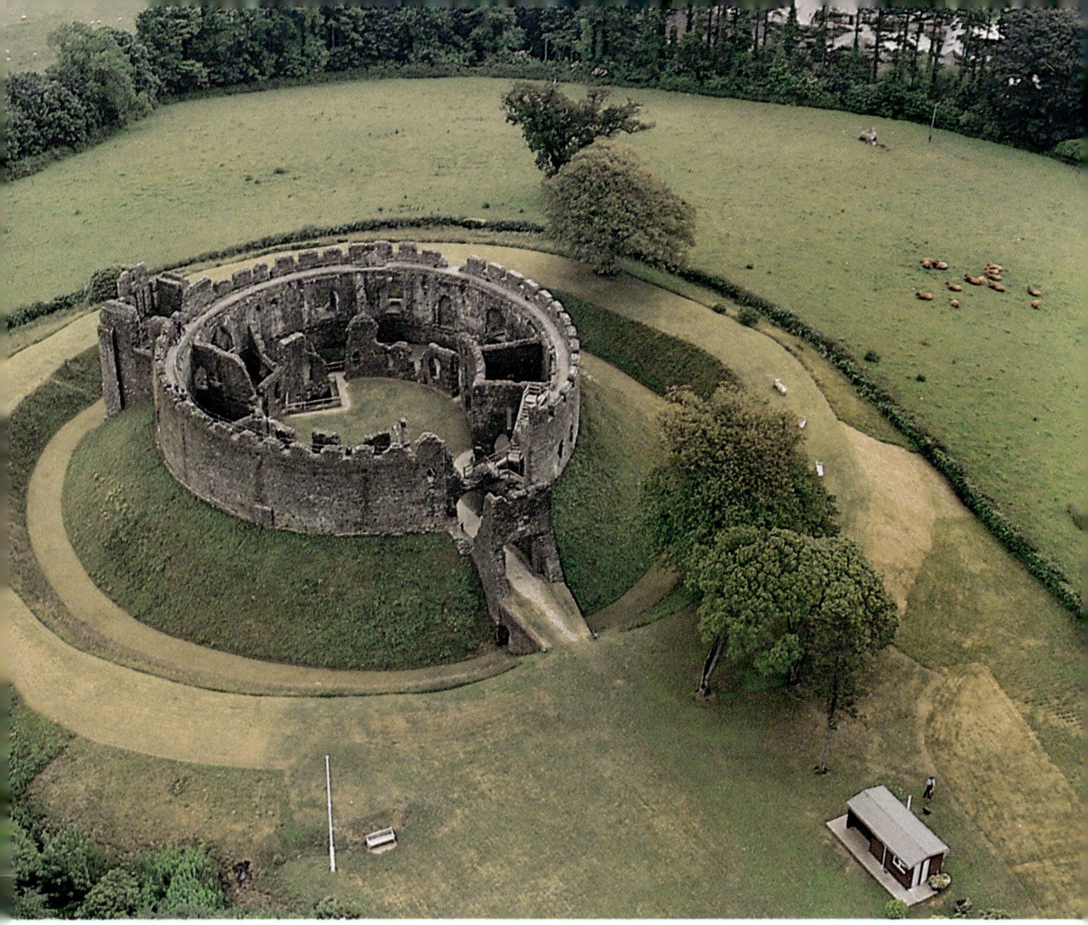

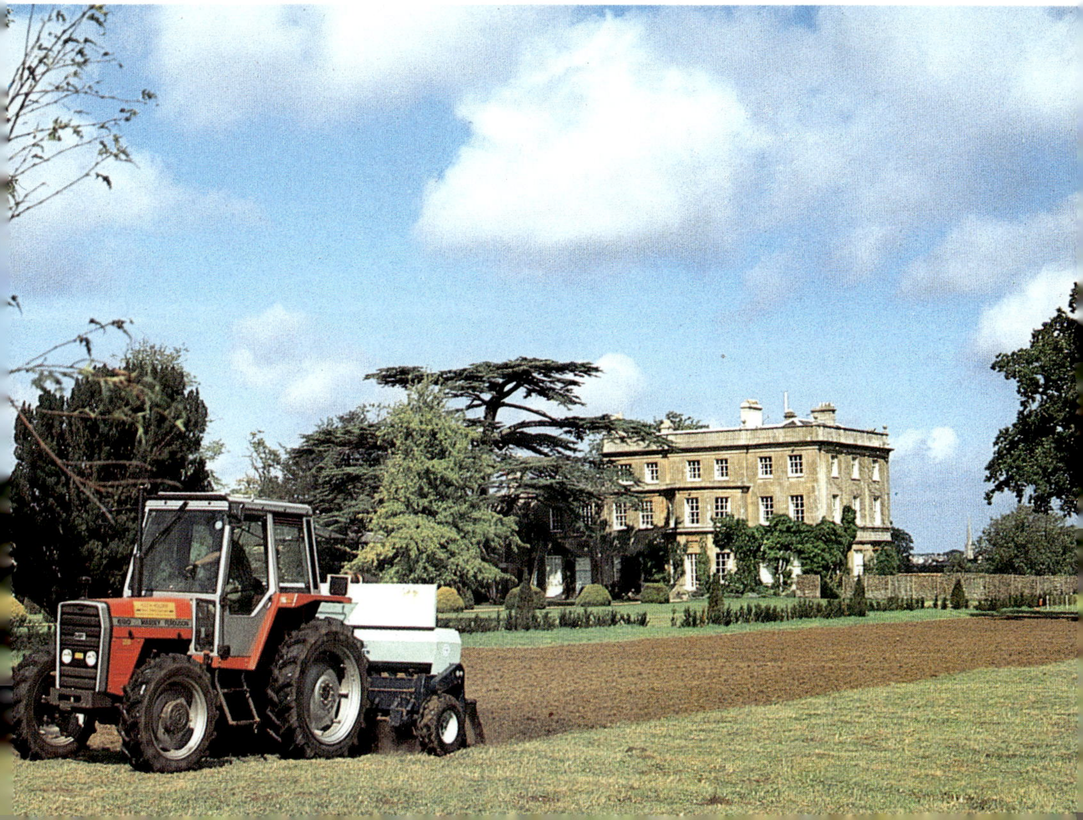

*The Prince of Wales with John Higgs visiting the Cornish woodland he has set aside as a
butterfly sanctuary.*

*The Prince of Wales speaking at a tenants' dinner at Moretonhampstead, Dartmoor, holding
one of the churchwarden pipes smoked by the farmers after dinner.*

cup. It was Duchy treasure, and was despatched by waggon to the dying King William IV. Prince Albert placed it in the family museum in Swiss Cottage, Osborne, but for almost a century its whereabouts was a mystery. It was the late Queen Mary who, shown an early engraving of the precious object, recalled that her late husband, King George V, had on his accession selected the Rillaton gold cup from plate at Marlborough House for transfer to Buckingham Palace. The King kept the cup on his dressing table, using it as a repository for his collar studs! From the ancient grave in the barrow between the Hurlers stone circle and the Cheesewring, the cup has come full circle to a place of honour among the antiquities now in the British Museum.

This is the Duchy territory over which Michael Hooper rides daily on horseback. 'There are no short cuts. Farming here will stay traditional for as long as we can stick the costs,' he says. Haymaking was good in 1986, on lowland pastures but to Michael and Margaret, spring appears to be getting later each passing year: 'It was nearly the end of May before we could stop taking feed to the cattle.' Neither feels in any way remote, or cut off from the rest of the world. The year, for them, is a long, nonstop affair, with little or no relaxation. No barley barons live hereabouts.

Critics complain that the Duchy these days resembles a feudal estate run by big business, that the rents are too high to encourage traditional farming. But in the time-honoured way of any father, the present Prince will want his son to inherit a flourishing concern, which has been run in a business-like way. Much money has been invested in Cornish farms: and if the title, Duchy of Cornwall, has a Ruritanian ring about it, then its royal owner and Steward, his staff and his tenant farmers, most certainly do not.

A Dartmoor bog in the Duchy-owned forest, disliked by the walkers but beloved of the naturalist. (John Clements)

CHAPTER FIVE

DARTMOOR

Helen Harris

Surveying the broad expanse of Devon countryside on a clear day from distant points in the south, east, north and west of the county, one's gaze is inevitably drawn to the distant heights of Dartmoor, rising from the surrounding plains and foothills in remote and challenging grandeur. In winter they may be white with snow, but in summer a greenness develops and produces darker shades as herbage responds to the frequent shedding of mist and rain brought on Atlantic airstreams. An early hunting ground of Saxon kings, Dartmoor became subject to forest law under the Normans. The term 'forest' used in this sense does not necessarily imply that the area was one of woods and trees. A royal forest has been defined as 'a certain territory of woods, grounds and fruitful pasture, privileged for wild beasts and fowls of forest, chase and warren to rest and abide there in the safe protection of the King, for his delight and pleasure.' The 'territory' was subject to forest laws whose origins, like those of common rights, are lost in antiquity.

Dartmoor is specifically referred to in a charter of 1204 when, following petitioning by the people of Devon – over the whole of which forest law had been extended in the twelfth century – and their agreement to make considerable payment, King John granted a charter of disafforestation in respect of the county 'up to the metes and bounds of Dartmoor and Exmoor'. The same charter provided that rights regarding the moor, to which Devonians had become accustomed, were to continue.

In 1239 the Forest of Dartmoor and manor of Lydford were granted by Henry III to his brother, the Earl of Cornwall. Thus the area changed legally from a forest to a chase, although for convenience the term Forest continued to be used to distinguish it from the county of Devon. On the Earl's death in 1300 the Forest reverted to the crown (Edward I) and remained so until, on 17 March 1337, King Edward III granted to his son, Edward the Black Prince, amongst other possessions 'the Castle and Manor of Lydford, and the Chase of Dartmoor'. Since then the Forest, as it continues to be known, has remained a part of the Duchy of Cornwall, vested in the sovereign's eldest son.

For nearly two centuries before the charter of 1337, Dartmoor had, in

Lydford Castle, the infamous Stannary prison for Dartmoor where, according to the old rhyme, Lydford law hanged a man first and tried him afterwards. (Western Morning News)

fact, been of value to the crown because of an attraction more tangible than hunting. Tin is first recorded as being recovered on Dartmoor in the mid-twelfth century. The bonanza that followed, in which for half a century Dartmoor tin production rose well above that of Cornwall and of any other European country, brought considerable revenue to the king. This increased notably with the imposing of tighter regulations and new tolls following the report of commissioners in 1198. However, after the year 1200 the Dartmoor boom subsided. Although Dartmoor tin production continued intermittently, reaching its peak in 1524 and surviving even into the present century, it became of increasing insignificance compared with the far higher rates achieved in Cornwall, and the early supremacy was never regained.

Whilst tin working on Dartmoor brought certain benefits to the crown, and later the Duchy, for those dependent on farming for their livelihood, the activities of the tinners must at times have caused great inconvenience and antipathy, particularly in view of the Stannaries' judiciary which set the tinners apart from aspects of the manorial system.

In 1240 an official perambulation was carried out to define (mainly by natural landmarks) the bounds of the Forest in the centre of Dartmoor, and the neighbouring commons, comprising those of the surrounding border parishes, twenty-two of which share a boundary with the Forest. The moorland area within these parishes constituted the 'commons of Devon', claimed as a 'parcel of the Duchy of Cornwall' since its creation. The whole area covers around 200 square miles.

From about the same time a number of farms became established within the Forest, known as 'ancient tenements'. Such freehold development was not unusual in a forest, and provided it caused no interference with hunting was even advantageous to the lord for duties that were entailed in return for certain privileges. The ancient tenements of Dartmoor were held by copyhold of inheritance (a kind of freehold), and in return for rights which included free grazing in the Forest, turbary (turf cutting) and stone-taking, tenants were required to attend the manor courts at Lydford and assist in the annual drifts of cattle to Dunnabridge and Creaber Pounds. At one time there were thirty-five ancient tenements, with, in some cases, two or three being grouped together at one location.

Within the parishes surrounding the Forest certain farms were said to be 'in venville', a term derived from the Latin *fines villarum*. Occupiers of such properties, besides their grazing rights on the commons of Devon, were entitled on payment of a very small rent to free daytime pasturage in the Forest, and later by a further small payment also by night. They might also have from the Forest 'all that may do them good save green oak and venison' but were subject to the restrictions of levancy and couchancy in being allowed to graze no more stock than they could support on their farms in wintertime. For the people of Devon as a whole (excluding the inhabitants of Barnstaple and Totnes) – so-called 'foreigners', 'wraytors', or 'strangers' – common rights were limited to free pasturage only on the commons of Devon, and for a small fee also in the Forest. The rights of the last group gradually fell into disuse and have long since ceased to apply.

In early times animals agisted on the Forest were placed under the care of a hired herdsman known as the priour, and accounts for fees were rendered by the forester. But in 1842 the system changed when the Duchy ceased its own collection of agistment fees and leased the four quarters of the Forest to 'moormen'. The moormen, usually farmers, in this capacity were lessees and, unlike the priours, not employees of the Duchy. They took in stock to pasture through the summer months and kept charge of them on behalf of their owners, collecting and keeping fees and paying a fixed rent to the Duchy. Often some areas were sub-let to others.

Livestock being sent up to the moor in spring would commonly be taken over by the moorman at some customary meeting-point in the in-country, and proceed by an accustomed route. With cattle then being kept much longer before finishing than now, herds would always include numerous waywise members that would lead the novices, and, with calmer conditions then prevailing in the countryside, the treks would usually be uneventful.

The moorman, on horseback, would probably have one or two helpers, plus dogs. Once on the moor the stock would be driven out to an area of favourable grazing where they were to be 'laired'. Once depastured on the lair, the animals, although not confined, would not normally stray far. Nevertheless, regular watch had to be kept and any wanderers sought and returned to the right grounds.

On certain dates fixed by the Duchy – and until 1843 heralded by the early-morning sounding of a horn – 'drifts' were arranged when the moor was thoroughly searched and all cattle or ponies driven to a point where any depastured illegally could be sorted out. The strays were secured in the respective pound (Creaber for the north quarter, Dunnabridge for the east, south and west) until redeemed by owners on payment of fines and watering charges. Any not claimed were forfeited to the Duchy and auctioned. The centrally situated circular Dunnabridge Pound, of around two acres, which can be seen north of the Two Bridge-Dartmeet road (SX 646746), was the last to survive in use, until 1940. Developed on the site of a pre-historic Bronze Age enclosure, its use as a pound is documented from the 1300s. The substantial walls have undergone rebuilding and maintenance at various stages and are still preserved in good shape, with the pound-keeper's shelter just inside the gate.

In recent years the system of moormen, or agisters as they came to be

Dunnabridge Pound, the two-acre enclosure between Two Bridges and Dartmeet used for centuries for impounding stray animals rounded up in the annual drift. (Helen Harris)

known, has largely lapsed. Only in the south quarter does it still apply, where the agister who leases from the Duchy is Mr John Edmunds of South Brent, the fourth generation of his family to be so involved since 1843. Now, when the moor is stocked throughout the year (because of modern developments that make this possible) his clients are nearer-dwellers, farmers with rights on commons but not on the Forest. They pay Mr Edmunds for grazing but look after their stock themselves. Today stock may be put on the Forest in one of three ways: if their owner has a right under the Commons Registration Act; because stock are taken in by an agister; or by direct licence from the Duchy.

Until a forbidding edict in 1796, holders of ancient tenements, where the father and grandfather had been in previous continuous occupation, claimed on succession the right to enclose a 'newtake' of eight acres. After this date, however, the term newtake acquired a very different meaning. In the late eighteenth century enthusiastic if not avaricious eyes were regarding Dartmoor and in the current growth of agricultural developments optimistic 'improvers' arrived with hopes of taming Dartmoor's seemingly unexploited potential. The Duchy, which had apparently become somewhat disinterested in the moor, made grants to numerous individuals of acreages for enclosure.

One of the first grants was to a Mr Gullet who in 1790 started enclosing land and constructing new buildings on the site of the ancient tenement at Prince Hall. These were later bought by Mr Justice Buller whose total enclosures mounted to 2,000 acres.

Another notable pioneer was Mr (later Sir) Thomas Tyrwhitt. Born in Essex in 1762, Tyrwhitt when studying at Oxford had become a friend of the Prince of Wales (later King George IV) who made him Secretary. Tyrwhitt arrived on Dartmoor in 1785 and began creating an eventual 2,300 acre estate within the Forest, building a house which he named Tor Royal, and other farmhouses and cottages, and enclosing land for farming. In 1786 he was appointed auditor to the Duchy and later, after several years as a Member of Parliament, rose to become Lord Warden of the Stannaries.

Tyrwhitt envisaged great possibilities for the improvement and productivity of Dartmoor, with corn, flax and root crops and plantations of trees. The turnpike road across the moor from Tavistock to Moretonhampstead was under construction and he furthered communications by improving and forming other local routes. Cottages and the Plume of Feathers Inn that Tyrwhitt built near intersecting roads were the beginnings of the village that he hoped would become a thriving community, and which he named Prince's Town – soon to evolve as Princetown. In this rigorous situation 1,400 feet above sea level with 80–100 inches annual rainfall, prospects were doubtful, but in 1805, aware of the shocking conditions in which Napoleonic war prisoners were confined aboard hulks at Plymouth, Tyrwhitt conceived the idea of a prison on the moor. With the Prince's approval work proceeded, and soon French prisoners, and later Americans (from the war of 1812) were

Princetown village with Dartmoor Prison to the right and North Hessary television mast on the tor above. (Helen Harris)

accommodated. After the prisoners departed, for some years from 1815 the prison stood empty and Princetown's trade sank into depression. Tyrwhitt then proposed a horse-drawn railway to provide connection with Plymouth, to bring up lime and sea sand for the land, coal, timber and other goods, and to take down granite from the nearby quarries, peat and agricultural produce. Opened in 1823, the Plymouth & Dartmoor Railway helped to some extent, but was never a paying proposition. Tyrwhitt died in 1833. In 1850 the prison was re-opened, as a civil prison, and so it has remained – the mainstay of Princetown's commercial livelihood.

Much reclamation and wall building was done in following years by convict labour to add to the proliferation of farming ventures – some quite small – that had sprung up in the area. Gradually, however, it was realised that cultivation of the moor was not easily practicable. In the 1880s, following opposition from those concerned for Dartmoor's wildness and beauty and commoners' complaints of interference with rights, enclosure was stopped. It had amounted to 15,000 acres since 1820.

Reactions to enclosure did not deter the Duchy from continuing to grant

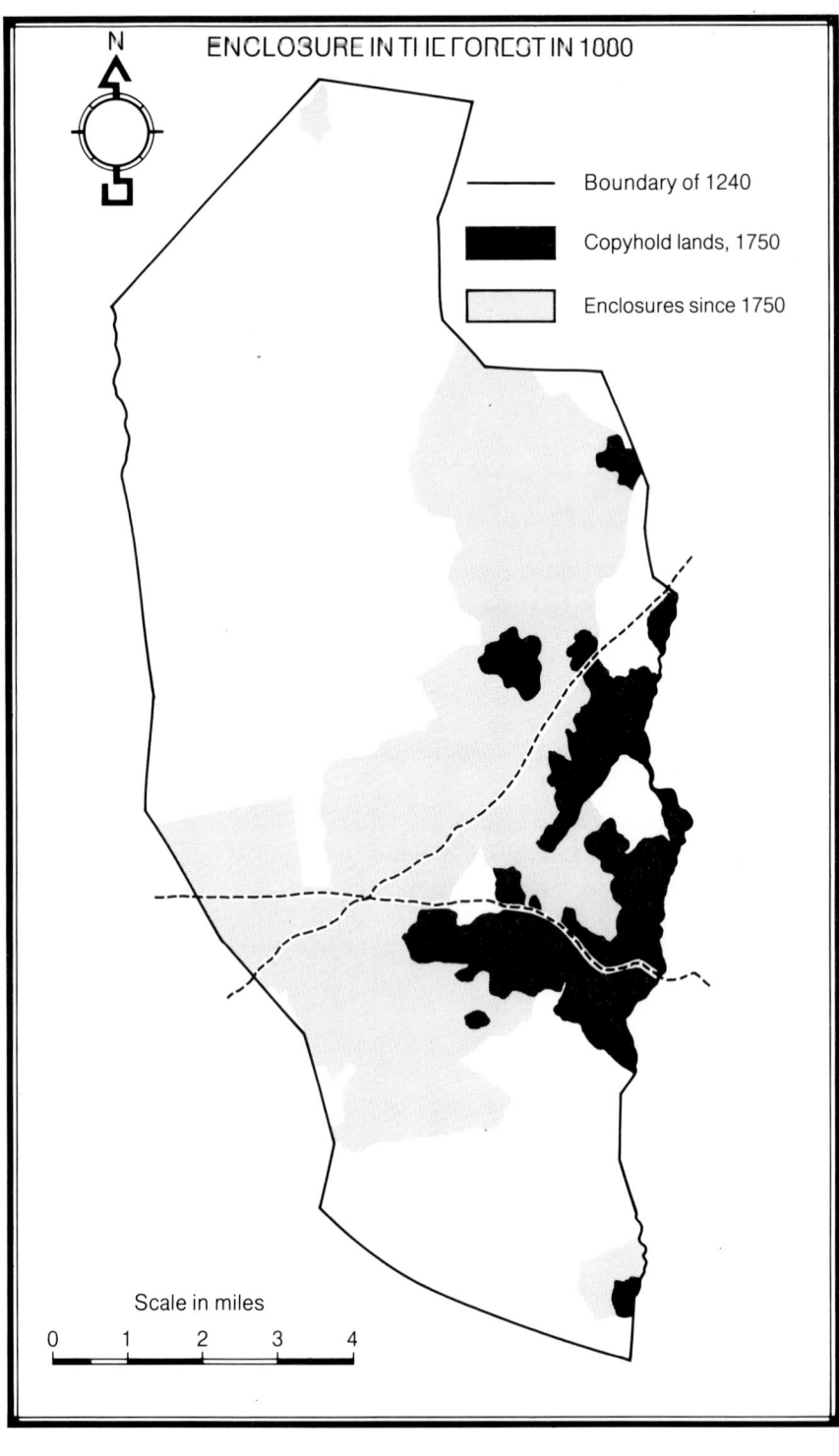

ENCLOSURE IN THE FOREST IN 1000

N

Scale in miles

0   1   2   3   4

Boundary of 1240

Copyhold lands, 1750

Enclosures since 1750

licences to individuals or companies for industrial activities such as mining, granite extraction and commercial peat cutting. In 1844, with the encouragement of the Prince Consort, even a gunpowder factory, known as Powder Mills, was established beside the Cherry Brook, and continued in operation until 1897. Duchy intentions undoubtedly were both to reap some return – if only meagre – from the bleak upland, and also, as befitting the responsibilities of royal ownership, to impart benefit either to Dartmoor dwellers or to national life in general.

So it was that in 1875, following army manoeuvres on Dartmoor in 1873 and application by the War Office, the Duchy agreed to the establishment of an army camp and artillery range in the northern sector of the moor near Okehampton. Soon summer training camps became regular routine and by 1895 the entire north quarter of the Forest was licensed by the Duchy for military practice. This pleased Okehampton tradespeople but caused concern to the commoners whose animals had to be driven from the ranges at firing times (leading to applications for compensation), and to the public whose access became restricted and endangered.

Development of the Okehampton range, and subsequent acquisitions of other portions of the moor for training, proceeded – although at times contested – up to the 1939–45 war, which caused more extensive requisitioning. After the war the government announced its intention of retaining a considerable area of Dartmoor for military training. This was met with strong protests, and a public enquiry was held in 1947. But the military won the day, although the proposed area was reduced and certain concessions were made.

Opposition to these activities has been maintained, notably at the Defence Lands Enquiry of 1985 when the Countryside Commission, the Dartmoor National Park Authority and various amenity bodies spearheaded by the century-old Dartmoor Preservation Association, all urged that military use is incompatible with the conception of a National Park (which Dartmoor was designated in 1951), and that there should be a phased withdrawal of the military presence from Dartmoor. The DPA, citing damage to Dartmoor's terrain and ancient monuments – despite Duchy stipulations – and danger caused to the public, has repeatedly appealed to the Duchy to cease reissuing licences to the Ministry of Defence. This the Duchy – pressed undoubtedly also from other directions – has so far declined to do, although renewals have been for shorter terms than those sought by the Ministry.

Acknowledging that the problem of such use of 24,000 acres of Dartmoor is a major issue for many people, and a matter of national concern, the Duchy in its Dartmoor Report of 1983 states that it: 'fully recognises the desire of

Enclosures on Dartmoor

Powder Mills near Postbridge, a nineteenth-century gunpowder works whose disused buildings have been restored and adapted as small industrial workshops. (Helen Harris)

many of those concerned for the welfare of Dartmoor to see an end to military training on the moor. It also recognises the problems associated with using a large area of the National Park for this purpose.' The report continues:

> The Duchy would in fact be very pleased if at any stage the military are able to withdraw. Its position, however, remains as it has done for some years in that so long as the government of the day requires the Dartmoor training area it will continue to lease it to them in the national interest. At the same time the Duchy will continue to do its best to ensure that the covenants under the Department's licence are complied with. It also supports the Nature Conservancy Council's proposals for regular scientific monitoring.

It must be true that the Duchy's Dartmoor estate is run more efficiently and sensitively now than at any time in its history, which has included periods of neglect. Consolidation stems from the nineteenth century when the buying of ancient tenements began in return for negotiated tenancy

112

agreements, and over the last two hundred years other properties have been purchased. Many replacement farmhouses were built around 1900, while early this century substantial areas were sold to the Forestry Commission.

Today, 70,000 acres of Dartmoor are owned by the Duchy of Cornwall, forming almost one-third of the National Park. Good relations exist with the National Park Authority, the Duchy fully accepting the national parks' statutory objectives of enhancing natural beauty and promoting enjoyment by the public, although emphasising the further commitment to the economic and social life of the community. Of the total area, 50,000 acres comprise unenclosed land which, in recent years, has been the subject of local hearings by a Commons Commissioner to decide the rights of many applicants under the Commons Registration Act. The remaining 20,000 acres consist of twenty farms on enclosed land, leasings to the Forestry Commission, Water Authority and the Home Office, and other tenancies of commercial premises, houses and cottages. The Home Office letting is in respect of Dartmoor Prison, its associated dwellings and the prison farm – a total acreage of 1,660 that makes it the Duchy's major Dartmoor leaseholder.

In the agricultural climate of the 1970s and early eighties, and with the classification of Dartmoor as a Less Favoured Area within the European

A 1974 view of Okehampton Battle Camp, base of military training exercises and live firing on Dartmoor. (Western Morning News)

Economic Community, many tenant farmers have sought to take advantage of grants to which they had become entitled for improving productivity. Before this recent decade the Dartmoor estate had for fifty years been left to a comparatively easy-going system of management, which led to declining economic activity and depreciation of fixed capital, with many farms being ill-equipped to sustain rising costs. Whilst the Duchy raised its rents, schemes were therefore embarked upon, and on several farms large new buildings have been erected by the estate for housing livestock and storing fodder and machinery. These concrete structures, whilst valuable to the farmer (and often replacing ugly tumbledown shacks), by no means enhance the Dartmoor landscape, although weathering and tree planting should soften the impact as time passes.

Caring concern for the landscape and environment is nevertheless one of the Duchy's important stated guidelines, although it has been criticised for encouraging tenants to pursue intensive rather than 'traditional' farming systems. Changes in the grant system may in time bring about a degree of reversion. Meanwhile the Duchy expresses itself open to constructive suggestions on the implications of these issues, and it supports conservation management agreements for tenants whose economic viability is affected by environmental considerations.

A piece of traditionalism which the Duchy has, however, reinstated and updated is the holding of regular 'audit dinners'. In the past tenants paid their rents personally, twice a year – at Lady Day and Michaelmas. Following the Michaelmas morning payment, held at the Two Bridges Hotel, tenants were invited to remain for the midday audit dinner. The practice lapsed a few years ago, but has recently been revived, separated now from the actual payment system and held every two years as a social occasion. Transferred to the evening, and with wives also included, these combined events for the Duchy's Dartmoor, east Devon and Somerset estates are now held at other suitably accessible venues. An important custom still retained is the provision for the men of fine long-stemmed churchwarden pipes for smoking after a meal. Made in clay by a Bristol firm, and ordered by the Duchy a gross at a time, they are laid on the table before the meal across the top of the cutlery, together with small pots of tobacco. The pipes are lit after the toasts, and are kept afterwards as notable mementoes.

During the present century Dartmoor's potential for recreation has again come to the fore. The former reserve of medieval kings and princes for pleasures of the chase is now an area that annually draws thousands of people in search of challenge or relaxation from the confines of modern life.

Not that Dartmoor has been overlooked in contributing to the sporting pleasures of present-day princes. For some of the dukedom of Edward, Prince of Wales (later King Edward VIII) his horses were kept and bred at Tor Royal, and the Prince was an occasional visitor. Equine activities there are recalled by Lt Col David Hurn, whose father was the stud manager. The work with horses began in 1917, for breeding packhorses for the army. Two notable Welsh cob type stallions, Grey Shales and Black Shales, were crossed with Dartmoor ponies for suitable pack animals, and about fifty mares ran on Tor Royal newtake. This enterprise ceased with the ending of the war, but soon afterwards the stables were in use again. Travelling abroad, the Prince was presented with an Arab stallion called Dwarhka, and this was brought to Tor Royal and used on Dartmoor mares with great success, particularly in producing children's riding ponies. One of the most famous offspring to Dartmoor breeders, and figuring in many pedigrees, was named The Leat, the result of a union between Dwarhka and Kitty – previously the carthorse of a Princetown fishmonger. Numbers and types of horses increased as Prince Edward toured the world and received gifts that included Argentinian polo ponies, Mexican broncos, and the noted Kinlark from Australia, and in the 1920s the breeding of thoroughbreds was started.

Besides wintering the polo ponies and sending them to Windsor each year, the Prince's hunters were kept at Tor Royal. They had to be schooled for jumping and got fit annually for 1 November – opening meet date – for which they would be dispatched by train, usually to Leicestershire. At least two big horseboxes were kept for them at Princetown Station, and the horses provided a memorable sight as they were led from Tor Royal, resplendent in rugs embossed with the Prince of Wales' feathers. Six horses used in Trooping the Colour ceremonies were also based at Tor Royal and during training these had to be accustomed to noise by all available hands banging drums and rattling tins. A favourite mount of the Prince was a large black horse called Victory.

On one or two occasions the Prince rode to hounds with the Dartmoor Hunt, and he also participated at its point-to-point at Wrangaton on 18 April 1928. He stayed overnight with Lord Mildmay of Flete, and as *The Western Morning News* reported 'that he has been able to make the long journey down to South Devon from London for the express purpose of competing in just one event has created a great deal of pleasure'. In the event, a three-mile chase over stiff country and fly fences, the Prince rode his horse Miss Muffit – previously hunted with the Belvoir – in a field of thirteen from all parts of the country. For nearly two circuits he led, but was beaten at the last fence by a Cornish-born gelding, Ladder, owned by Mr T. P. Lawry and ridden by Mr C. H. Hext. Subsequently, when weighing him in, the clerk of the scales, Mr Edward Coulton (this writer's grandfather) remarked that the winner was an exceptionally good one, to which the Prince modestly replied 'It doesn't take a damned good rider to beat me'.

Over a hundred horses were kept at Tor Royal in its hey-day, with twenty to thirty men employed. Although the house (built by Tyrwhitt but now Duchy property) was kept up, with housekeeper and chauffeur in residence, on his few visits the Prince and his party stayed at the then Duchy Hotel (now a prison officers' hostel) in Princetown. Eventually the system's con-

Edward Prince of Wales, unhatted, exercising one of his horses at Tor Royal in the 1920s.
(Picture lent by Lt Col David Hurn)

siderable expense became realised and in 1931 the stud was closed down. After some time Tor Royal was let for farming.

Today, hunting, shooting and fishing rights are reserved to the Duchy on both tenanted and unenclosed land, registered rights of common claimed for sporting rights having been disputed by the Duchy at the Commons Registration hearing, and the objection upheld by the Commissioners. With the consent of the Duchy the estate is regularly hunted over by four hunts converging on Postbridge, the Duchy being aware that all tenants may not agree with fox hunting but considering that both farming and hunting are traditional and must be allowed to co-exist. Fishing is let by licences to the general public through the South West Water Authority.

As is generally known, the present Duke of Cornwall, Prince Charles, is very highly aware of the needs of conservation in all its aspects. When in 1980 the Duchy was setting up its study for the 1983 report, *Future Management of the Dartmoor Estate*, a firm wish was expressed for closest co-operation with the Dartmoor National Park Authority, and the study committee included the Authority's assistant officer. Both Duchy and National Park accepted the likelihood of differences of opinion and interpretation of the report's final recommendations, since interests involved in the management of a landed estate do not necessarily coincide with the objectives of a national park. Both may differ from those of people who derive their livelihood from the moor, and from the decisions of other bodies, for example, in some instances of government grant approval for farming schemes. But good relations were established. In publishing the report the Duchy warmly thanked the NPA for the very great help and assistance its officer had provided and stated: 'A working partnership has been forged which both parties intend to build on in the future.' For its part, the NPA has recently noted with appreciation the Duchy's 'increased co-operation noticeable over the last few years'.

Better understanding seems also to have been achieved between the Duchy and the Dartmoor Preservation Association. Differences still exist, with the DPA particularly concerned about the policy of allowing continued military training on the moor, about agricultural developments including fencing by farmers, and regarding access to newtakes. But the DPA welcomed the Duchy's initiative in producing its report, and at a subsequent amicable meeting with the Duchy Secretary, the late John Higgs, when, with representatives of the Ramblers' Association also present, matters concerning footpaths were discussed, much common ground was found to exist, and the Duchy's hope of 'building bridges' was truly begun.

The Duchy of Cornwall is advised on conservation by the Nature Conservancy Council and in 1982 Prince Charles initiated a long-term management plan to encourage wildlife on Duchy lands. In it are included two specified Forest Nature Reserves on Dartmoor, Wistman's Wood and Black Tor Copse – high-altitude remnants of ancient pedunculate oak forest.

To promote local employment and as a means of maintaining otherwise redundant buildings, in 1981 the Duchy in conjunction with the Council for Small Industries in Rural Areas entered into a scheme to convert disused farm and other buildings to workshops for small enterprises. Premises in the Princetown area, former stables at Tor Royal, and buildings at Powder Mills have so far been converted and businesses established, including a farrier, a woodworker and a blacksmith.

Also in the interests of both conservation and job opportunities, the Duchy is supporting a project by the Bridge Community Programme Agency in which fifteen young people are being taught in the rebuilding of stone walls under the Youth Training Scheme. Heather management and trial work towards improvement are currently being considered by a liaison committee of Duchy and National Park representatives, while the Duchy has recently appointed its own project officer – a former National Park ranger – to deal with matters of public concern, including footpaths and camping rights.

Prince Charles himself takes a deep personal interest in Dartmoor affairs. As Duke of Cornwall he spends time on the moor, visits tenants, and in February 1983, in order to gain first-hand experience, worked for five

Yardworthy, Chagford, where Prince Charles spent a week on farm work in 1983. New buildings (right), added to the more traditional structures promote increased productivity and convenience. (Helen Harris)

rigorous days on remote Yardworthy Farm, staying in the house with Mr and Mrs Fred Hutchings. He worked alongside their son Wilf on the full range of jobs, including helping to milk the cows at 7am and 5.30pm, and participated in fencing for sheep folding, hedge and wall building, dung spreading and log-loading.

Whilst in aspects of public encroachment involving political decisions the landlord's royal status necessitates his maintaining a relatively aloof position, there is no doubt whatever about the Duchy's increasing sensitivity to public opinion, and of the Prince's desire for understanding and co-operative harmony in all matters concerning Dartmoor.

CHAPTER SIX

THE ISLES OF SCILLY

Clive Tregarthen Mumford

The elements for unease were built into the Duchy–Isles of Scilly relationship from the very early days. It was, perhaps, inevitable. A tiny, remote, disadvantaged group of islands thirty miles adrift in the Atlantic, of limited acreage (total 3,964), overpopulated and of largely unfavourable economic circumstances were owned by what islanders saw simply as an 'outsider'. By their very nature islanders, fiercely independent, distrust and even resent 'outsiders'. When there is a smack of autocratic privilege about that alien ownership, as in the case of the royal Duchy, a feeling of grievance is born. No appraisal of Duchy–Scilly affairs down the years would be honest if existence of this age-old divide, now happily fast being bridged, was ignored.

The Duchy's association with the islands was, almost without exception until modern times, conducted through a lessee (more often than not an absentee represented by a steward) the first of whom was Dreux de Barentin, a soldier from the Channel Islands. The shadowy Middle Ages suggest a succession of Blanchminsters followed by an undistinguished smattering of Coleshills, Danvers and Whittingtons. The only sure fact to emerge from this vague inaugural period of the Duchy's dealings with Scilly is the grinding wastedness of the remote archipelago and its inherent lawlessness.

In the mid-1500s Leland saw St Mary's as 'a poore Town and a meately strong pile but the Roues of the Buildings in it be sore defacid and woren.' Little wonder that this rocky appendage to the toe of Cornwall was regarded as a worthless possession by the Duchy and in the light of the owners' disinterest it is not surprising that the turn-over of fifteenth and sixteenth-century tenants was a regular one. Leland goes on 'Few men be glad to inhabit these islettes for al their plenty for robbers by the sea that take their catail by force . . . .' Hardly an attractive landowning proposition as appreciated by the tenants who held Scilly in fee of the Honour of Launceston as a 'foreign rent' for 300 puffins or 6s.8d. – and equally lacking in value for their successors, the monks of Tavistock Abbey, who later held the islands in 'mortmain' (dead hand). This was a medieval way of saying 'forever'. But on the Dissolution Scilly reverted to the Duchy.

It was the lawlessness of Scilly – and the growing awareness of its strategic value as opposed to its capital worth – which in the mid-sixteenth century brought to the islands their first notable Duchy lessee. The Lord High Admiral, Thomas Seymour, who had taken possession of the islands in 1547 and schemed to marry the Princess Elizabeth, plotted to take over the state and used Scilly as a base for his operation, linking with pirates. He was executed for having 'gotten into his hands the strong and dangerous Isles of Scilly where he might have a safe refuge if anything for his demerits should be attempted against him.' When Sir Francis Godolphin, member of a famous Cornish family of landed gentry, was given the lease in 1570 the Duchy was determined Scilly should never again be used against England, rather that it should be fortified as a valuable defence against the imminent Spanish threat.

Sir Francis, who found Scilly 'a bushment of briars', leased it for thirty-eight years for £20 a year and undertook to provide justice, enlist his tenants in time of war and draw munitions from the Tower of London (the nation's armoury). But his first major deed was to build Star Castle as the islands' main fortification (Scilly had been an Armada rendezvous point in 1588). Started in 1593 it was completed with commendable expedition and economy the following year and still dominates the capital of St Mary's, Hugh Town, from its hill-top. It was a symbol of Scilly's change to a defence-dependent society.

The Duchy's desire for closer links with Scilly as evidenced by the Godolphin landlordship – he was a prominent royalist – continued through successive Godolphin lessees and through the islands' notable performance on behalf of the crown in the Civil War. Initially overrun, like mainland Cornwall, by the parliamentarians (and controlled by them in the interregnum) Scilly, under Sir John Grenville of the *Revenge* family redeclared for the royalists and it took a parliamentary fleet under Admiral Robert Blake to force a surrender.

Scilly and the Duchy were never again to enjoy such close relations until 'direct administration' in 1922. For the next two centuries later Godolphin lessees and their successors through marriage, the Osborne, Duke of Leeds family, favoured remote control from the mainland, their affairs often being conducted by unscrupulous agents. It was, perhaps, in these parlous times that any resentment at landlordship was born, whether Duchy or Duchy-appointed lessee. The measure of order introduced by the first Godolphin gradually disappeared as hard times fell on an overpopulated group of islands until by the early nineteenth century they were lurching from one annual crisis to the next as the begging bowl and mainland grants battled to bolster a subsistence economy. The establishment of peace in 1815 was a body blow to an economy totally dependent on Star Castle and its garrison – and in 1831 the Duke of Leeds, finally exasperated by his albatross holdings, surrendered the lease and ended a 260-year run of Godolphin–Osborne control (interregnum excepted) of Scilly.

Tresco Abbey, the home Augustus Smith built for himself in the Isles of Scilly. The famous gardens are to the left. (Frank Gibson)

Into a depression of want now strode a reforming colossus in a Hertfordshire squire, Augustus Smith. Not for him the absentee role practised by his predecessors. A political liberal who in the islands' context became a benevolent autocrat, he took the lease of Scilly from the Duchy in 1834 for 99 years or three lives and made his home there – on Tresco. He undertook to pay a fine of £20,000 on possession, £40 per annum and £5,000 on improvements over six years, which included the building of St Mary's parish church and the new quay. He was also responsible for clergy stipends.

Augustus, who came to be known as 'The Governor' faced a daunting task. Not long before he signed the lease (flirting at the time with an alternative venture in Ireland), the Duchy surveyor, Edward Driver, had visited Scilly and recorded a melancholy story. All was chaos! Leases were often held by verbal agreement alone; in some cases ground rent had not been paid for years; there was sub-letting and the inevitable confusion which followed the

121

custom of dividing up a small holding among sons when a father died. The islanders were fractious and unco-operative; lawlessness in the form of wrecking and smuggling hung in the desolate air.

This legacy of waste of the absentee Godolphin–Osbornes was swept away by the most competent, certainly the most socially conscious, man ever to hold the lease of the islands since the Duchy landlords came to Scilly. He transformed the islands from a wilderness of pauperism to a community of full employment and order with a thriving economy. He deported population surplus to requirement; he encouraged piloting and shipbuilding (free trade legislation gave a huge fillip to foreign trade); he restored order to farm tenancies; he introduced compulsory education, anticipating the Forster Act. He built roads, the pier, the church. Rent audit day was held twice yearly at Star Castle, historical headquarters of the islands. Inevitably islanders saw his modus operandi as high-handed, even ruthless and as a result an enduring resentment of 'Old Caliban' (as he was known by the less respectful) and his successors at Tresco Abbey was born.

But so reduced were circumstances when Augustus arrived that a painless rehabilitation was plainly impossible. John Stuart Mill recognised Augustus' feat: 'There is a prosperity of a kind, undoubtedly,' he said, 'but it is paternal government. I detest paternal government.' Scillonians wholeheartedly agreed. Paternal the Duchy was not, considered Augustus, in its relations with the new lessee. Throughout his correspondence there are repeated outbursts against 'that d . . . Duchy'. Augustus nursed a conviction of ill usage. Insecurity was at the root of it. Changes in the Duchy hierarchy saw an old ally in Sir George Harrison succeeded by a less sympathetic figure in Mr Gardiner. What Augustus had done for Scilly – and spent on his own account on renovation – appeared to be ignored by Gardiner who appeared to be more concerned in extracting revenue from the islands than endorsing Augustus' renovating crusade.

'In consequence all kinds of irritating points were perpetually being raised' wrote that admirable biographer of Augustus, Elizabeth Inglis-Jones, 'and the Proprietor's rights to this and that questioned, the Duchy claiming every source of income and emolument that was not specifically mentioned in the lease.'

Augustus feared for his lease agreement. The 'three lives' format was threatened and Augustus was looking to successors to continue his work and recoup some of his immense capital outlay. The Duchy of Cornwall Management Act realised his worst fears. Now he was faced with the awful possibility that, should the two other lives expire before him, on his death Scilly would revert to the Duchy, his heir inheriting no reparation for his expense. From this moment on 'minor annoyances and disagreements were continually cropping up to aggravate his sense of ill-usage . . . by the "damned Duchy".' He more than once threatened to cut his losses and leave. But his heart was now thoroughly imbedded in Scillonian granite. In 1864 he relinquished his old lease and was granted a new one for another thirty-one years.

Augustus Smith, architect of modern Scilly, and a fortuitously inspired choice as lessee by the Duchy, died in 1872 (oddly enough at the Duke of Cornwall Hotel, Plymouth). The latter's property had appreciated un-imaginably in fewer than forty years. Augustus' epitaph could have been *Inveni lateritiam, marmoream relinquo* (I found it brick, I left it marble).

As in the case of the earlier Godolphins the Smith governorship of Scilly burgeoned into a dynasty. Augustus' nephew, Thomas Algernon, inherited the lease although Augustus had in his will first directed the lease should be returned to the Duchy provided it paid £20,000 down and £3,000 a year for its remaining twenty-three years. The Duchy declined and after some uncer-tainty (at one stage an advertisement in *The Times* declared Tresco Abbey and Island to be let for a term or by the year) Thomas Algernon Dorrien Smith took over.

Thomas Algernon, a soldier by profession and a horticulturalist by leaning, has gone down in Scillonian history as the man who launched the flower industry, still hugely important in the islands' economy. Tresco Abbey remained the seat of administration through his period and when he died in 1918 he was succeeded by his son, Major Arthur Algernon Dorrien

Picking off the heads of daffodils on Gugh, a necessary operation when a flower field has gone too far into bloom. Agnes with its slipway is in the background. (Molly Gill)

Smith. There were fourteen years left of the original lease but wartime austerity was proving debilitating. The flower industry had been hard hit in World War I and many island homes were in bad states of disrepair. In 1920 Major Dorrien Smith surrendered the lease and two years later took out a lease solely for Tresco and the uninhabited islands.

Into the vacuum moved the Duchy to assume direct administration of Scilly first-hand for the first time since its association with the islands began some six hundred years previously. It was a unique event in Duchy history. Save for Tresco, where Major Dorrien Smith's successor, Commander Tom, and his grandson Robert the present incumbent, maintained control, the one-tenant system of the Godolphins, Osbornes and Smiths was dead. Now it was the Duchy direct with no 'middle men' cushioning any dealings between owner and 'owned'.

Through their first-ever Land Steward in the islands, Mr Jeffery, the Duchy took up residence appropriately at Scilly's historical headquarters, Star Castle. Leading up to and during World War I much of the island housing had fallen into disrepair (one of the reasons why the Dorrien Smiths surrendered the lease was that renovation costs loomed cripplingly large) and the Duchy immediately constructed a workshop complex in Hugh Town, St

Edward Prince of Wales at Pelistry on St Mary's where farmer 'Tommer' Tregear created a farm by stone moving. The Duchy Secretary, Major McCormick, imperiously holds up one finger to tell the photographer only one picture is permitted. (Gibson)

Mary's with rehabilitation to the fore of their thinking. A significant part of run-down Hugh Town housing stock was pulled down and reconstructed and general material improvements in the islands embarked upon. All the sub-tenants of the Dorrien Smiths now became direct Duchy tenants. Some found the new arrangements unacceptable and left the islands, but there were newcomers waiting to become Duchy tenants.

Generally the transition from the Smiths to the Duchy was a smooth one. The flower industry, hard hit in the war when food took precedence over bulbs, took some time to get back on its feet. In 1925, for instance, the flower export figure was only 600 tons, the 1896 figure, while the potato trade was also depressed. The Duchy helped islanders to get over the bad patch. They converted the old lifeboat house on St Mary's into a bulb-treating station to eradicate eel-worm pest, which at the time was a major threat; and they introduced an agricultural expert in Mr Gordon Gibson who advised island farmers and researched deeply into ways of improving their lot. Edward Prince of Wales visited the islands and a few new tenants were brought in from Wales, suffering then in the great depression of the twenties.

On the smaller, more geographically-disadvantaged off-islands of St Agnes, Bryher and St Martin's there was, and still is, a certain feeling that the smallholder tenant has a harder row to hoe than his counterpart on the main island of St Mary's (the latter now reverting to its former central role previously usurped by Tresco under the Dorrien Smiths). Everything there was that little bit more costly; transport, freight, the fundamental business of getting flowers to the St Mary's steamer, let alone to mainland markets.

Until recently all the off-islands, save Tresco, had no mains electricity, private generators (spelling costly freight import of oil) providing their power. The Duchy has always recognised these very real problems but was in the classic cleft stick when seeking a solution. Across-the-board physical improvement and expansion would mean radical change, possibly destructive of the off-island character.

The off-islands are the essence of Scilly, St Mary's being more 'main-landish'. The landlords' assistance was careful, always aimed at ensuring stability. Generation upon generation of the same families farmed these islands; the inappropriate lease-seeker, who might so easily create an imbalance, both social and physical, in this sensitively poised world, was studiedly refused. Had the landlords' intention been to make the off-islands a purely economic portfolio they would almost certainly have been irretriev-ably ruined — and Scilly seriously affected as the later holiday traffic leant heavily on the attraction of unspoilt, uncommercial offshore-island natural-ness.

In recent years the Duchy has tackled off-island problems more positively. Compensation was offered to tenants who had erected their own houses (as opposed to the Duchy itself); new long leases were granted to tenants agreeing to spend an approved sum on improvements. Rent reviews were arranged. Concerned for the livelihood of the off-island farmer, the Duchy imposed a rent (by the acre) lower than on his St Mary's counterpart. As the islands' Land Steward, Col Ian Robertson says, 'You've got to be a certain type, a person who wants to live on an off-island. We get masses of applications – you need a self sufficient sort of chap.' For the off-island way of life the penalties are higher costs and less profit than on St Mary's.

A picture of the miniscule off-island world the Duchy owns – unique in its estate – can be gained from the following statistics. As opposed to the main island of St Mary's (total acreage 1,554, population 1,488, 30 farm tenancies, 59 Rent Act tenancies and 72 leasehold and others), St Agnes (366 acres and 62 population) has 9 farm tenancies over 5 acres, 2 Rent Act tenancies and 13 leasehold and other tenancies. St Martin's (586 acres and population 81) has 11 farm tenancies over 5 acres, one Rent Act tenancy and 24 leasehold and other properties. On Bryher (327 acres and 63 population) the list reads 4, 5 and 14. There is no room for the big operator. You have to be a special sort of person to live there . . . 'Giant' St Mary's is only 5 miles by 3!

The most far-reaching act in the Duchy's sixty-odd years of direct administration took place in 1949. It sold the freehold of Hugh Town on St Mary's, a reform which was to be of the utmost significance. Post-war ex-servicemen-councillors were challenging the old order and intolerant of privilege, however well it was used. Relations with the Duchy, who reserved a right to an unelected seat on the island council and whose former lessee, Major A. A. Dorrien Smith, was their nominee as chairman, became strained in the oft-baulked search by the council for land for council house expansion.

A momentous letter, later withdrawn, was written to the King. Whether this was a major, or merely contributory reason for the resultant sale is debatable. Changed public attitudes had also been noticed at the Duchy Head Office in London.

In 1949 the Duchy announced it was selling Hugh Town, St Mary's: 170 houses, 18 shops, 3 hotels, 2 bank houses, the steamship company office, post office, Roman Catholic Church, power generating station and cinema, along with 20 boat houses and other stores and open spaces (keeping beaches, except Porthcressa, and foreshores). The move represented a fundamental break with history. A two-tier island now came into being, freehold alongside leasehold. The council naturally welcomed the expansion of their jurisdiction, but recognised the dangers. A public meeting highlighted the problems the authority faced in the application of the Town and Country

Hugh Town and harbour, St Mary's, with Star Castle in the background (right). The Duchy sold off its freeholds in the town in 1949. (Gibson)

Visitors are now the main source of island income: the Queen Mother touring Tresco gardens in 1962 accompanied by the late lessee, Cdr Tom Dorrien Smith. (Gibson)

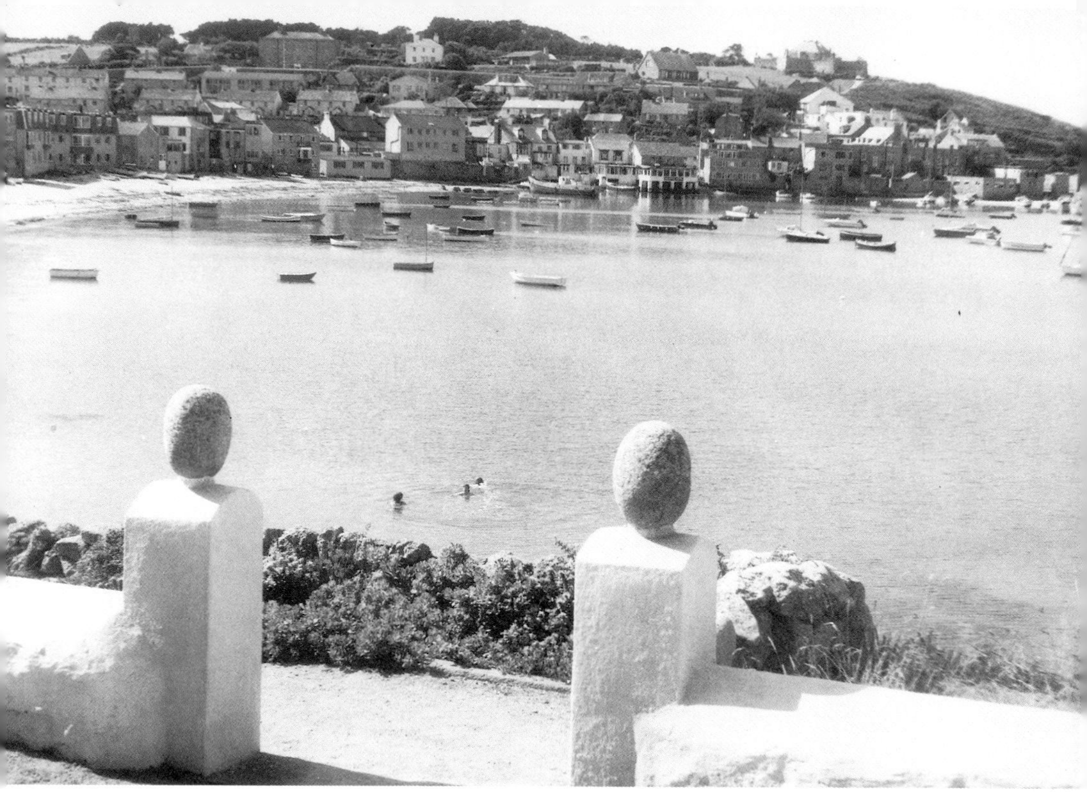

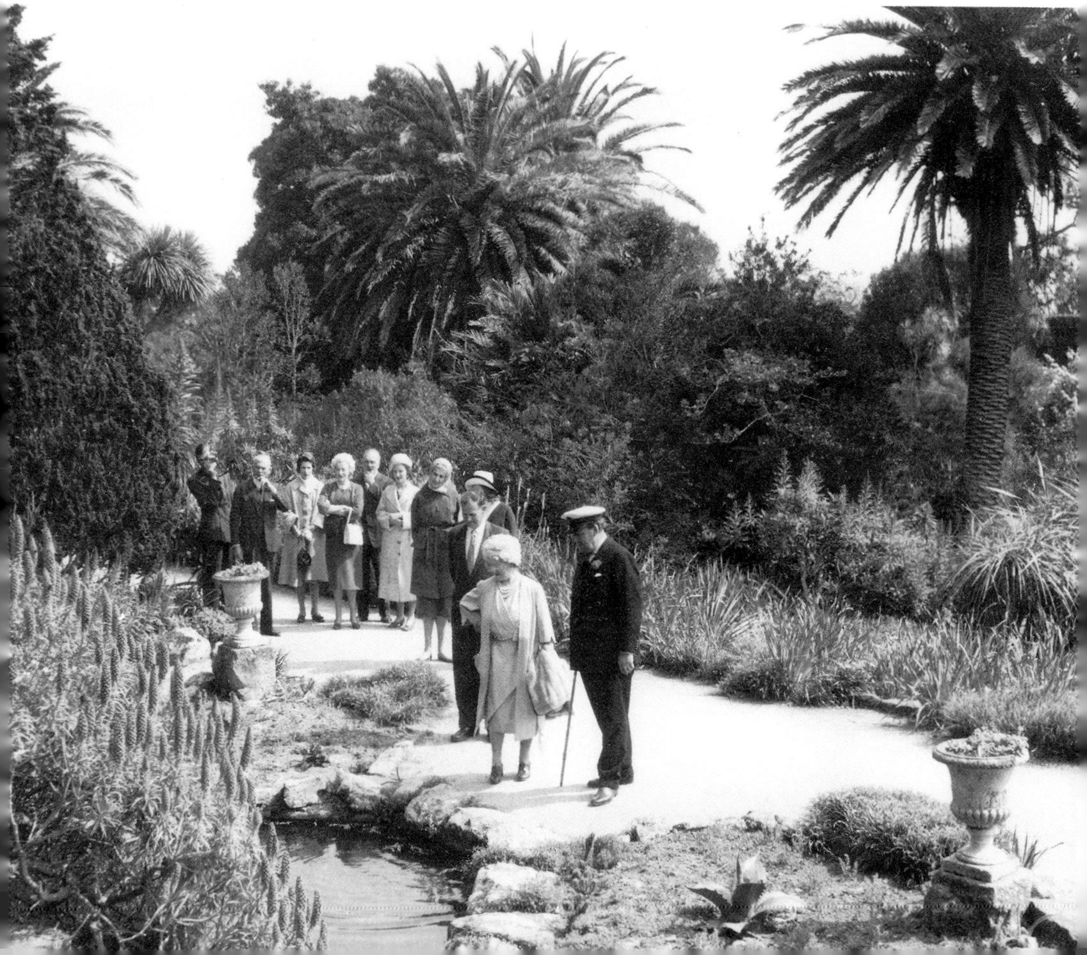

Planning Act, some of the properties needing renovation. A deputation was sent to London to see the Lord Warden of the Stannaries, Sir Clive Burn. The council feared the exploitation of the freed properties by 'outsiders', and the costs that might be required by law for the housing repairs. The seeds of today's tourist-based economy were sown. It was the era of the Welfare State. Paid holidays brought the hitherto remote islands within the range of the ordinary man and his family. The new householder celebrated his new-found status by 'taking in visitors'. Thus was established the holiday trade.

Save for a council estate at Old Town, Hugh Town remains the lone freehold enclave in Duchy-owned Scilly. The off-islands stay almost wholly in the ownership of the Duchy as policy, although the schools and churches have been sold. The dangers inherent in free-market off-island forces in speculative hands are obvious. However on St Mary's the sale of some leasehold housing outside Hugh Town has been taking place, albeit slowly. 'It's our policy to divest,' says the Land Steward. But government restraint on council purse strings has hindered any process of municipalisation. At present the Duchy owns a third of Scilly's housing stock. Broken down there are 70 farm tenancies, some with cottages, and with rents agreed every three years between farmer and landlord; 70 Rent Act tenancies with a fair rent assessed by the Rent Officer and then negotiated between tenant and the Duchy; and 120 leaseholds. With differing lengths of lease and levels of rent 'it's a marvellous mixture', says Col Robertson.

While tourism is, without dispute, Scilly's economic staple (the Duchy recognises the two-strings-to-the-bow need in the islands by permitting the catering for and taking in of visitors via a licence system on both farm and leasehold properties and has, with council approval, allowed farm chalets on the off-islands), land let for farming remains the prime concern. In recent years the Duchy has taken steps to assist this major islands' industry whose natural climatic advantages are under threat from international market forces and the big mechanised combines of the mainland.

There has been close liaison with the Ministry of Agriculture and the islands' NFU; in the last two years a Duchy Farm Tenancy Agreement has been re-drafted following negotiations with the NFU ('Trying to listen to the voice of the other side' as Col Robertson says); there has been rent-free support for the experimental station at Trenoweth on St Mary's; Prof John Marsh, an agricultural expert from Reading University, is being funded by the Duchy to undertake a study for island farmers on both farming methods and marketing. The Duchy has made it a policy to try and keep full employment on the land, achieving this by preventing the amalgamation of holdings with the inevitable drop in employment; it has launched an extensive programme of shelter-belt tree planting against the winds that damage the flower industry. But the major injection in recent years by the Duchy has been in the new Farm Buildings Improvements Scheme. A five-year 'one off' scheme, it aims to improve up to forty sets of farm properties at financially advantageous rates. The scheme, involving a large capital commitment, is the first direct Duchy input into the farming sector on the islands in its history.

Scilly, so different from other mainland Duchy districts, maintains this difference in the matter of maintenance, insurance and repairs to and of its farm properties. All costs are borne by the tenants, not landlord. The reason is not difficult to see. There are fifty-seven sets of farms. In their total acreage on the mainland there would, perhaps, be only four or five holdings. Four sets of repair bills, insurances etc are more acceptable than fifty-seven. As a result of this extra cost to the farmers, Scillonian rents are less than on the mainland.

With assistance has come a hardening of business attitude. 'Without

Prince Charles sets off on a bicycle tour of Tresco with the present lessee, Robert Dorrien Smith. (Gibson)

doubt people over the years had seen the Duchy as a soft touch' wrote the late Duchy Secretary, John Higgs, in a 1985 article in *The Times* entitled 'Not all cream from the Cornish Duchy'. Scillonian tenants have since 1980 good reason to remember his words. Rents on St Mary's – at the Duchy housing estate at Launceston Close in Old Town and elsewhere – have in four years trebled, even quadrupled. 'The rents bore no relation to existing mainland values' said Col Robertson. Farm and house rents were 'appallingly and artificially low'. Robertson admits that getting a fair rent has been painful but feels the Duchy has managed to preserve a 'soft face despite what might appear a hard-nosed operation'. 'Enormous' amounts had been spent over the past five years in repairs and renovations. The new business approach adopted in the mid-seventies by the Duchy had at last crossed the water to Scilly. Even now the Duchy does not make a profit on the islands, although the capital value of its holdings is considerable.

Rent rises and hard-nosed business notwithstanding, the Duchy's relations with the islands' council remain cordial. Two or three joint meetings are held a year, usually when Prince Charles or the Duchy Secretary are on the islands. Many much less formal contacts are made as necessary. A recent initiative which shows the Duchy's concern, over and above that of a landlord's obligation for a unique community (which brings Prince Charles as Duke of Cornwall on annual, sometimes more, visits to the islands despite his busy international schedule), is the Moss Report. In 1984 the Duchy jointly with the local council commissioned a land use and community development study by a firm of consultants, Graham Moss Associates. It minutely examined every facet of island life, producing a blueprint for the future economic well-being of Scillonians. The council has adopted the Moss Report as general policy and at the time of writing has fifty-nine articles nailed to the EEC door in Brussels as part of an Integrated Development Operation (IDO) for European funding. This groundwork for Scilly's future prosperity is an eloquent indication of the co-operation existing between the two authorities in the common objective of securing the islands' future welfare.

The Moss Report recommended a Duchy withdrawal from the ownership of public service-type utilities, in particular the pier and harbour on St Mary's and the islands' airport. In the report's opinion they should not remain in private ownership. Already negotiations are in progress for the transfer of the former although the Duchy is not pressing the issue. The council does now lease the airport at a peppercorn rent. Finalisation of these transfers along with more of the Duchy Rent Act housing stock will ensure the Duchy's islands' portfolio is put on a sounder financial basis.

To some islanders this handing over to the community is seen cynically as a landlord ridding himself of his liabilities (the quay is in poor condition, the airport operation financially hard-pressed). Some go further and suggest that these are the initial shots in a phased Duchy 'pull out'. The Land Steward refutes this view: 'The Duchy is staying without a shadow of a doubt.' However he hints that the extent of their future involvement with the islands will depend on circumstances.

The formation in 1985 of yet another Moss Report suggestion, the islands' Environmental Trust, lends some weight to those who sense, rather than have evidence of, a pending Duchy disengagement. Apart from a brief to conserve archaeological and terrestrial areas and protect island wildlife, the Trust is due to take over – on a ninety-nine-year lease at an annual rental of one daffodil a year – all the 2,000 acres plus untenanted land in the inhabited islands, and all the uninhabited islands as well. To some this looks like a preparation for a possible Duchy departure which, they say, could see Scilly administered by a mainland-based Land Steward. The Duchy sees the setting up of the Trust (like 'Moss', endorsed by the council) as a positive move for islanders' benefit: a chance for Scillionians to 'run their own show'. Sensitively it has overseen the formation of an all-Scillonian set of trustees, thus knocking on the head the fears that 'mainland experts' would tell islanders how to run their affairs. This has helped to win islanders' confidence. The charitable status of the Trust opens up attractive avenues of funding, too.

Other Duchy-involved schemes in the islands are the CoSIRA workshops programme (to date there are four on St Mary's and one on St Agnes with others planned) and the historic bringing to the off-islands of mains electricity. Completed in 1985 and officially switched on by Prince Charles himself in April 1986 during another of his increasingly regular trips to Scilly, this £3½ million power scheme was financially assisted by the Countryside Commission and Duchy via a grant to the South West Electricity Board to underground their own and British Telecom cables, thus improving the value of the off-islands for the Duchy by retaining their natural environment as well as helping the inhabitants themselves. And the Duchy is operating a loan scheme for tenants who have found rewiring and connection charges too onerous.

Tresco, the second largest island in Scilly, retains its historical apartness. It is a private estate held by Robert Dorrien Smith on a one-hundred-year lease from the Duchy. The private, some say neo-feudal, ownership is very much evident. A landing charge is levied; dogs have to be kept on a lead; cars are banned. Mr Dorrien Smith, who took a new lease in 1979 on the death of his father, Commander Tom, runs the estate on hard-headed business lines. The lessee, like his antecedents going back to Augustus Smith, has a home at Tresco Abbey and has introduced Timeshare properties and a helicopter link with Penzance. Tresco also boasts a top-class hotel, the Island Hotel, and its world famous botanical gardens laid down a century and a half ago by Augustus. Tresco, deposed from its position as capital of Scilly following the lease changes in the twenties, is still very much 'Smith land'.

In a fast-changing Scilly where mammon is being chased in a way islanders' ancestors would not understand, the influence of the Duchy, with its feudal undertones still detectable, appears to some a quaint anachronism. But any thinking Scillonian – age-old, in-born prejudice notwithstanding – would not relish the prospect of the closing of the 'house on the hill' that is the Duchy HQ, the striking of the fifteen-bezants flag, the selling of the royal bungalow, Tamarisk, or the termination of contracts for the tiny band of fourteen island staff ranging from the harbourmaster to maintenance men and part-timers. For the Duchy's departure would rob the islands of a priceless bulwark against Scilly's most potent enemy – exploitation and over-development. It has been the Duchy down the years who by careful, wise (at times paternal, true) landlordism has protected the islands from the tinsel fate of so many mainland beauty spots. It has been the buffer against speculation. By holding a tight rein and imposing strict, often at times high-handed disciplines, it has guided the islands along an economic tight rope in a balancing act between social responsibility and profitability.

One trusts that the islands' council, left alone without the practical and moral backing of a Duchy, would be able to muster sufficient backbone to ward off the seductive attentions of the developer.

If the Duchy was to reduce its commitment in the islands tomorrow, it could have no more honourable epitaph, despite some of the shortcomings of their lessees down the centuries, than that of knowing it had succeeded in protecting Scilly's greatest asset, the natural state. Without it the tenor of life in the islands would be threatened.

Prince Charles on St Martin's in June 1985 inspected the progress of the off-islands mains electricity scheme. Behind him (right) is the then Duchy Secretary, John Higgs (later Sir) and the island Land Steward, Col Ian Robertson. (Duchy)

CHAPTER SEVEN

KENNINGTON

Nicholas Long

For the West Country passenger arriving by train at London's Waterloo Station, the view from the train window is, for the most part, bleak and uninteresting, although relieved by an occasional glimpse of the river Thames and the Houses of Parliament. Therein, it might be said, lies the dilemma that has faced many holders of land on the South Bank of the Thames; so near and yet so far from central London.

Much of the immediate area from Vauxhall to Waterloo is bound up in the fortunes of the Duchy's manor of Kennington which formed part of the original grant under the Charter of Woodstock in 1337. The manor, the Duchy's only urban holding, at that time comprised some two hundred acres in two principal holdings with several detached portions. The main holdings were, to the north, the lands known as Prince's Meadows (the area today around Coin Street and Stamford Street, to the east of Waterloo Bridge) and to the south the Kennington estate, an enlarged triangle roughly bounded by Kennington Lane, Harleyford Road and Kennington Park Road. The Kennington estate contained the Manor House (known also as Kennington Palace) on a site to the west of the junction of Kennington Road with Kennington Lane. Between the two lay the manor of Lambeth, land held by the Church and in which Lambeth Palace stands. Within the manor of Lambeth were several detached portions of Duchy-controlled land.

In 1337 the area was remote to the then settlement of London, which was gathered around London Bridge. The main London–Brighton road, the former Roman Stane Street (now Kennington Park Road), marked the east boundary of the Kennington estate and the Kingston Road (now Kennington Lane), meandered through the estate. Virtually all the land was agricultural, being meadow and pasture. The manor was managed by stewards until 1516 when a lease of 21 years for the lordship of Kennington was granted to Sir John Pulteney. From that time, the greater part of the manor was held on lease by one or more tenants. In 1531 Henry VIII ordered the demolition of Kennington Manor House and used its materials in the erection of the new Whitehall Palace. The accounts of the period refer to payments for the digging of a dock near 'Faulxe Halle' for the loading of barges and for the

Sir Charles Chaplin pointing out no 287 Kennington Road, where he lived with his family in part of the house, about 1912, during a January 1975 visit to London. (Duchy)

wages of the workmen in pulling down the house.

The lease passed successively between noblemen, many of whom are commemorated in local street names. The Clayton family was to have a long association with the manor, being tenants of the demesne lands from 1661 until 1834. Local street names reflect the Duchy or Cornish associations, Stamford, Stannary, Orsett and Newburn for example while yet others, Cardigan and Chester, remember the Duke of Cornwall's other titles. The estate's pub names provide clues; the Black Prince and the Duchy Arms are direct associations whilst the White Hart stands on the edge of the ancient White Hart Field.

In January 1616 John Norden surveyed the manor of Kennington, com-

Wistman's Wood, a survival of the primitive forest that once covered Dartmoor. (Roy Westlake)

134

The Isles of Scilly from the air, St Mary's in the foreground looking north.

Mesembryanthemum, or Hottentot fig, growing on St Helen's in the islands. (Frank Gibson)

(Overleaf) *A corner of Tresco Gardens in the Isles of Scilly.* (Frank Gibson)

piling a list of tenants, giving an indication of the value of the holdings and much other valuable information. The purpose was to provide the Prince's Council with vital information on which to base their future management policies. From the survey, Kennington is seen as still being a largely agricultural estate, with growing pockets of commercial activity (such as brick making and ship repair) mostly along the riverbank. A little later soap and candle making were to become important local industries.

London was slowly spreading on the north bank of the Thames but Southwark remained the only area on the south side of the river to be built over, clustered around the approach to London Bridge. Crossing the river elsewhere was by boat, the river being the most vital commercial artery in seventeenth-century London.

It was by river that many visitors reached the New Spring Garden created at Vauxhall in 1661. A rival attraction to the Spring Garden at Charing Cross (which then became known as the Old Spring Garden), the gardens were to become a principal attraction for almost two hundred years. They were to feature extensively in contemporary accounts; Pepys noted in his diary in 1662 being rowed across the river and mentions the 'abundance of roses' and 'the cakes and powdered beef and ale', also complaining that he was overcharged. Even before the end of the seventeenth century, the Spring Garden had become notorious as a place of assignation. In *Amusements* by Tom Brown in 1700 reference is made to the garden as being a haunt 'where both sexes meet, and mutually serve one another as guides to lose their way, and the windings and turnings in the little wildernesses are so intricate, that the most experienced mothers have often lost themselves in looking for their daughters.'

The gardens were to enjoy a revival in 1728 when Jonathan Tyers took the lease of the site for thirty years at £250 per annum. He reconstructed and improved the gardens, re-opening on 7 June 1732 with a Ridotto Alfresco, an extremely popular entertainment at that time. The event was attended by the Prince of Wales (George II's son, 'poor Fred', who was to die before his father), the evening lasting from 9pm until 4am, admission costing one guinea. The Prince of Wales was to become a regular visitor and it was not unknown for him to oblige with a song – to the entertainment of all.

Tyers worked hard to make the gardens successful, increasing their beauty, attracting artists, including Hogarth, to paint pictures in the buildings within the gardens, erecting statues and generally improving the standard of entertainment. He died in 1767 leaving the gardens to his four children, his son Jonathan managing the gardens until his death in 1792. The business was continued by his son-in-law Bryant Barrett who sold the gardens in 1821 for about £30,000 to the London Wine Company. The building of the railway to Waterloo in 1847 was to seal the fate of the gardens and in 1859 the land was sold for redevelopment. Today the only reminder of the gardens is the manager's house on the corner of Kennington

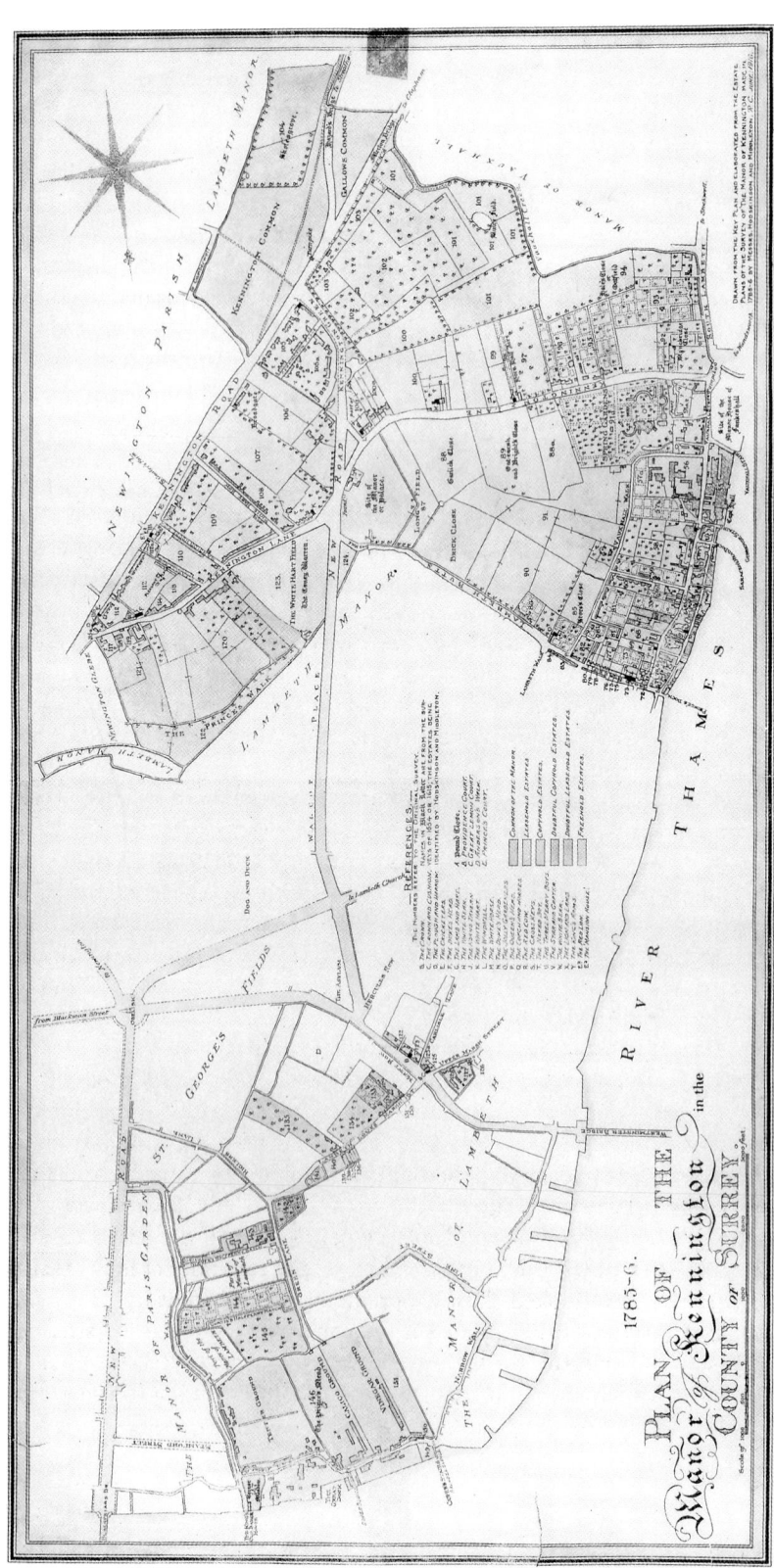

Manor of Kennington, 1785–8

Lane and St Oswald's Place. The site of the gardens is again an open space, although without the character of the Spring Garden, having been cleared by Lambeth Council using compulsory purchase powers.

Another garden, the London Botanic Garden, was opened on Duchy land at Prince's Meadows in January 1779. The garden, which lasted for about ten years, was open to subscribers who, for one guinea a year, were entitled to walk in it and use the library. William Curtis, the proprietor, was forced to close the garden in 1789 and move to new premises in Brompton on account of the smoke and effluent in the area. The pollution problems of the Prince's Meadows are reflected in the Middleton survey of 1785 which stated there were '70 dwelling houses with warehouses, dyehouses, storehouses, account-ing houses, brewhouses, coachhouses, carthouses, stables, sawhouses, cranes, sheds, wharves, yards, gardens, fields, ponds and canals, containing in all nearly 29 acres'.

Much of the area to the south (now containing the South Bank complex and not Duchy land) also contained breweries, potteries, shot-works and other industrial premises. Most remarkable of the local industries at that time was the Artificial Stone Manufactory of Mrs Eleanor Coade, where Coade Stone, a material virtually impervious to weathering and pollution, was made to a secret formula, production ceasing when the last surviving member of the family died. Other local industries included, in Lambeth High Street, the Doulton family pottery works. Potteries were also a feature of Duchy river-side holdings, particularly at Vauxhall, where Lambeth Delphware was made.

The opening up of the area south of the river was to come with the build-ing of bridges and roads. Westminster was opened on 18 November 1750. The following year the turnpike trustees were empowered to construct a road linking the southern approach to the bridge with Kennington Common. The New Road (Kennington Road) provided new development opportunities as well as improving communications. Vauxhall Gardens, for example, became a carriage-ride away from central London. Building along the New Road did not start until the late 1780s when the terrace, Chester Place (now 233–291 Kennington Road) was built. This long terrace of thirty houses, with a pediment over the three central houses in the group, is a remarkable tribute to the co-operation between Georgian speculative builders, many different builders contributing individually to a magnificent and unified whole. During the same period many other houses were built, among those surviv-ing being the Duchy's present local office at 155–157, Kennington Lane. The later terraces in Kennington Lane (nos 113–147, on the north-east side now owned by Lambeth Council) provide the only reminder of how much of the estate must have looked throughout the nineteenth century.

The century was to bring further bridge and road building, significantly for the Duchy, Vauxhall Bridge in 1812 and Waterloo Bridge in 1817. Harleyford Road, linking Vauxhall Bridge and the Camberwell New Road followed in 1818. London was beginning to spread rapidly with ribbon development along these new roads. By 1840, Kennington was almost completely built over. In 1810 the Duchy had granted a lease of the Prince's Meadows estate for 99 years to Messrs Thomas and John Leit who built over the land, including the cottages remaining in Duchy and Roupell Streets.

In 1845 Kennington's most famous landmark, the Oval cricket ground, (now the home of the Surrey County Cricket Club) came into being, lying at the southernmost point of the modern estate. During the seventeenth and eighteenth centuries the land formed part of the Clayton holding, records variously showing the growing of fruit and asparagus. On the termination of the Clayton lease, in 1834, a 99-year lease was granted to William Otter, the minister of St Marks (and later Bishop of Chichester). Otter appears to have intended building a house for the minister and developing the remainder to provide an endowment for the living. This plan lapsed because of objection from the Duchy and Otter turned the land into a market garden. In 1836 he again tried to persuade the Duchy to permit him to build on the land. This time the Duchy was more amenable but during negotiations Otter died in 1840. His trustees subsequently could not agree terms with the Duchy.

Eventually in 1845, an alternative use was found, as a subscription cricket ground, the first match being played by the Montpelier Club in May 1845. This club was not successful but the Surrey Club, formed at the Horns

The tollgate, Kennington Common, shortly before its removal in 1865. In the background is St Mark's Church. (Duchy)

Tavern in the autumn of 1844, shared the ground, eventually becoming the sole lessee in 1874. Many improvements were carried out, including the rebuilding of the Tavern in 1877–78 and a circle of earth banks created around the ground. The pavilion was rebuilt in 1895–97 (architect: Thomas Muirhead).

A short distance from the Oval cricket ground lies St Marks Church, one of four so-called 'Waterloo Churches' built in Lambeth 1822–24. The church was built on a part of Kennington Common known as Gallows Corner. Among the executions to have taken place on the site were those of several Jacobites after the rising of 1745. The common belonged to the manor of Kennington whose tenants enjoyed rights to pasture cattle and horses during the summer months. The common also had a Speaker's Corner, large crowds gathering to hear popular preachers on Sundays. Gatherings of a political nature also took place, the most famous being on 10 April 1848 when some 25,000 supporters of the National Charter assembled to march on Parliament, a procession frustrated by 170,000 police and troops.

By 1850 the condition of the common had become such that the vicar of St Marks promoted a scheme to turn the area into 'a place of resort for respectable persons'. Powers were obtained and, with the support and encouragement of the Prince Consort, Kennington Park was created, opening in March 1854. As part of the laying-out, the 'model' dwellings sponsored by the Society for Improving the Condition of the Labouring Classes which had been built for and exhibited at the Great Exhibition of 1851, were re-erected in the new park.

Railway development in the area was advancing, the London and Southampton Railway's London terminal having been opened at Nine Elms on 21 May 1838. This station, remote from central London, was reached by boat from an adjacent pier, not a very practical arrangement. With short-distance passenger traffic increasing, the company, now the London and South Western Railway, obtained powers in 1845 to construct an extension to a new terminus close to Waterloo and Hungerford Bridges. The extension was to weave a careful path from Nine Elms avoiding a gas works, Vauxhall Gardens and Lambeth Palace and crossing twenty-one roads to Waterloo Station. The railway, with four tracks, was contained on a brick viaduct of arches, designed to minimise disturbance in an area already built up; nonetheless, over seven hundred homes needed to be demolished. The line was opened on 11 July 1848.

The Duchy, in 1854, acquired from the LSWR a group of houses in Vauxhall Row; the properties were in poor condition and a scheme of improvement was put in hand, the buildings becoming known as the Vauxhall Model Lodging Houses. This appears to be the Duchy's first direct involvement with the provision of housing in south London. The development of the area continued, building covering most of the back lands.

In 1861 an experimental horse tram line was laid between Kennington

Gate and the south side of Westminster Bridge. It only lasted a year but a regular horse tram service was to come seven years later from the junction of Kennington Road with Westminster Bridge Road, southwards, dividing at Kennington Gate into routes along Brixton Road and Clapham Road. The stabling and tram depot for this line was built at Kennington Cross on a large site extending back to Cardigan Street (the site of the former Manor House).

A major improvement in public transport of even greater significance to the development of London was the opening, by the Prince of Wales on 4 November 1890 of the City and South London Railway, London's first deep tube railway. A station for the line was built in Kennington Park Road, the distinctive dome of which (housing the lift machinery) remains today.

The modern history of the Kennington estate starts in the early 1890s with the abolition of copyhold and demesne tenures and the opportunity for the first time, for the Duchy to acquire reversions of land and redevelop on a larger scale. By this time, the estate had degenerated to a slum with buildings for the most part run-down and in generally poor condition. Kennington had not escaped the population drift from the inner suburbs to the newer, more commodious suburbs such as Norwood, Penge or Purley. The better-off classes had all but deserted Kennington; the residents of Kennington, as shown in Charles Booth's *Descriptive Map of London Poverty* of 1889 were mostly at the lower end of the social scale being, generally, 'poor' but with pockets of 'comfortable' and 'very poor: chronic want'.

The Duchy was concerned about the conditions in which many of its tenants lived. A start was made in 1893 by building several tenement flats of a pattern to become familiar on the estate. Designed by the Duchy's local surveyor, each tenement accommodated one family per floor in suites of rooms with kitchens and external WCs. The first houses were in Sancroft Street on the Kennington estate and more followed in Chester Way (a simple brick cartouche between 7–8 Chester Way commemorates the year of construction, 1894), Cottington Street, Courtenay Street, Kennington Lane, Kennings Way, Newburn Street, Orsett Street and Aquinas Street on the Prince's Meadows estate. The later flats were self-contained and internal WCs provided. In Stamford Street, on the Prince's Meadows estate, the Duchy converted several terraces of houses into flats, schemes which proved very successful.

The employment needs of the area were not overlooked in the rebuilding, provision being made, for example, for stabling and storage of hansom cabs (in Courtenay Street, now the 'T. S. Griffin' building). The Duchy misjudged the rapid decline of the hansom cab following the introduction of the motor-taxi; by 1908 the building was redundant and a further use being sought. Another commercial scheme was the building of a blacksmith's shop off Kennings Way. This scheme was more successful and continued in regular use until the mid-1960s.

144

The conversion of the horse tramways to electric operation in 1903, (Kennington Road was part of the first route to be electrified – the Prince of Wales opened the line on 15 May) heralded a new era. For the first time the ordinary person could travel to work at a fare he could afford by a frequent and reliable means. Land prices and rents throughout London increased substantially as a result of electric tramway construction.

By 1908, the Duchy had in prospect several reversions, yielding relatively large parcels of land for redevelopment. Still there were problems, with still later reversions making comprehensive redevelopment difficult. As early as 1898, a report on the rebuilding of the triangular site bounded by Chester Way, Kennington Lane and Kennington Road revealed that there were 148 houses on the site of which 71 were on lease for lives depending in the aggregate on 37 different lives. (It was to be almost forty years before the area was fully rebuilt.)

The Old Tenants' Hostel, now known as Woodstock Court, Kennington, built in 1914. The inner courtyard can be seen through the archway. (Duchy)

During the summer of 1909, the Keeper of the Records, Walter Peacock, toured new housing projects in German cities. Another member of the party was Stanley Adshead, recently appointed Professor of Civic Design at Liverpool University. About a fortnight after their return Peacock contacted Adshead and, on behalf of the Prince of Wales, invited him to prepare a report on the Kennington estates with a view to rebuilding. Adshead proposed in March 1911 comprehensive redevelopment of the estate, in stages, commencing with the areas where land was available. He believed there was scope for attracting back the middle-classes to the estate by building the type of house or flat they would aspire to and letting at higher rents. The plans were grand in scale with crescents, squares and wide streets containing a variety of cottages, flats and shops. Kennington, in Adshead's vision, would be restored as a good-class neighbourhood.

While accepting many of Adshead's recommendations, the Duchy felt it had a much stronger duty to rehouse its existing tenants, mostly old and poor, with many living in miserable conditions, at rents they could afford. There was some urgency for new housing for the needy and the Prince's Council instructed that plans be prepared for the construction of fifty tenements in the Newburn Street area. This scheme, as eventually built, was the Old Tenants Hostel (now known as Woodstock Court) a two-storey block around an open courtyard.

The first scheme approved was the building of cottages in Denny Street; the architect was not Messrs Adshead and Ramsey but J. D. Coleridge, the cottages being adaptations of his successful design in Aquinas Street on the Prince's Meadow estate. Approval followed for the laying out and construction of Courtenay Square and the re-alignment of Cardigan Street. This work involved the demolition of a pair of the 1893 tenements: only nineteen years after construction, they were considered to be obsolete. Their facilities were inadequate and they would require extensive modernisation; demolition was justified as the cheaper option. Cottages were built in 1912–19 on the north, west and south sides of Courtenay Square and in Courtenay Street, adjacent to the square. The Cardigan Street elevation to the square was not to be built until 1919. In the newly laid-out Cardigan Street, cottage flats were built, being of the same overall external appearance as the cottages in the square but containing two flats, one per floor. A three-storey block of twelve flats was built on the corner of Cardigan and Sancroft Streets.

In Chester Way similar three-storey blocks were built in three groups. Along Kennington Lane were two further blocks, either side of the junction with Courtenay Street and a row of four shops with flats over. The later group of eighteen flats in Chester Way (Nos 1–3) – not completed until 1916 – were built to a higher standard with superior internal fittings and a central boiler providing domestic hot water to each flat.

Adshead had formed a partnership with another architect, Stanley Ramsey, on obtaining the Kennington commission, and continued his work at Liverpool University, being there for half the year. It is probable that Ramsey was responsible for much of the detailed work although Ramsey suggested it was collaborative. The Adshead and Ramsey buildings are in a restrained late-Georgian style, adapted to modern use, finished in ochre London stock brick with bands and panels applied to highlight the simple features of each terrace or block. The Kennington Lane frontages are finished in a reddy-brown Crowborough brick.

When surveying the area for his report, Adshead was much influenced by the Georgian character of Kennington. He realised the importance of continuing the scale and feel of the town rather than following the fashionable trend for the country, with rustic terraces as inspired by William Morris. Adshead's work at Kennington for the Duchy was to set a trend in the planning and execution of housing estates which is still relevant today.

A number of other buildings, designed by Adshead and Ramsey, were built as part of the general rebuilding. A bakery and shop was built in Newburn Street, the estate office was moved from Kennington Park Road to Kennington Gate (opposite the Oval tube station) where an elaborate frontage was created, and the vicarage for St Anselm's Church built. Construction of the church was started and halted in 1914, the foundation stone being laid by the Prince of Wales. A clearly distinguishable band remains in the brickwork at about the 4.8m (16ft) mark, reflecting the break in building which was not completed until 1933.

Perhaps the most remarkable building was the creche or babies' hostel in Black Prince Road, immediately behind Woodstock Court. This was inspired by Mrs Arthur Michelson, the wife of an Australian millionaire who persuaded the Duchy of the need for a local creche. Mrs Michelson took a lease on the building which was built by the Duchy and, after 1919, funded the provision of care for young working mothers and their newly-born children. War broke out shortly before the building was completed; it was almost immediately requisitioned and turned into a hospital. Mrs Michelson's enterprise is remembered in the name of one of the local authority blocks of flats opposite.

In the period following the war the Duchy endeavoured to alleviate some of the effects of local unemployment by further building projects. Work started in 1922 on the construction of Kennington Palace Court, a block of thirty-six flats, and continued in three phases over the next three years. Another scheme of this period was the building of a block of flats, 231, Kennington Road. This building forms the end of the terrace 233–291, Kennington Road, a successful achievement of compatibility through a thorough understanding of Georgian detail and design.

During the 1920s and early 1930s land disposals occurred, most notably the sale to the NAAFI of the site between Kennington Lane and Kennington Park Road, to the north of Kennings Way, and the sale of several significant sites to the London County Council. London County Council and Lambeth

Kennington Palace Court, built 1922–24 but reflecting the strong neo-Georgian feeling of the estate. (Duchy)

Council applied considerable pressure on the Duchy to improve the condition of much of its remaining poor housing. While respecting the Duchy's pre-war achievement, the lack of continuity was a great cause for concern. Among the sites sold were a strip of land to the south of Kennings Way on which flats were built, and several acres to the north and east of the Oval on which London County Council was to build blocks of flats, each named after well-known Surrey cricketers.

1930 was an important year with the appointment of Holroyd Chambers, a chartered surveyor, as Land Steward, the first appointment of an agent (in contrast to a direct employee) to manage the Duchy's local affairs. This arrangement was to prove successful and has been followed in other Duchy districts.

Chambers, who was to be Land Steward for thirty-four years, set about a further ambitious building programme in a further attempt to do away with the remaining slum property, several large blocks of flats being built in the period 1932–1938 including cottages and flats in Black Prince Road, Boyton House (Kennington Lane), Newquay House (Newburn Street), Restormel House (Chester Way), together with a house in Denny Street, Tamar House (Kennington Lane), Trevose House (Orsett Street) and also Climsland House (Aquinas Street, Prince's Meadows). These blocks, all designed by Louis de Soissons, provided modern housing to a high standard and were let at rents comparable to council-provided property. Of particular importance was Newquay House, the largest block built for the Duchy with seventy-six flats leading onto balconies and set around a central courtyard. During the 1930s a programme of modernisation for existing property provided an electricity supply and means of hot water. The estate survived World War II largely intact but some buildings were badly damaged. On the Kennington estate bombing in the Newburn Street area required the reconstruction of a shop and houses in the early 1950s.

The Prince's Meadows estate fared worse. A number of buildings were destroyed and in 1952 the Duchy sold the estate to London County Council. The area was to become, twenty-five years later, the scene of one of the most protracted planning battles in recent times. Local people backed by Lambeth Council succeeded in ensuring the Coin Street area was developed for housing and not, as was proposed, for offices and other commercial uses.

The biggest project of this time was the redevelopment by Southbank

A 1930s visit by Prince Edward to Kennington with his mother, Queen Mary. (Duchy)

Estates Limited on a 125-year building lease, of the Albert Embankment flour mills site with three large office blocks, Tintagel, Camelford and Alembic Houses. The development involved the demolition of the Vauxhall model dwellings as part of a road re-alignment.

Housing need was not overlooked, two blocks of flats with small bedsit or one-bedroom units being built in 1955 and 1963. Respectively, Rothesay Court (in Harleyford Street) and Carrick Court (in Kennington Park Road) were designed to accommodate professional single people, for which there was a great shortage of suitable accommodation. Both blocks have laundry facilities for residents and other amenities of special benefit for single people. The triangular site behind Kennington Cross bounded by Cardigan Street and Sancroft Street was comprehensively redeveloped in 1968 to provide a mixed scheme of houses, flats and studios set around a central communal garden, known as the stables site development (after excavations revealed evidence of stabling linked with Kennington Palace). On the main road (Kennington Lane) frontage an office block, Edinburgh House was built.

The most recent development, in 1977, comprised two blocks of flats and a sheltered housing scheme in Kennington Road. The sheltered housing, Rupert House, and one block, Elizabeth House, was let to, and is administered by, the Guinness Trust. The remaining block, Jubilee House, is managed by the Duchy. In the wider Kennington area redevelopment has continued, Lambeth Council and the Greater London Council embarking on large compulsory acquisition schemes. Tower blocks and sprawling council-owned schemes now surround the Duchy's estate, dwarfing and dominating the neighbourhood.

The modern manor of Kennington comprises some forty acres of mostly residential property in the area of Kennington Cross. Until the early 1980s the Duchy had remained as a provider of much-needed rental accommodation but rent controls and ever-increasing maintenance costs dictated the need for disposal. As properties become vacant they are being sold. The Duchy's change in direction has been the cause of much local concern as it has always been seen as a provider of rented accommodation in an area where it is in short supply. Many families have been Duchy tenants for generations and, potentially, it will not be possible for sons and daughters to look to the Duchy for a home. The solution might lie in the possibility of introducing new forms of tenure, with the tenants being their own landlords, and this is under investigation at Newquay House. Woodstock Court continues to provide sheltered housing for the local elderly.

The Adshead and Ramsey estate remains largely intact together with the de Soissons blocks, an impressive gathering of buildings now surrounded by local authority developments on a monumental scale. The estate provides a useful reminder for architects and town planners that it is possible to provide homes for a mixed inner-city population and to do so on a scale and in a manner that those who live there can respect.

A July 1986 visit by Prince Charles to Kennington: seen here talking to tenants of Newquay House. (Duchy)

CHAPTER EIGHT

EAST OF EXETER

Michael Havinden

About half the Duchy's agricultural estates lie in a triangle scattered between Bradninch in east Devon, Daglingworth near Cirencester in Gloucestershire and Dorchester in Dorset, with a detached outlier at Boverton on the south Wales coast just west of Barry. The majority of the estates are in Somerset and Avon. They comprise altogether some twenty-eight thousand acres and provide roughly two-thirds of the Duchy's agricultural rental income. There are twenty-one separate estates ranging from ancient holdings like Bradninch in Devon, and Mere in Wiltshire, which have been part of the Duchy since its foundation in 1337, to recent acquisitions like the Duke's residence at Highgrove near Tetbury in Gloucestershire (purchased in 1980).

For management purposes this large group of estates is divided in two. The Duchy's central district, with its headquarters at Bowhill Farm in Bradninch, run by John Hitchings, a land agent with many years of experience working for the Duchy, manages Bradninch and the five estates in south Somerset, lying between Taunton and Yeovil, in addition to Dartmoor and various foreshore rights. The remaining nine estates in north Somerset and Avon, with the six outliers in Dorset, Wiltshire, Gloucestershire and south Glamorgan, form the eastern district, which is managed on the Duchy's behalf by the firm of Smith, Woolley and Co in Bath. An agricultural enterprise of this size and variety naturally possesses a wide range of differing soils and natural environments, and can best be understood by subdivision into groups of estates. Each has its own system of farming and activities, such as forestry and rural industries, which have evolved separately, influenced and shaped by their individual histories within the Duchy.

EAST DEVON AND SOUTH SOMERSET

These six estates in the central district comprise Bradninch in Devon, and the Somerset estates of Curry Mallet, Isle Abbots, Isle Brewers, Stoke sub Hamdon and the former manor of Milton Falconbridge, lying in many detached pieces in the modern civil parishes of Long Load and Ash, which were anciently within the historic parish of Martock.

Bradninch is the Duchy's largest and most ancient holding in this group. It came in the original charter of 1337, and the Duchy still retains rather more than three thousand acres of farmland which is distributed amongst thirteen farms. Originally the ancient borough of Bradninch, about nine miles north-east of Exeter, belonged to the Duchy as well, but in 1986 only five houses and cottages were still held. The Duchy's farms lie on both sides of the town, but most of them are situated to the west of the town on the hills which rise to a height of 259m (847ft) at Christ's Cross on the western edge of the parish. These are typical Devon hills, usually a brilliant emerald in colour, smooth and rounded in shape, but quite steep in places. Much of the soil is derived from red sandstones; so that when some fields are ploughed they stand out dramatically amongst the rich pastures which predominate in this basically dairying region.

The Duchy has done much rearranging of its farms' sizes and boundaries in order to ensure that each one is an economic size (they average about 260 acres each), conveniently compact and with good access to roads. The

Bradninch Manor House: a 1936 visit by King Edward VIII. (Western Morning News)

thirteen surviving farms are a far cry from the seventy-one holdings which existed in 1854. Half a dozen cows milked by hand were an economic proposition in those days, but with modern milking machines and milking parlours, herds in excess of a hundred cows have become the norm. It has been Duchy policy to re-equip farms with running water and modern buildings suitable for dairying – though milking parlours have been purchased by the tenants themselves. Though dairying has been the mainspring of farming at Bradninch, the red land will grow a variety of arable crops, and three of the farms are not in dairy production. They rely on corn and sheep, or corn and beef, and with the arrival of quotas limiting milk production, further diversification away from dairying seems probable.

Although the general trend of Duchy policy has clearly been towards the creation of fairly large (but mainly family-worked) farms to maximise economic viability, there is also some anxiety about the elimination of openings in agriculture for young men of limited capital who are looking to make a start on a smaller holding. One of the farms at Bradninch was let some years ago on a thirty year lease to Devon County Council for its smallholder scheme. This farm has been sublet by the County Council to three smallholders. In continuance of this policy another Bradninch farm was recently reduced to about ninety acres to allow a young man an opportunity to start farming on his own account. It is the Duchy's policy to let this farm only to relations of existing tenants, a policy that may have to change if there is insufficient demand.

Legally the Bradninch farms are all let on annual tenancies, but since tenants have enjoyed security since 1947, and their heirs have had a right to succeed (provided they are suitable) under an act of 1976, the legal form of the tenancy bears little or no relation to the length of tenure, and in fact it has long been Duchy policy to maintain a long-term continuity of family tenancies. The Duchy charges more or less the average commercial rent in each district (which was between £40 and £50 an acre in Bradninch in 1986).

The Prince of Wales takes a keen interest in the development of the estate. He visits the farms regularly and knows all the tenants personally. He is specially concerned with the encouragement of wildlife through tree-planting, and has stimulated this by granting some exclusive shooting rights at Bradninch to his tenants in exchange for tree planting, pond digging, etc on their part. The response has been so enthusiastic that it is reckoned that over 200,000 trees have been planted – probably more than on any other estate in England. One tenant, John Berry, at Billingsmoor Farm in the extreme north of the parish, has won several national awards for his conservation work. The conservation effort and the management of their joint shoot has brought the tenants together socially much more than was previously the case, and has contributed to a sense of community and social cohesiveness on the estate which the Prince had always been concerned to foster.

A distance of some twenty-four miles separates Bradninch from its nearest

Wishay Farm, Bradninch, a traditional east Devon farm, tastefully modernised. (Duchy)

Somerset neighbour, the Curry Mallet estate, which lies on the edge of the Somerset levels about six miles south-east of Taunton. The north-western part of the estate lies on a low range of hills running north-eastwards from Hatch Beauchamp to Curry Rivel and separating West Sedge Moor to the north from the valley of the river Isle to the south. The Duchy farms slope gently southwards from a height of some 70m (210ft) down to the Fivehead river, a tributary of the Isle. The land here is only some 23m (69ft) above sea level, and liable to flood. Despite the gentle slope the general appearance is of a flat and rather bare countryside since the ravages of Dutch elm disease in the 1970s. A vigorous tree planting campaign is now under way, which will restore variety to the landscape in future years.

Curry Mallet became part of the Duchy in 1421 as part of the big exchange when numerous Somerset lands came as compensation when Isleworth in Middlesex was granted to Sion monastery. For a long time the tenants' lands were much dispersed and intermixed in a parish which was only partly enclosed. In a survey of 1771, William Simpson recorded that 1,277 acres were let on copyhold tenure to forty-three tenants, who also enjoyed rights of common grazing on West Sedge Moor and other commons. The vicar had nearly thirty-seven acres of glebe and there was a freehold estate belonging to the Pyne family of nearly 137 acres. It is this latter estate on which the ancient medieval manor house (much rebuilt in the sixteenth century) stands, and is now occupied by a descendant of the Mallets; thus rather concealing from the average visitor that most of the parish is a Duchy estate.

The land was described as 'very valuable' by the surveyor Thomas Davis in 1809, but it is regarded as mostly average in quality today. Enclosure and reorganisation of farms took place gradually during the nineteenth century, and the land was extensively under-drained by the Duchy about one hundred years ago. Today there are six farms ranging from about 250 to 400 acres in size. They are mostly mixed dairy and arable farms though one has no dairy and relies on corn and pigs. The farmsteads are sturdily built of the characteristic local blue-grey lias limestone. The Duchy also owns a few other houses and cottages in the village, but most of the 104 dwellings in the three scattered hamlets are owned by their occupiers or are council houses. The nature of the relationship between the Duchy and the inhabitants of Curry Mallet has been the subject of a special study commissioned by the Duchy and published in 1984.

Lying just to the east of Curry Mallet are the two parishes of Isle Abbots and Isle Brewers, built on what were once small, flat islands in a sea of marshes. Here the Duchy has four farms comprising about 820 acres in a very low, flat and watery landscape. They were purchased by the Duchy in 1862 and comprise three average-sized farms of about 250 acres and one smaller one of 70 acres. One of the larger farms is an arable farm, but the other two are dairy farms, one of which was completely re-equipped for dairying in the early 1980s. Although only a few miles from Ilminster, Isle Abbots and Isle Brewers have the feel of deep, lush and remote country.

Going eastwards the next Duchy estate is at Stoke sub Hamdon on the road to Montacute, just south of the A303. Here the scenery is very different. Stoke is a large, handsome village set on a hillside some 50m (150ft) above sea level overlooking the great plain of drained levels which stretches northwards to the hills behind Langport and Somerton. Much of Stoke is built of the beautiful golden limestone from the quarries at Hamdon Hill, which overlooks the village to the south. A great Roman earthwork stood on this site and its ancient quarries have been worked since Roman times. The only survivor belongs to the Duchy. Stoke is quite a populous village and has long had an important industrial as well as agricultural side to its economy. It too came to the Duchy in the exchange of 1421, but in reversion, so that the Duchy did not actually obtain it until the death of the sitting tenant, Sir John Tiptoft, in 1443. The land is very good at Stoke and the traditional system of arable farming in strips in open fields was long continued and the remains of the strips are still visible today. A map made by William Simpson in 1786 shows hundreds of such strips in the open fields to the west and east of the village. Enclosure took place gradually during the nineteenth century, but as late as 1890 there was still some strip farming in

Caseberry Farm, Bradninch, set in the rolling east Devon countryside. (Duchy)

King George VI receiving a line of Duchy tenants on his 1937 visit to Stoke sub Hamdon.
(Western Morning News)

the Great Field. The small farms that were characteristic of earlier periods have also been gradually amalgamated and in 1986 the Duchy held only two – one a dairy and mixed farm of 416 acres, and the other a smaller, but specialised arable farm of 112 acres, which concentrates on blackcurrant and potato production.

The Duchy also owns about fifty houses and cottages which are let to local people, but which are gradually being sold off. There were four small glove-making factories in the nineteenth century and the trade is still active in Stoke. The Duchy lets its quarry on Hamdon Hill and has kept it open because it is the last remaining source of the fine stone which is still needed for repairs to the decorative doorways and windows of many local houses and churches dating from Tudor and Stuart times. Ham Hill is now a country park run by Yeovil District Council, and the one-third of it owned by the Duchy is let to the Council rent-free. A new development has been the con-version of redundant farm buildings into workshops for local craftsmen, which was tastefully done in 1985 at the former North Street farm.

The final estate in this southern Somerset complex is the former manor of Milton Falconbridge situated on the lowlands between Martock and Long Sutton. It consists of one unit, Falconer's Farm, of about 225 acres. The farmstead is situated on a slight rise in the hamlet of Milton, and its lands stretch northwards in a scatter of detached fields towards the River Yeo in the floodlands of the Levels. Like Stoke sub Hamdon, Milton came to the Duchy in 1421, in reversion, on the death of Sir John Tiptoft in 1443. Various parts of the manor were enclosed piecemeal prior to the Parliamentary act of 1810, when the remaining 212 acres in three common fields were finally enclosed, although the common meadows along the river Yeo were not included; and still have common rights attached to them. The ancient stones demarcating the different strips, or 'doles', still remain. The enclosure did not lead to rationalisation, and the Duchy farm is still much inter-mixed with lands belonging to Winchester College. It is, however, gradually being consolidated by exchanges and sales of land and will eventually become a somewhat smaller but more easily worked unit. It is a dairy and mixed farm.

NORTH SOMERSET

The Duchy has three estates in north Somerset which stretch in a line north-eastwards from Shepton Mallet. They include lands in Shepton Mallet, Stratton-on-the-Fosse, and Laverton, a tithing in Lullington parish, north of Frome. They are all in the eastern district, and are managed from the office in Bath. The Duchy acquired half the manor of Shepton Mallet in 1421 as part of the Isleworth exchange but over the years has sold off nearly all its land in the town; so that its present estate consists of three farms on the north side of the town, stretching up the steep Mendip scarp, and a scatter of miscellaneous pieces of land to the south of the town, which are mostly let to

The fields of Stoke sub Hamdon, lying to the north of the village. Tenants' lands formerly lay in hundreds of small strips in this still unenclosed field. (Duchy)

neighbouring farmers, but which could become available for urban development if Shepton Mallet were to expand southwards. Scattered small urban properties are still in process of being sold.

The farmland is divided into two fairly substantial dairy farms, of around 200 acres each, and one smaller mixed farm of about 130 acres. The land at Shepton lies on the southern scarp of the Mendips and is not of very high quality. It rises to about 270m (about 800ft) at its northern extremity, making for a fairly exposed location. A few miles to the north-east, over the crest of the Mendips, lies the estate at Stratton-on-the-Fosse, another manor acquired in the 1421 exchange. The Duchy has four farms here situated in a line on the east side of the Fosse Way, the former Roman road over the Mendips. Stratton is on the northern edge of the Mendips as they slope gently towards Radstock. It is chiefly celebrated for Downside Abbey and school, which stand imposingly to the west of the village, but which are not on Duchy land. The Duchy's farms are all dairy farms, and contain some good land and have been well equipped with new buildings. Two of them are of substantial size (about 275 and 200 acres) while the other two are between 110 and 140 acres. The Duchy has sold nearly all its residential land in the village over the years, which may account for its rather mixed architectural appearance.

About eight miles to the north-east of Stratton is Laverton, a remote hamlet lying in gently rolling country on the eastern edge of the Mendips as they slope down to the valley of the little river Frome. The Duchy has rather more than 1,000 acres here, which also came in 1421. There are three substantial farms of between 350 and 280 acres, and two smallholdings (of 60 and 40 acres) formerly let to Somerset County Council which have now reverted to the Duchy. The farms are dairy and arable and the house of one of them, Manor Farm, which is just to the north of the attractive little Norman church, is dated 1627. It has mullioned windows and a fine, vaulted, plaster ceiling inside. Laverton is remote but has a well-cared for and prosperous look. Just north of Manor Farm, there are the remains of an ancient limekiln, where the farmers used to burn the local limestone before spreading it on the land as quicklime, to neutralise soil acidity, which is surprisingly prevalent on soil overlying limestone.

THE AVON ESTATES

The county of Avon is a new creation which only came into existence in 1974, so the six estates here, which all lie to the south of Bath, were once in Somerset; and one of them, at Farrington Gurney, straddles the new county boundary. Four of these estates, at West Harptree, Widcombe in Sutton-Stowey parish, Farrington Gurney and Midsomer Norton lie close to one another in a line stretching from west to east, on the northern slope of the Mendips. This was formerly in the Somerset coalfield, where the Duchy once had some prosperous mines, all now closed down. The other two estates, Newton St Loe and Englishcombe lie adjacent to one another, although unconnected by roads! They form a large block of land on the south-western outskirts of Bath.

At West Harptree, an attractive village in rolling country, just outside the coalfield, the Duchy received half the manor in the exchange of 1421, but past sales have reduced its holding there now to under 200 acres, all of which is let in scattered pieces to local farmers. There is neither a Duchy farm nor Duchy houses in the village. At nearby Widcombe, which also came in the 1421 exchange, the Duchy has three dairy farms – two largish ones of between 250 and 320 acres and one smaller one of 120 acres. They lie in pretty country to the south-west of the Chew Valley Lake, a large reservoir for Bristol, which was created in the 1950s and flooded some of the Duchy's land. Some of the land at Widcombe is fairly good, but where the farms climb up the steep scarp of White Hill the land can only be used for rough grazing and woods.

The village of Farrington Gurney stands about three miles east of Widcombe. An important centre of coal mining since the seventeenth century, one of its first mines was started in 1635 by John Mogge, who had been bailiff of the Duchy's estates since 1618. The ancient stone-built village

The late Sir John Higgs, Secretary to the Duchy (1980–86) leaves Falconer's Farm, Milton, Martock, Somerset, suitably fortified with farmhouse cider. (Duchy)

was much extended eastwards in the nineteenth century by the construction of new cottages for the miners who worked Farrington Gurney colliery, one of the most important mines on the Duchy's estates. This mine was sunk in the 1780s and was worked until 1922. Fairly extensive remains are still visible to the east of the village. One was converted into a barn and the colliery offices have become dwelling houses. After 1922 the Duchy assisted the unemployed miners to start two co-operative mines, one of which, called Marsh Lane Colliery, survived until 1949. Some fifty men worked there and were visited by Prince Edward when he was Duke of Cornwall in 1934. He went underground in one of the coal tubs, and no one remembered that the pit had no washing facilities until he re-emerged. One of the miners' wives came to the rescue with soap and towels.

Farrington's narrow and densely built-up village street forms part of the A362 main road from Radstock to Bristol, and endures heavy lorry traffic. A by-pass has become necessary and the Duchy has recently sold forty-three development sites to allow this to be built; but some twenty cottages, a public house, a garage and a restaurant remain part of the estate. In addition there are three largish farms (in the 200–300 acre range) and two small-holdings which are let to Avon County Council. There is some good red land at Farrington and the farms produce potatoes and cereals as well as milk. There are some visible remains of coal mining, but they are surprisingly unobtrusive considering how long Farrington was a leading coal-mining area.

Just east of Farrington is Midsomer Norton, where the Duchy lands also date back to the 1421 exchange. There are a little over 1,000 acres here, including a good mixed dairy farm of nearly 300 acres at Chilcompton, purchased about 1960. Midsomer Norton was also an important coal mining centre. It expanded from a village into a small town in the nineteenth century until it joined up with its eastern neighbour, Radstock. The Duchy had three important mines here – Old Welton, Clandown, and Welton Hill. All are now closed down, but their remnants have left the Duchy with a scatter of industrial and commercial sites, on the edges of the town, although it no longer possesses any property in the town itself. Old Welton colliery, on the eastern edge of the town, was worked from about 1783 to 1896, and little of it now remains, but a DIY commercial premises occupies part of its surface buildings. Welton Hill colliery, a little to the north-west of Old Welton, was active between 1813 and 1896, and the sites of its three shafts are still visible. The colliery manager's house at the pithead remains in use, but the Cow Inn, where the miners once refreshed themselves when they left the pit, is now derelict. The last of the Duchy mines was at Clandown, which was worked from 1811 to 1929. The site may be seen on the right-handside from the A367 road from Bath as it descends steeply into Radstock. It is now leased by the Duchy to a concrete block works. In all, the Duchy has five small industrial sites in Midsomer Norton, as well as two fairly large dairy and mixed farms (between 230 and 380 acres) north of the town.

About seven miles north-east of Midsomer Norton is Newton St Loe, the Duchy's largest estate in the eastern district, and the only one in which virtually the whole of the village is owned. The Newton estate comprises about 4,800 acres, and is one of the newest in Duchy ownership, a large part having been bought from the Temple family in 1941. The Temples, who had invested a good deal of money in improvements and amenities, were glad not to see the estate dismembered. It lies adjacent to the Duchy's lands in Englishcombe and the land is fairly good, so that it doubtless represented an attractive investment opportunity.

The stately mansion at Newton St Loe was described by Pevsner as one of the finest eighteenth-century examples in Somerset, the 'noble reticence' of whose Georgian style, in cool Bath limestone, 'is characteristic of the School of Bath' – though its architect is unknown. It was built in the early 1760s, was leased to the City of Bath in 1945 on a long lease, and now houses Bath College of Further Education. Nearby is an ornamental lake and the much-restored remains of the keep of the thirteenth-century castle of the St Loe family, while on a hill to the west is the iron age fort of Stantonbury. There are fourteen farms at Newton, ranging in size from under 200 acres up to nearly 600. Eight of them are dairy farms, while the other six concentrate on cereals and beef, with a few sheep. These are all fairly conventional types of farm, but one has an unusual feature – Priston Mill Farm, where a traditional water-powered mill is still in use and growing increasingly popular as a supplier of stoneground wholemeal flour. A mill was recorded on this site in the Domesday survey of 1087. The present buildings date from the eighteenth century and the pitch-back water-wheel from about 1850. There are very few such working mills still in existence.

On a hill to the east of Newton is the ancient village of Englishcombe with its venerable Norman church looking westwards down the valley towards the brook separating it from the lands of Newton, and down which part of the ancient earthwork, the Wansdyke, runs. An historic landscape survey has been done here to guide conservation work. There are two large dairy and mixed farms in this hilly parish of 640 and 730 acres each, which came in the Isleworth exchange of 1421. A former wagon shed has been turned into a craft workshop, and several barns have been sold for conversion into houses. Englishcombe stands like a rampart of rural peace against the bulging suburbs of Bath along its eastern border.

WILTSHIRE AND DORSET

The Duchy has two largish estates in these counties, one at Mere in the south-west corner of Wiltshire, part of which extends into north Dorset near Gillingham; and one in south Dorset, at Fordington, which stretches round the southern and western sides of Dorchester.

Newton Park, Newton St Loe, near Bath: the eighteenth-century mansion (left) is leased to Bath College of Further Education whose associated buildings are to the right. (Cambridge University)

Mere, Wiltshire: a view of the town looking south from the castle site. (Kate Havinden)

The ancient 'castle, manor and hundred of Mere' was part of the Duchy's original grant of 1337, and had previously belonged to the Earl of Cornwall, King Henry III's brother, Richard. The castle, of which only the imposing hilltop site now survives, was built about 1253. It was situated on a steep-sided hill overlooking the little grey-stoned market town from the north, from which there are extensively magnificent views in all directions. It had a hall, a chapel and six towers and commanded one of the main roads from London to Exeter (now the A303) which formerly passed through Mere. From its ramparts the great scarp of the Wiltshire downs could be overseen to the north, while to the east, west and south stretched the extensive plain occupied by the former Gillingham forest, with the hills of Shaftesbury and the Dorset downs in the distance to the south. The castle had decayed long before 1660, when the rector said 'here was anciently a castle' and the site has now been landscaped and is let to the Mere parish council for a playground and place of recreation. Mere has a large ornate church and many fine houses and inns of the Tudor and Stuart period reflecting its former prosperity, but the Duchy now retains only a few houses in the town. It has, however, some 3,800 acres of land let out in farms and smallholdings. There are four dairy farms on the heavy, former forest land to the south of the town, ranging from 120 to 280 acres; and they are adjoined by another two farms of similar size over the Dorset border in Gillingham. These, along with about 400 acres let to the Dorset County Council for five smallholdings, were purchased from the Crown estate in 1862.

North of Mere the Duchy has four more cereal and beef farms (one of about 600 acres, and three of about 300 acres) which stretch up onto the downland scarp. In addition about 850 acres to the east of the town are let to the Wiltshire County Council for another eight smallholdings. All this is a far cry from the ancient system of farming in Mere, when numerous tenants with small farms enjoyed extensive common grazing rights in the forests and on the downs. Sixty of them signed a petition opposing an act of Parliament which authorised the enclosure of 840 acres of pasture and meadow in 1807. Its passage was met with riots in 1810 and it was not until 1821 that the enclosure commissioners were able to complete their award. The downs are indented by a fine series of ancient terraces, known as strip lynchets, and the Duchy is concerned to preserve the ancient monuments and amenities in this area. One specially fine hillside of natural pasture is protected by covenants against the use of chemical fertilisers and sprays, and sports a magnificent carpet of wildflowers in the spring and summer.

Some twenty-eight miles south of Mere is Fordington, where the Duchy has about 3,000 acres of fairly good land on the gently rolling chalklands to the east, south and west of Dorchester. This too is an ancient estate, having been acquired by a grant of 1342; though Maiden Castle hillfort was added much later in 1913 and two farms, Clandon and Ashton, were acquired more recently. Ancient systems of farming survived for a long time in the great open-field of Fordington, with its estimated two thousand arable strips (known locally as 'lawns') and common grazing rights. A survey of the manor by John Norden in 1612 showed that there were eighty tenants, mostly farming twenty to thirty acres apiece. They could not only graze their livestock on the surrounding downs, but had the right to take them in the summer to another Duchy manor (now sold) at Hermitage, twelve miles north of Dorchester in the ancient forest of Blackmoor, where grazings were lusher than on the dry chalk downs. Another survey of 1650 showed that there were still sixty-eight tenants who could each keep three cows and 120 sheep on the commons. All their farmsteads were in Fordington village. The old open-fields were not finally enclosed until 1873, by which time the tenants had been reduced to about a dozen. Today, farming is very different. The Duchy lands are let to only five farmers who occupy mixed dairy and corn farmsteads created after the enclosures in the old open-field. Three have between 700 and 800 acres apiece, while another has some 400 acres.

The Duchy has had special problems with its land at Fordington, because owing to a flood plain to the north of Dorchester, the town could only expand by spreading onto Duchy land to the west, south and east; and this difficulty has been compounded by the recent plan to build a by-pass round the south of the town. This will not only cut some Duchy farms in half but will also pass through the remains of an ancient Roman aqueduct, to the north-west of the town, which the Duchy has some responsibility for preserving. For a long period the Duchy was reluctant to sell land for urban development, which thus occurred only slowly in the late nineteenth and early twentieth century. This led to over-crowding in Fordington village, which had become a suburb of Dorchester; and to strained relations with the town. This problem has now been overcome, and the Duchy is gradually selling land to allow the town to expand. This is also a profitable policy for the Duchy, which by selling land can provide itself with investment funds for acquiring equities and urban commercial properties, and hence reduce what was perhaps once an over-reliance on agricultural land.

A further problem for the Duchy is its ownership of Maiden Castle hillfort, which it is committed to preserving and protecting. Here it is caught between the conflicting pressures from the public, who want better access and facilities for visitors; and the archaeologists, who are anxious lest improved access will multiply visitors, causing damage to the site, as happened at Stonehenge. It will require sensitive diplomacy to please both parties.

The Duchy does not own any property in the old town of Dorchester, but still retains some fifteen cottages in Fordington as well as a foundry, a cash-and-carry store, an industrial site and a miscellaneous collection of grounds let to the town for sports, clubs and allotments, etc. Fordington is an interesting place; one of Dorset's most famous inhabitants, the novelist Thomas Hardy lived there; and by its ownership the Duchy has stamped its mark indelibly on the town of Dorchester and its environs.

GLOUCESTERSHIRE AND SOUTH GLAMORGAN

The three estates here are all relatively recent acquisitions. Daglingworth near Cirencester was purchased in 1959, while Boverton in south Glamorgan, which the Duchy farms in partnership with a Welshman, and Highgrove, the Prince's residence and home farm, were bought in the early 1980s. It was one of the peculiarities of the Duchy, when Prince Charles inherited it, that none of the recent Dukes had established a residence in it, since the medieval castles had decayed hundreds of years ago. Prince Charles wished to live in the Duchy and this meant that a suitable residence had to be bought. Eventually, Highgrove House and park, about two miles south-west of Tetbury in Gloucestershire, comprising 363 acres, were purchased in 1980; and as the Prince's enthusiasm for farming grew, an adjacent farm of

The mighty Iron Age fort of Maiden Castle, Fordington, Dorset, important not just for its antiquity and archaeology but also for the wild flora its grassland supports. (Cambridge University)

some 400 acres was bought in 1984. An amalgamated home farm of some 700 acres was established in 1985.

Prince Charles has taken a very active part in planning the type of farming to be pursued and with the help of a farmer, John Pugsley, a member of the Prince's Council, a system has been developed in which a herd of about 105 Ayrshire cows will produce milk, with an emphasis on production from grassland and a minimum of bought-in concentrated food; while about 420 acres of land will be devoted to arable crops. In addition a flock of 400 ewes, sixty young dairy cattle, and forty-five beef calves will be kept.

It is well-known that Prince Charles is interested in organic farming as well as conservation, but speculation that the farm is being entirely run on an organic system is incorrect. Most of it is a conventional commercial farm, but some eighty acres have been set aside for a trial scheme of rotational non-chemical farming in which a variety of legume fodder crops, grasses and arable cash crops will be grown, with a view to testing the system both practically and financially. The long-term object is to run a profitable farm, but also to show that consideration can be given to the interests of wildlife and to explore the possibility of a significant reduction in chemical inputs, as well as contributing to the visual improvement of the countryside.

The Duchy's Wildlife and Landscape Advisory Group has visited the farm and an active programme of improving existing woodlands, and extending them wherever possible has been launched. Trees will be planted in corners of fields and in patches of waste land. Hedgerow trees will also be encouraged and hedges, which had previously been neglected and become overgrown, will be properly laid.

The arable land will produce cereals and break crops such as rape, peas, linseed and beans. A grain store to hold 850 tonnes is being built and corn-drying facilities are being included. The Prince insisted where possible that all equipment, buildings and machinery should be of British manufacture, but this produced some frustrating headaches. It soon became obvious how few of today's successful agricultural machines are British made. Purchases of second-hand machinery helped to solve the problem, but the decay of British manufacturing remains an unwelcome and unpalatable fact, the effects of which were perhaps not expected down on the farm.

It is clearly going to take several years before the experiments, innovations and improvements at Highgrove fully mature. Prince Charles has explained on television how much he enjoys engaging in farm work, and how he had spent several periods working on various Duchy farms. He clearly derives great enjoyment and satisfaction from addressing the perennial and timeless problems of farming and conservation.

The Duchy's second estate in Gloucestershire is at Daglingworth, atop the rolling Cotswold plateau, where slightly more than 1,100 acres were purchased in 1959. This is a pretty village of traditional Cotswold limestone houses, where the Duchy has two farms on quite good land. One is a beef and cereal farm of slightly over 600 acres and the other a dairy and mixed farm of some 250 acres. There is also a thirty-six acre smallholding, about six cottages in the village, a stone quarry, and about 120 acres of woodlands.

Finally there is Boverton, a very fertile estate of some 700 acres on the south Glamorgan coast which was purchased by the Duchy in 1983. Here an experimental partnership scheme has been introduced on 350 acres, under which the Duchy has entered into partnership with a Welsh farmer. The Duchy has put up one quarter of the capital for this mainly arable farm, and takes a rent plus one quarter of the profits.

A new development for the Duchy has been the purchase of some farms in Lincolnshire. A farm of over 900 acres of good fenland near Spalding was bought in 1985, as was another farm of some 750 acres on the rolling upland country near Ancaster. These Lincolnshire farms represent a move towards the cereals sector of farming and a lessened reliance on dairying, and help to give the Duchy a more balanced spread of properties.

DUCHY INFLUENCE ON VILLAGE LIFE

In most of the villages Duchy influence is fairly limited since its contacts are mainly with its farming tenants, who form only a small part of the village population. However in two villages, Curry Mallet and Newton St Loe, the Duchy influence is more noticeable; at Newton because the Duchy owns almost the whole of the village, and at Curry because Duchy plans for residential development were opposed by certain of the residents, leading to a special study of Curry Mallet's problems in 1983.

This study was commissioned by the Duchy and carried out by Dartington Institute, a research organisation which is part of the many rural and rural-related activities financed by the Trustees of Dartington Hall, near Totnes, Devon. For the past twenty years or more the population of Curry Mallet had been falling (it fell from 341 to 286 – or by 16 per cent – between 1961 and 1981), opportunities for employment in the village in agriculture were greatly restricted and, outside farming, were virtually non-existent. The result was that most of the population worked in Taunton or nearby villages, and it had been Duchy policy for some years to sell off redundant farmhouses and cottages. There was also a need for new bungalows for elderly residents, and possibly for homes for urban dwellers who wished to retire to Curry Mallet. Consequently the Duchy decided to sell one of its houses which had a small orchard attached to it, and to apply for planning permission to build some new houses in the orchard.

This was opposed by a group of residents who felt that the site was inappropriate, and perhaps more fundamentally, that the Duchy's plans would change the nature of the village community in ways which they disliked. They seem to have felt that important decisions were being taken over their heads. In response to their petition to the Prince's Council, the Duchy decided to make a thorough study of the needs and desires of the parishioners as a guide to their long-term development plans. A survey was made of every household (104 in all) and it soon transpired that there was a large measure of misunderstanding about the Duchy's attitude to the village, as well as some inevitable divergences of views about how they wished to see the village develop in future.

It was fairly clear though that the majority of the parishioners were worried, both by the decline in the size of the population and by its changing age structure, since in 1981 50 per cent of the population of Curry Mallet were over forty-four years of age compared with 42 per cent for Somerset as a whole and 37 per cent for England and Wales. Most of them thought that

The Prince of Wales talking to his tenants, Mr and Mrs R. Doble at Lyddons Farm, Currey Mallet, Somerset.

The Prince of Wales with tenants of one of the workshops created for rural industry at North Street Farm, Stoke sub Hamdon. (Council for Small Industries in Rural Areas)

(Right) *Rolling farmland at Mere in Wiltshire, part of the eastern estates of the Duchy.* (Roy Westlake)

(Overleaf) *A Dartmoor view from Combestone Tor, looking towards Loughter Tor.* (Roy Westlake)

the Duchy took little interest in the parish and that its policy could not be influenced by their wishes; but most of them also favoured an increase in houses in the village, and hoped tht the Duchy would somehow be able to increase jobs within the parish. As a result the Duchy decided to go ahead with its plans for housing development; and hoped that the mechanism of consultation and co-operation between itself, the Parish and District and Rural Community Councils, and the inhabitants which the study had generated, would break down previous mistrust and open a new era in relationships, in which the Duchy would be more sensitive to the villagers' needs, while also being conscious of their desire to maintain their independence, and avoid a sense of being patronised. Clearly the Duchy is being asked to perform a rather delicate tightrope-walking act here.

At Newton St Loe, no specific problems have arisen, but the village's location, a few miles to the west of Bath just off the Bristol road, makes it a particularly attractive site for potential suburban development. The Duchy's policy is to try to sustain the village as a viable rural community and not to allow it to become merely a dormitory suburb of Bath. To this end new houses, which would be out of character with the village have not been encouraged, and the Duchy has helped to renovate the village hall. The former estate yard has become the headquarters of the south-western region of the British Trust for Conservation volunteers, and fishing rights and boat houses on the river Avon have been let to local clubs. Land has also been leased to Saltford golf club for its course. It is always difficult for rural communities to sustain themselves when they are close to large towns, but since Newton is a particularly attractive village, the Duchy has thought it right to do what it could to maintain its character.

FORESTRY

Woodlands in these two Duchy districts are mainly to be found at Daglingworth and Newton St Loe, where there are about 300 acres in all. In neither case are they on sites suitable for high-class commercial production of softwoods (pines and larches, etc), so the Duchy has adopted a long-term policy and is managing the woods with a view to maximising the growth of a range of hardwoods (oaks, beech, ash, etc). These have long-term value and in the short-term add to the amenity of the landscape and encourage the conservation of wildlife. The aim is to remove dead and weak timber and to improve the woodlands by a consistent and steady policy of replanting with sound and healthy trees.

SMALLHOLDINGS AND WORKSHOPS

The Duchy has been an active supporter of the various county council smallholder schemes and on many of its estates it has leased land to the councils for sub-letting to suitable smallholders. The aim now is probably more to regard such holdings as 'starters' where young people of limited capital may gain experience before moving on to larger farms, than as long-term farming enterprises in their own right; though no doubt this would be subject to variation in different localities. Clearly, although the general thrust of Duchy policy has been to amalgamate farms into larger sizes in order to increase their viability, there has also been a concern to try to ensure that smaller farmers receive some encouragement, and that the 'farming ladder' is not entirely eliminated.

The workshop programme is designed to tackle a quite different aspect of rural life – namely the reduction in village population as farming increasingly mechanises and employs fewer people; and simultaneously the problem of what to do with redundant farm buildings as farms are amalgamated. The rise of the 'self-sufficiency' and small-business movement, coupled with a certain reaction against big city life, has helped to create a demand for craft and industrial workshops in pleasant rural surroundings which the Duchy has been able to go some way towards meeting.

In the eastern district, there are five workshops at the former Street Farm in Highgrove, three in the old estate yard at Newton St Loe, two at Stratton-on-the-Fosse and one at Englishcombe. In the central district, development has been concentrated at the former Halthaies farm at Bradninch, where there are four workshops, and at the old North Street farm at Stoke sub Hamdon, where eight new workshops were opened by the Prince of Wales in October, 1985, and where another six are planned. This is a most attractive conversion of a fine Ham stone farmstead in a village street. Altogether the Bradninch and Stoke workshops provide employment for over fifty people, and comprise a surprising range of activities. On the manufacturing side, products include furniture, printed plastic and fabric articles, marquees and tarpaulins, Windsor chairs and educational toys and jigsaws. Some of these are exported as well as being sold throughout the United Kingdom. Businesses providing services are also very varied. One firm provides a cookery training base, two others are involved with graphic design, another specialises in interior design and wallpapers, while yet another provides educational software for computers, which are sold world-wide. One of the designers is a cartoonist with an international reputation, and design work is carried out for a wide range of national and international clients.

These new developments, encouraged by the Duchy, have helped to sustain village life by activities outside the traditional agriculture-related aspects. They provide a heartening new perspective, and the prospect of arresting the steady decay of rural life which has been such a depressing feature of the past century. It has been said of the Duchy that the managers of its affairs have to steer a difficult course between striving for a profitable commercial operation, without neglecting their responsibilities to increase the welfare of the many people who live and work on the Duchy's estates.

Farm buildings at North Street Farm, Stoke sub Hamdon, redundant as a result of farm mergers and now converted into workshops for modern crafts and small businesses. (Duchy)

This is not always an easy task, but the vitality of the smallholding and workshop schemes, as well as the more traditional farming activities, suggests that this difficult job can be successfully accomplished.

CHAPTER NINE

FORESHORE AND FUNDUS

Tony Carne

Three hundred and thirty miles of coastline and fifty-eight miles of river combine to give the county of Cornwall one of the strongest and most scenically spectacular natural boundaries in Britain. Of this boundary, three fifths of the foreshore, the coastal and estuarine land between the high and low tide marks, is owned by the Duchy of Cornwall along with twenty miles of fundus, the navigable river bed of the Tamar, the fundus of most of the other Cornish rivers and some in south-west Devon too, with accompanying strips of foreshore.

The last few decades have witnessed a gradual change of use of many of these assets of the Duchy. Beaches where for centuries fishermen toiled all year round over nets and boats, where farmers drew sand and seaweed, now lie deserted during winter but are crammed during the few summer months with the prostrate bodies of sun-seekers packed 'like pilchards in a mawn'. Similarly, creeks and harbours which once handled vessels from places as widespread as Newcastle and New York now shelter countless pleasure craft. The traditional industries of fishing and seaborne traffic are virtually dead and have been replaced by the brash young leisure business.

The foreshore is traditionally owned by the crown as a regality, unless otherwise disposed of, as in the case of the Duchy of Cornwall. In Cornwall the foreshore varies, from a broad expanse of sand at Polzeath to a narrow, near vertical, strip of rock at Land's End. But however extensive the foreshore, the same rights are conveyed by ownership, a feudal relic which today is assuming a new significance.

The Right of Wreck was once jealously guarded and enabled the Duchy to claim all shipwrecks, flotsam and jetsam found on the foreshore. In the days of primitive sailing ships this was far more lucrative than now. In the year 1296/97 one item alone provided the Earl of Cornwall with £40. The Right of Wreck was difficult to enforce and was frequently conveyed to the local lord of the manor or the Duchy's officer in Lostwithiel, the Havener, who supervised foreshore and fundus.

If a wreck occurred the lord, or Havener, would have to move swiftly if he wished to claim his rights before the local population could get their hands

The beach at Polzeath on the north coast of Cornwall, part of the Duchy's foreshore, crowded with holidaymakers in the summer of 1977. (Western Morning News)

on it and spirit it away. In 1342/43 the Black Prince claimed to have lost £1,000 and again in 1345, he complained that wrecked goods, including silver valued at 2,000 marks (the mark, common unit of medieval currency, had the value of 13s 4d), had been stolen by people on the spot. If wreckage was salvaged by others the lord would claim half of its value but again he would need to be quick, and many a cask of wine failed to reach its rightful destination intact due to 'spillage when dropped on the rocks'.

The reason why Cornish lawlessness over wrecking was so much worse than elsewhere was largely due to the county's remoteness from any seat of government, with only two ports, Saltash and Padstow, deemed large enough to warrant Admiralty jurisdiction. Plunder of wrecks got worse during the eighteenth century with the tinners having a frightful reputation for violence. Lawlessness was also associated with smuggling; a seaboard population engaged upon smuggling was unlikely to be sensitive over the ethics of wrecking. A reliable witness, Dr Borlase, has left illuminating accounts of wrecking in Penwith. On sighting a vessel sailing close to the shore the tinners would leave their work and follow her around the coast, waiting for her to strike. A crowd of two thousand was not uncommon; one of four thousand was reported at a Sennen wreck in 1838. The wreckers would be armed with axes and 'could cut a large trading vessel to pieces in one tide and cut down anyone who opposed them.' Borlase had seen half-dead men stripped of their clothes and valuables. Nor was it only the lower classes who were responsible. At a wreck at Looe in 1751, customs officers tried to form a guard of townspeople but, instead of helping, they rushed to get out their carts and fill them with cargo. Wreckers were seldom brought before the law and wrecks were regarded as a gift of the gods, providing riches as well as a break in monotony.

Lawlessness did not always prevail and the unfortunates who had taken to the rigging of a wrecked ship were frequently the subjects of heroic rescues. With the generally evil reputation of Cornish longshoremen it is not surprising that some shipwreck victims were sceptical of rescue. In the 1850s a Liverpool ship was wrecked on Bryher in the Isles of Scilly and as the rescuers approached the desperate crew were seen to grasp staves to defend themselves. The bodies of shipwreck victims who perished were often treated unceremoniously and were either buried in the cliffs, or on the beach above the high water mark. Their bones are still uncovered during spring tides or landslips. Not until an Act of 1808 were shipwreck victims buried in a parish churchyard. On one such occasion, when a young curate had anxiously enquired of a wrecker as to what action should be taken about a corpse which had just been washed in, the only reply he received was 'Sarch 'ees pockets'.

The use of the term 'wrecker' must not be taken to imply that vessels were deliberately lured ashore by the showing of false lights. There is not evidence to support this, nor was anyone ever brought before a court of law charged with such an offence. Nevertheless, in the Malicious Damage Act of 1861 clauses were included, specifically for Cornish wrecking, which dealt with the showing of false lights and the masking of lights or buoys. When this Act was replaced by the Criminal Damage Act of 1971 the myth was still so prevalent that these clauses were retained. One wonders what the Cornish MPs were doing at the time of its passing.

Wreckage was sometimes salvaged from 'just offshore', beyond the low water mark. In such cases the lord (or Havener) would claim way-leave on items carried over his foreshore. The same rules applied to goods purchased at sea and landed on a beach, when one-fifteenth of their value would go to the owner of the foreshore rights. In the eighteenth century wreckage commonly consisted of barrels of tar, casks of wine, driftwood, boats, anchors and cordage. Not only did it provide the inhabitants of poor coastal parishes with luxuries such as silks and brocades but with essentials also. Many wrecked ships' timbers still serve as lintels, beams, and joists.

With so many shipwrecks on its exposed shores, Scilly wrecking stories are legion; this one illustrates its hazards. Georgie, of St Agnes, found a barrel, a tidy little keg containing fat, very carefully packed and quite watertight. He took it home and shared the fat amongst his friends before his sister, with whom he lived, used some to bake some cakes for tea. It was just ten minutes after teatime that a very distressed Georgie appeared, staggering down Duck Street from Higher Town gasping, 'Doant 'ee 'ate it! Doant 'ee 'ate it! Sister's mortal ill! Sister's mortal ill!' Some of the fat was later sent away for examination. It was gelignite.

Wrecking nowadays means little more than the gathering of driftwood. The scale of wrecking was enormously reduced by the advent of iron ships, bigger vessels and improved navigational technology, but the most significant difference for wreckers in the twentieth century is that it is the coastguard, as receiver of wrecks, who has to be dodged rather than the lord of the manor.

Whilst technology has reduced the frequency of shipwreck, it has also put wrecks which were formerly inaccessible within the reach of the underwater archaeologist. In October 1973 an underwater search by members of the Nautical Archaeological Section of the Plymouth Sound branch of the British Sub-Aqua Club made a discovery which initiated the exciting 'Catharina Project'. Protruding from the mud botton in 30.5m (100ft) of water off Drake's Island was a ship's bell. Markings on the bell revealed a name, *Die Fraumetta Catharina von Flensburg*, a date, 1782, and that the vessel was a brigantine. The Duchy, owners of the Right of Wreck, granted a licence to excavate, and rolls of reindeer hides were raised which, after being sealed in anaerobic condition in the silt, were found to be almost perfect. Many interesting artefacts were also recovered including a solid silver shoe buckle. The hides were all sold to a leathercraft factory in Falmouth to be fashioned into a variety of quality leatherware with some of the proceeds being used to finance the project.

Included in the Right of Wreck were whales and other fish cast up by the sea. This also was formerly far more lucrative than today, when whales, porpoises and tunny were not uncommon sights on beaches after gales. A whale caught in Mounts Bay in 1354 was ordered to be taken to Sonning in Berkshire for the household of the Black Prince. Sturgeon are still royal fish and should be presented to the Duke, but nowadays they frequently seem to be caught 'just offshore' and are several days old when brought in, although recently one did find its way into the Aquarium in Plymouth. Today this Right of Fish is more of a liability than an asset as the removal or burial of the carcass is often involved. Not long ago, a dead whale stranded at Tregantle created a big stink when the army dynamited it and plastered half a mile of cliff with decaying fragments. All fish landed on the foreshore was subject to landleave. In fishing ports this was usually claimed by making a levy on the number of boats registered in the port.

The reign of King John saw an important development in the fishing industry, one which was to be of major economic significance to Cornwall, the salt-curing of pilchards by a method introduced from Bayonne. The fish were cured in cellars, known locally as palaces on account of their size, and the process used salt imported mainly from Guerande in Brittany which was subject to an import tax. The vast bulk of fish was exported to France and Italy although salt-cured pilchards remained a staple part of the Cornish winter diet until well into the present century.

In Elizabeth's time there was a rumpus in Sutton Pool following the imposition of a large levy by Plymouth corporation on the pilchard industry to pay for Drake's fort on Plymouth Hoe. The merchants already paid dues to the Duchy (the cellars were built upon Duchy fundus) and the extra charges were too much. So they moved to Cawsand Bay to build new cellars free from the controls of Plymouth. The citizens at least could not have been sad to see

The village of Kingsand on the Cornish shore of Plymouth Sound. The pilchard cellars built by the merchants of Plymouth in late Elizabethan times to escape the taxes imposed on them in Plymouth can be seen along the foreshore, notably at Martin's Cove, the first white-roofed building past the houses. (Western Morning News)

Porth Navas, a side creek of the Helford river where the Duchy has control of the fishing, and the home of the Duchy Oyster Farm. (Western Morning News)

them go for the stench must have been appalling. In 1870 the vicar of St Ives was quoted as saying that the smell of fish there was sometimes so strong as to stop the church clock. The levying of landleave upon fish was further complicated during Elizabeth's reign, and again in Cromwell's time following the suppression of piracy. This enabled fishermen to venture from inshore waters to the deep-sea grounds without fear of abduction, and land their catches at ports other than their home ports.

Traditionally the Duchy has control of the fishing on the Camel, Helford, Fal, Fowey, Tamar, Avon, Salcombe, and Dart rivers and estuaries by boat, net and weir. Fish weirs, now gone, usually consisted of nets supported by poles strung out at right angles to the river bank and used to catch fish on the ebbing tide. Oyster fishing in Cornwall is believed to date back to Roman times. Pollution has closed the Lynher fisheries at Saltash but the Duchy oyster farm at Porth Navas on the Helford is very much a thriving concern.

Despite a recent setback caused by the disease *bonamia*, the farm is now under new management and produces nearly a quarter of Britain's oysters. The fisheries are leased to Len Hodges, a fourth-generation oyster fisherman who has three assistants. Oysters are trawled from the Helford, Frenchman's Creek and the Fal by sailing boats and brought to Porth Navas where they are graded (1 to 5) according to size and put into aerated concrete tanks to purify themselves. A large, No 1 oyster may take from five to seven years to grow and will sell at five for £3. They are packed into boxes with seaweed and sent by rail to London from Falmouth. Undersized oysters are used to re-seed the beds.

In addition to oysters, mussels and clams are also farmed. The clams are sent from Southampton and spend four months being purified before selling at five for £1. A similar farm exists at Mevagissey, where what is little more than a cemented-up crack in the rocks has been leased to a fisherman as a crab tank. Locally caught spider crabs are kept in it before being shipped out in eight-ton lorry loads. Other leases for use of the foreshore rocks have been granted at Penzance, Marazion and Mousehole for tidal swimming pools. These are run by the local councils, although some are now disused. There are several lifeboat slipways also for which a 5p per annum peppercorn rent is paid.

Freehold ownership theoretically confers rights upon the owner which extend from the centre of the earth, to the height of the heavens above. So, at Hayle, wayleave has been granted to certain individuals permitting them to 'pass through the corridor' and enabling them to continue mining activities under the sea. Rights of easement have been granted at Porthcurnow for submarine cables to come ashore and also over the Tavy where a gas main crosses the river. Similar situations exist with the chains of the Torpoint ferry which lie upon Duchy fundus and with the Tamar bridges. British Rail leases the area of fundus which the central pier of the Royal Albert Bridge sits upon. Plymouth breakwater was built on the Duchy fundus but was recognised as Admiralty freehold property in 1811. The Breakwater Fort also stands on the fundus and will be recognised as Duchy property when it is no longer required by the Ministry of Defence. In the Isles of Scilly undersea power cables have recently been laid from St Mary's to the off-islands. This has led to serious repercussions for the inter-island ferry service, which had depended upon the revenue from carrying diesel generator fuel to remain economically viable. Their future is now uncertain.

Tin streaming, once a major Cornish industry, is now virtually extinct and confined to amateurs. The last licence to be issued was to a streamer who collected ore-bearing rocks from the foreshore at Cligga Head. Not far away, at Penhale, a military training area is leased to the Ministry of Defence, and Newquay frequently hosts international surfing contests. With so many varied activities taking place on the foreshore it is scarcely surprising that there are conflicts of interest. On major holiday beaches such as Widemouth

Bay, Polzeath and Par chaos could easily develop, were activities not properly regulated. Problems concerning the granting of concessions for car-parking, ice-cream sales and deck chairs, together with segregation and safety of bathers, surfers, canoeists, water-skiers, sand-yachters, dogs and naturists, are normally left to the lessees. These include local authorities, hotels, or the National Trust, which leases 52 of the Duchy's 228 miles of coastline. But, despite this, the Duchy office at Liskeard continues to be plagued throughout the summer months with phone calls from irate residents, which can be either complaints about fouling by dogs or queries about 'the Duchy position over nudes on beaches'.

Edward Prince of Wales on a visit to the Duchy Oyster Farm at Porth Navas, accompanied by Major McCormick. (Western Morning News)

The reign of Henry II saw the revival of tin streaming on Dartmoor and Bodmin Moor which gave rise to the extension of foreshore and fundus rights on certain rivers. Tin coinage towns away from the coast, Ashburton, Tavistock and Bodmin needed a port which, for security's sake, was normally situated upriver, close to a castle. This led to the development of Totnes, Saltash and Lostwithiel, all long ago superseded by newer ports at the mouth of their estuaries. Lostwithiel, which became the Duchy's administrative centre, was ironically destroyed as a port by the very industry which had created it when the sand and gravel washed down from tin streaming silted up the river. After 1400, sea-going vessels were unable to navigate that far upriver and port activities were transferred to Fowey, where a harbour board was incorporated in 1869 and port facilities much expanded. Ancient fishing rights on the Fowey were extended upstream beyond tidal limits and were curiously defined as to 'soe farr as two oxen yoaked can goe and pass'.

Ships' harbour dues (keelage) were collected at the Stannary ports. At Saltash these amounted to one shilling for every English ship and two for a foreign keel that anchored in the Hamoaze. (After the Armada Spanish ships had to pay seven shillings.) Dues were collected by the Corporation who leased the right from the Duchy. A similar situation existed on the Camel with the Padstow harbour commissioners, and on the Dart where Dartmouth Corporation were empowered to appoint a water bailiff in 1511. Mooring rights at Looe are in the hands of a private individual.

Coinage dues were also collected on the Stannary rivers which, not unnaturally, some tinners sought to avoid paying. This was the origin of Cornish smuggling whereby unstamped ingots of copper and tin (and bales of wool) were smuggled out of the country concealed under barrels of cured pilchards. Before the establishment of harbour commissioners the Duchy Havener at Lostwithiel collected dues, but, as this gradually became more difficult, the right was leased out.

During the Middle Ages the Duchy collected petty customs dues in eighteen Cornish harbours. Some of these harbours are very small, a reminder of how small the vessels themselves were until after 1600, when the development of the East India trade necessitated the use of larger vessels. Some of the smaller harbours, such as Portwrinkle, continued to pay Duchy dues on pilchards up until the 1780s. After a history of boom and slump, the fishing industry, and particularly large-scale inshore fishing finally succumbed in the nineteenth century to overfishing and pollution. Fish are fastidious. As industrialisation increased the waters became more and more polluted so that the last Cawsand Bay seine net was sold in 1855 as the fish shoals ceased to appear in the approaches to Plymouth. The extent of the pollution may be illustrated by considering Millbrook Lake where a property developer, despite protests, has excavated a medieval causeway which gave access to the river at all states of the tide. Upon examination the excavated material was found to be partially composed of waste from a copper smelter which had existed nearby in the 1870s. When the waste had been dumped it had contained a significant proportion of arsenic. Its effect, together with all the other smelters in the Tamar valley, upon fish stocks can be readily imagined.

At intervals throughout its history the Duchy's policy of leasing assets has changed, according to circumstances, and at times assets have been sold off. This happened during the Regency period and during the latter years of the last century. The policy has now reverted back to the traditional leasing and licencing. If a lessee wishes to make extensive developments then a long lease of fundus is granted. Seven, fourteen, twenty-one or even thirty-one year leases are not unusual, with an upwards rent review every two years or so. If an individual wishes to carry out activities upon a limited scale then a licence would be granted. A licence would be granted for a pontoon, a lease for a permanent jetty.

The recent upsurge in popularity in boating, with the consequent demand for moorings, illustrates how the Duchy seeks to safeguard local interests by leasing control of assets into local hands. Traditionally, mooring upon Duchy fundus was free. The increased pressure upon mooring spaces in the 1970s led to chaos, particularly when boat owners from London and the Midlands realised how advantageous West Country mooring rates were and flocked to take advantage. With over five thousand boats mooring on Duchy ownership each year, harbours soon became jammed, with saturation point reached on the Helford causing congestion and damage to boats swinging in too close proximity. This situation was not aided by the false assumption amongst holiday-home buyers that mooring rights accompanied adjacent property ashore. Now a waiting list for available moorings is in operation.

The situation was badly in need of regulation so the Duchy started to introduce rents for mooring spaces which are still far cheaper than elsewhere. On the Tamar the operation of ascertaining the number of boats and the names of the owners mooring on Duchy foreshore and fundus was carried out from the Princetown office which also issued licences. Help was given by the Ministry of Defence who later took a lease of the river Tamar from its confluence with the river Tavy down to the limits of ownership south of the breakwater. The MoD then became responsible for managing the moorings, including their allocation and licensing. Deep water mooring on the Tamar costs £40.25 (£35 + VAT), which on the Hamble would be in excess of £100, and rents will continue to be reviewed upwards according to market trends. Naturally the sudden introduction of rent caused much resentment amongst local boatmen who, for generations, had enjoyed free mooring. In some cases the Duchy has encouraged the formation of local groups, an example of which is the Millbrook Lake Mooring Association which acts under the auspices of the parish council. Millbrook Lake has been leased by the Association which, in turn, sub-lets mooring spaces to its members. In this way locals are not squeezed out by wealthy strangers and the moorings are properly regulated.

The moorings problem is not so intense on the Camel estuary which has been leased out to the Padstow harbour commissioners, established in 1844 to control navigational safety and to preserve trade, by developing facilities and dredging which was paid for by dues. Here also there is a need for control over conflict of interest, between dredging for fertiliser and building sand, para-gliding, water-skiing and wild fowling. The Duchy also owns rock, sailing and golf clubs.

The Isles of Scilly, apart from the freeholds of Hugh Town sold off in 1949, are owned entirely by the Duchy. The pier and harbour remains Duchy property, and a full time harbour-master and boatman are employed, although transfer of ownership is currently being discussed.

The Waters of Tamar were originally part of the Honour of Trematon and were leased out to the Mayor and Corporation of Saltash, although Sutton Pool had by 1275 eclipsed Saltash as the premier port on the river. Over the years the Duchy had 'farmed' Sutton Pool and much land had been reclaimed for cellars and jetties, frequently upon Duchy mud, without permission. Following the Restoration, Lord Arundel was swift to act to re-assert Duchy rights over structures erected on Duchy fundus. Several owners of cellars and jetties, much to their dismay, suddenly found themselves to be Duchy tenants and throughout the seventeenth and eighteenth centuries there were endless lawsuits over Sutton Pool with the Duchy attempting to exert its authority and extract its dues. By the early nineteenth century the Duchy had had enough and, to avoid further trouble, the Prince Regent decided to lease the harbour to the Sutton Pool Company (now the Sutton Harbour Improvement Company) for £6,000 under the Sutton Pool Act of 1812, for ninety-nine years. It was finally sold to the Improvement Company in 1891. The Duchy retains the right to appoint one member to the Board. It still owns the Cattewater, up to Laira Bridge, and part of Hooe Lake. An area of fundus has recently been leased to Plymouth City Council for a new 300-berth marina at Queen Anne's Battery on the Cattewater, which opened in 1986. A similar lease has been granted to the Mayflower Marina at Ocean Quay, at the entrance to Stonehouse Pool on the Hamoaze. The Waters of Tamar extend to the limits of Plymouth Sound which are bounded by a line drawn between Penlee Point and the Shagstone. Shipping here enjoys the cheapest bunkering in Europe along with free anchorage and shelter.

Catharina von Flensburg is not the only wreck owned by the Duchy in Plymouth Sound; others range from a Lancaster bomber which crashed into the breakwater following a raid over France in 1944, to the 3,500 ton P & O liner, *Nepaule*, which struck the Shagstone and sank in December 1890. The wreck of the *Glen Strathallen* lies just south of the Shagstone, outside Duchy limits; she was scuttled deliberately in 1970 and is used as a training wreck by Plymouth Ocean Projects Ltd of Fort Bovisand. Commander Bax of the diving school has been granted licences for diving in four areas of the Sound and other wrecks are being investigated.

A *1938 aerial view of Sutton Harbour, Plymouth, showing how quays and warehouses have been built out across the Duchy-owned fundus. Now the area on the right is a massive yacht marina.* (Western Morning News)

The Duchy owns the fundus of all the rivers flowing south out of Dartmoor to the Channel with the exception of the Yealm and the Erme. It may have had early ownership but in each case powerful landlords lived on the banks of these rivers and were probably able to acquire the river rights in early times. The Avon is one of Devon's most beautiful rivers, and, with some small exceptions as at Bantham beach, completely uncommercialised. The neighbouring landlords, Evans Estates, have allowed no development along its banks and the Duchy owns the fundus up to Aveton Gifford.

(Overleaf) *An aerial view of Dartmouth Harbour, where the Duchy rights are now leased to a harbour authority, again showing the pressure for yacht moorings.* (Western Morning News)

Fishing rights are administered by the South West Water Authority who have a 'fixed engine' salmon trap at the weir, kept open to allow unrestricted passage of the fish.

Much of Salcombe has, at one time or another, been built upon Duchy foreshore and recent sales of property have been heavy. With sixty per cent of the dwellings now holiday homes it is not surprising that there has been heavy pressure on moorings which are controlled by the lessees, the South Hams District Council. Accretion and derelictions of the Salcombe foreshore have given rise to many boundary problems. In the past boundaries have been marked either by a fixed line on a map or by the limits of tidal flow. Anomalies have arisen where adjacent properties have had boundaries fixed by different methods and over the years the tidal extremities have varied.

As a legacy of the tin trade the Duchy controls the whole of the river Dart although the Waters of Dart are administered by the Dartmouth Harbour and Navigation Authority and include the fundus and some foreshore extending up to the head weir at Totnes. The Duchy has the right to appoint one member to the board, an amalgamation of two former bodies which up until 1970 had separate control over the upper and lower waters. The Authority was established in 1975 under an act of Parliament whereby the Duchy leased the right to manage the river and its moorings and to collect harbour dues by the water bailiff. Before this both parties collected dues, which during the last century had involved considerable trade of coal in and wool out, and which led to a series of misunderstandings and arguments with the Mayor of Dartmouth. Leases have been granted for three marinas in areas not managed by the Authority and there are plans under consideration for a proposed new port at Noss.

Duchy ownership outside the four main south Devon rivers included areas of Brixham and Torquay harbours, and foreshore and fundus fronting Paignton. Most has now been sold off and all that now remains is the area of fundus adjoining Paignton beach. Some of the details of the sales make interesting reading. For instance in 1869 a half of Torquay beach was sold to Sir F. Hesketh for £100. The other half was acquired by the local Board of Health in 1890 for £896. Nine years later Brixham harbour was sold to the UDC for £104 and similar sales of foreshore and fundus were made during this period in Cornwall.

No longer does the Duchy dispose of assets which are capable of providing income. A new commercial awareness is apparent, which is characterised by tackling the problem of encroachments. Many are long standing, over a hundred years old and which have since become part of the scenery. Some are massive; Brixham breakwater, for example was erected upon Duchy fundus which was never conveyed. The more recent have been served with encroachment orders, and are being required to negotiate their rights to be there, and will need to be granted either leases or licences. When steps are taken to deal with encroachments, local reaction is often hostile and has been violent. It is not limited to the seashore; in the early years of this century a Land Steward set out to deal with encroachment on Dartmoor by farmers at Sticklepath. A near riot followed and the police had to be summoned to ensure his safety. Action has to be taken on over a hundred encroachments on Duchy fundus in south Devon alone.

A recent survey of the south Devon foreshore and fundus has been made by boat but the increased pressures of the 1980s have meant that more up-to-date methods are needed, and aerial photography now helps keep track of potential encroachments.

And so, after six hundred and fifty years, the foreshore and fundus of the Duchy of Cornwall has reached a time of great change. After adjusting to the changes of the twentieth century it must now look ahead to the twenty-first, a century in which the burgeoning leisure industry can be expected to dominate our rivers and beaches in ever more exotic and multifarious forms, from the height of the heavens to the depths of the seas.

CHAPTER TEN

MINING

Roger Burt and Michael Atkinson

The Duchy of Cornwall has for centuries gained substantial financial benefit from the existence within its boundaries of heavily-mineralised lands. In the counties of Devon and Cornwall, almost every commercially important metalliferous mineral has been mined, including tin, copper, lead, silver, zinc, arsenic, manganese, cobalt, tungsten and iron. The Duchy also received royalties on the mining of coal in Somerset, and on the quarrying of clay and stone throughout the South West. Although, in the role of land-owner, the Duchy had a strong interest in the mining of most minerals, its longest and most fascinating association with the mining industry was the control and administration which it exercised over the extraction of tin ore from the twelfth to the early nineteenth century. The study of the Duchy as an institution rather than a geographic entity is therefore more closely tied up with the development of the tin mining industry than that of any other metal.

In order to understand not only the Stannary system of tin working by which the Duchy governed the industry but also the economy of mining in general in the South West, it is important to understand the nature of metal deposits and the problems encountered in working them. Metal mining has always been a risky, speculative and unpredictable activity, the vicissitudes of which have only been tolerated in the hope of large profits which on occasion resulted. Even on a small scale, mining or streaming was not a dependable or constant source of income. However, since the ores once found and extracted were extremely valuable, tin mining especially attracted the attentions of speculating traders, miners, smelters and the revenue-seeking Duchy officials. Whilst the former hoped to profit from the actual working or processing of ores, the aim of the Duchy was to maximise its income from royalties and taxes by fostering and protecting its mineral empire. The unpredictability of mining stemmed from the occurrence of ores in roughly vertical veins, or lodes, which varied in depth, width and consistency and which were remarkably difficult to locate.

The geographic spread of tin ores within the south-western peninsula is largely influenced by the granite intrusions which form the moors such as

194

An old photograph of Coinagehall Street, Helston, its name a reminder of the town's importance in Stannary days. (Western Morning News)

Dartmoor and Bodmin Moor. Indeed, the boundaries of the individual Stannaries corresponded to these wild upland tin-impregnated regions because it was on these moors or in the valleys emanating from them that medieval technology was able to extract tin ores at the surface. At the beginning of the nineteenth century, copper and tin production was centred in the west of the region, notably in the Camborne-Redruth districts. Later, from mid-century, other important deposits were to be developed in east Cornwall and west Devon. Lead, silver, zinc and iron ores were less significant in terms of value but nevertheless were worked at many sites in the South West, mainly in the nineteenth century. However, some rich silver/lead deposits were worked from a much earlier date in Bere Alston, Combe Martin and the Mendips. The mining of coal in Somerset, an industry which developed from the mid-seventeenth century to a peak in the early twentieth century, involved Duchy interest as owners of estates in the area. Although never a major producer of coal, the Somerset mines provided substantial royalty dues to the Duchy.

The Duchy of Cornwall received an income from mining both as a land-owner and also from the receipt of dues owed to the crown under the Stannary system. The right to receive such dues was transferred in 1338 from the crown to the newly-established Duchy of Cornwall.

THE MEDIEVAL TIN INDUSTRY

The documented history of tin working in Britain commences in the twelfth century although it was undoubtedly worked before that date. Its prehistoric use in the making of bronze would naturally have involved small-scale working of tin (and copper) ore in the South West, the area being the only source of tin in Britain, but prior to Saxon times there is little evidence of exploitation. The exact origins of the Stannary system are as yet unclear but it would seem that at the time of the formal laying out of the rights of both the Duchy and the tinners around AD 1200, the basic elements of the system were already in operation. In 1198, William de Wrotham overhauled the Stannary system to yield greater revenues to the crown and described its operation. The charter of King John of 1201 laid down in detail the rights and privileges of the tinners, as well as establishing local Stannary admini-stration, and in 1305 Edward II confirmed these privileges in a further charter. The system thus laid down formed the basic structure of the industry until the abolition of coinage in 1838 and the Vice-Wardens' courts in 1896.

The Stannary system (the term being derived from the Latin for tin — stannus) was designed to nurture and control the industry for the benefit of the crown or Duchy. Under its terms the Duchy received dues from all tin produced in the South West, both on and off its own property — 30d per hundredweight for Devon and 5/- for Cornwall on first-smelt tin and, after 1198, a further 1 mark per thousandweight on the second smelt — and reserved the right to purchase all tin and resell it on its own account. In the early fourteenth century, the two taxes were replaced by one 'coinage' tax, of 1s 6¾d per cwt for Devon and 4s per cwt for Cornwall, on finished metal as a result of improved smelting techniques removing the need for two separate smelts. The right to purchase all tin, or pre-emption, was rarely exercised because of the opposition it drew from tinners and traders. However, some dukes took advantage of it.

In return for providing substantial funds to the Duchy, the tinners were awarded privileges which were defended against anyone who tried to remove or reduce them. A Lord Warden of the Stannaries was appointed, but the running of the administration was placed in the hands of two Vice-Wardens covering Cornwall and Devon. Four Stannaries were established in Cornwall (Blackamore, Foweymore, Tywarnhaile and Penwith & Kerrier) and four in Devon (Chagford, Tavistock, Ashburton and, from 1328, Plympton) and

Medieval tin-streaming (above) *and simple ore dressing process using a wooden buddle. From* Agricola, Georgius, De Re Metallica *(1556, New York edition 1950)*

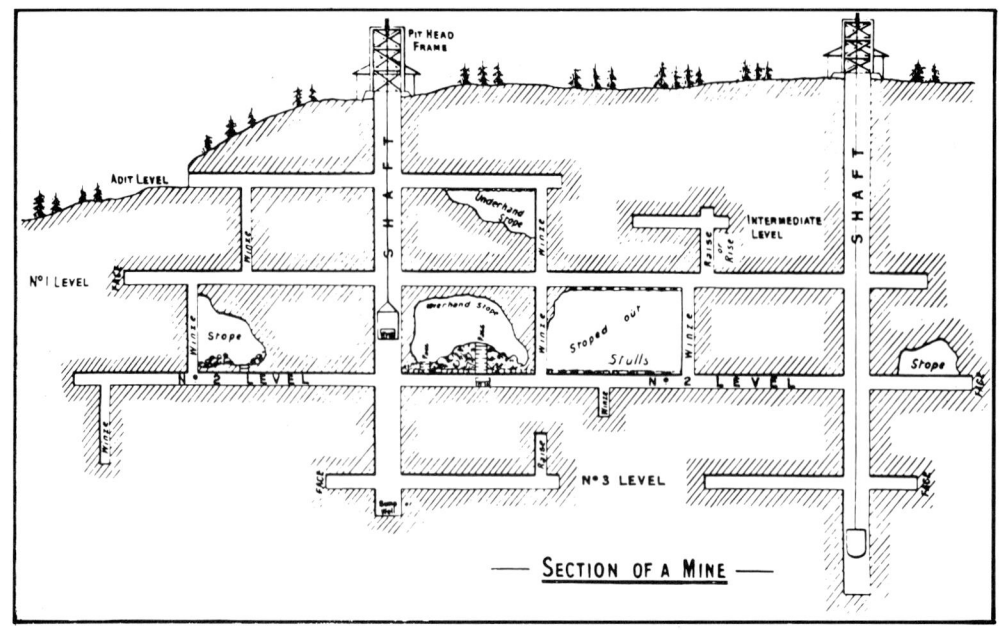

Section of a typical deep metal mine

within these areas the tinners had their own laws, customs and judicial system. A tinner was exempt from serving in the armed forces. He could leave his feudal lord, stake a claim (bounding) without permission from the owner of the soil, divert water to extract the ore or power waterwheels, dig peat for fuel and despoil land and rivers without fear of redress. In all cases except extreme criminal acts such as murder, he was tried and punished not by the crown's court but by his fellow tinners in local Stannary courts. If found guilty, they could be either fined or incarcerated in Stannary gaols at Lydford or Lostwithiel. On occasions, the tinners assembled at a Parliament or Great Court, which on Dartmoor meant meeting on the moor at Crockern Tor, to consider issues of general concern. Such was the importance of the revenue raised from the Stannaries that whenever complaints regarding tinners were made, for example for silting up harbours with waste carried down rivers from tinworks, or spoiling farming ground, the Duchy or crown always defended the tinners.

The physical evidence of the medieval tin industry can still be seen. Piles of rounded stones, large areas of depression and grassy tips, remains of blowing houses and the occasional grinding stone or granite mould are all relics of centuries of tin working. A recent study of the Dartmoor tin industry has identified over 800 separate tinworks and about 100 definite

198

mills where the ore was processed. Although Dartmoor was originally the leading producer it was soon far outstripped by Cornwall. Therefore there were certainly a far greater number of sites in the South West as a whole.

Until the fifteenth century, the working of tin and other ores was normally undertaken on the surface. Initially, the tinners would simply work the very rich tin ore which had been washed from the lodes and deposited in river valleys, the working of such alluvial deposits being known as streaming. Since water was essential for separating the ore from the waste, tinners were given wide rights to divert rivers and streams to the working site. Complaints were common. For example, in attempting to limit possible damage to other interests, the Convocation or Parliament of Tinners of Cornwall enacted that 'Whereas Streaming Tinners under a Pretence that they have a right by Virtue of the Charter to turn Water and Water-courses, whereas and as often as Need shall require for the working and searching of Tin, and thereby disturb and spoil Pot-waters running to Men's Houses, and also divert Water from ancient Mills, and likewise disturb and spoil running Waters out of Malice', the practice was illegal and punishable by fine claimed in the Stannary court, or when malice was involved by forfeit of 'the Sum of five Pounds to the Use of the King, or Lord Duke of Cornwall'.

The power of water was also essential to the next stage of extraction. Having exhausted the tin ores that had been washed down into the valleys, the tinners traced the ores back to the parent lode in higher ground. They tried various means for this exploration, including searching for tin-stones or shodes, tracing vegetation patterns, digging exploratory pits or hatches and even divining. Once located, the lode was worked either by opening hand-dug trenches along its length or by diverting water over it from streams or reservoirs. These techniques resulted in deep trenches, or beamworks, following the outcrop of the lode. Many examples of these may be seen all over the South West, particularly on Dartmoor.

Streamed tin was sufficiently pure to allow immediate smelting without being upgraded or 'dressed', but most ores had to be pounded to fine particles and washed before smelting in order to remove waste material. The crushing of ore was performed using several methods – grinding stones, mortar and pestle and, later, stamps. The latter survived into the present century and consisted of long wooden rods with weighted heads, powered by a waterwheel. The washing of ore was a relatively simple affair involving the sifting of ore and waste in a flow of water to separate out the heavier tin particles. Smelting was initially a two-stage process – firstly, the ore was rough smelted at or near the tinworks and, secondly, it was refined at a smelting centre designated by the Stannary Warden. In the fourteenth century, the two processes were replaced by the blowing house, a small and rudimentary building equipped with a hearth and a bellows powered by a small waterwheel. They have often been referred to as Jews Houses although the association of the Jews with the tin trade has not been established.

The power of the crown and Duchy was most in evidence at the Stannary towns on Coinage Day. All tin had to be taken to the Stannary town for assay and sale and, of course, payment of dues to the Duchy. The Coinage Day was attended by Duchy officials who weighed and tested each block, involving the striking off of a corner for sampling – hence the term coinage, after the French coin for corner. The sale attracted merchants from all corners of Europe and from the London Pewterers, who formed the main domestic market. A reasonably accurate picture of the change in fortune of the tin-producing areas can be gleaned from statistics of tin presented for coinage. In the twelfth century, Dartmoor was the leading producer but a gradual move westwards occurred into west Cornwall. In the fourteenth century, the main Stannary towns were Bodmin and Lostwithiel, but by the sixteenth century, these had been replaced by Helston and Truro. In 1663, Penzance was appointed as a Stannary town to handle the increasing output from the far west.

The system of Stannary administration of tin production survived intact until 1838 when, largely due to its inability to meet the demands of a larger, more integrated industry which resented payment of dues 'to supply a revenue for the Heir Apparent' and the physical inconvenience of being compelled to delay sale of tin until a Coinage Day, the coinage dues were abolished and the Duchy compensated by an annual payment by the Treasury from the Consolidated Fund.

NEW MARKETS AND NEW TECHNOLOGY

The medieval mining industry was essentially small-scale and primitive. Whilst the methods of production remained simple and inexpensive and the market for the ore limited, it was perfectly feasible for the Stannary system based on small producers and close control to satisfy needs. It could even be argued that Stannary law protected rather than hindered mining and smelting interests for it ensured the concentration of activity within the Duchy. In the early eighteenth century, it was suggested that copper be brought under Stannary administration to confine smelting to the South West.

The expansion first of copper, then of tin mining, from the eighteenth century was stimulated by new uses for the metals and made possible by new mining technologies. Although the result of this renewed activity in tin mining in the early nineteenth century led to the end of Duchy control, the general expansion of mining benefitted the Duchy when mines lay upon their estates.

For centuries, tin had been used for ornamentation, jewellery, funeral furniture and in some dyes and glazes, but its principal uses had been in alloys for printing type, bronze and most important pewter. None of these markets showed a potential for marked expansion – indeed, the main

Remains of ore-crushing machinery at Gobbet Mine, near Hexworthy: one millstone of a crazing-mill, replaced by stamps in the late sixteenth century.

Water-powered stamps at the Golden Dagger Mine, south of the Warren House Inn, Dartmoor: a 1937 picture of a mine worked intermittently from the 1860s until 1914, on the site of much earlier workings.

domestic market, the Pewterers, had virtually disappeared by the nineteenth century with the replacement of pewter by pottery. Until the rise of the tinplate trade, the Cornish tin industry faced a difficult time, aided only by the East India Company contract for regular supplies of tin to China in the late eighteenth and early nineteenth centuries. The development of tinplate for canning, storage etc, provided a major new demand in the nineteenth century. Tinplate works had been established in 1720 at Pontypool in south Wales and a gradual expansion benefitted Cornish mining and smelting. However it was in the mid-nineteenth century that Cornwall, and to a lesser extent Devon, derived greatest benefit from the Welsh tinplate industry. By 1870, over three-quarters of Cornish tin was being used in tinplate making.

Copper had long been used for ornamentation, kitchenware and the manufacture of bronze, but the expansion of copper mining in the eighteenth century was based upon the development of the brass industry, mainly in the Bristol area. The introduction of copper sheathing of ship's hulls and a general increase in the use of copper for boilers, vats, pipes etc, was also very important. The beginnings of the Cornish copper boom seem to lie in the abolition of the monopoly of the Mines Royal and the Mineral and Battery Works over copper mining and smelting in 1689, and is commonly associated with the figure of John Coster. In the 1680s Coster established a copper smelting works at Redbrook, in the Wye valley, and in the early eighteenth century took over and greatly improved the Chacewater mine in Cornwall. In 1717, the first copper smelter was established at Swansea, initiating a long period of interdependence between south Wales and the South West which involved the shipment of metallic tin, copper and iron ores to south Wales and the return shipment of coal to fuel the steam engines at the mines. The mutual advantage of this system was not accepted in the South West, for there were a number of attempts to establish copper smelting works in Cornwall in the eighteenth century, notably at Hayle. However, the economics of the trade so favoured south Wales that all the Cornish ventures failed. The expansion of copper mining was abruptly interrupted in 1768 when the huge Anglesey deposit was discovered and only revived when the best deposits were exhausted in the 1790s. The heyday of copper really came in the nineteenth century, with huge profits being made by the main copper mines, such as Devon Great Consols, United, Consolidated, Dolcoath and South Caradon.

The market for lead and iron ores also expanded but in neither case was the South West a major producer. Lead was used for guttering, paint manufacture, glass making, pottery glazes, printers' type and pewter – most of these markets expanded with the general expansion of the British economy. Iron ore mining was unusual in so far as it was mainly confined to the middle decades of the nineteenth century, with ores being sent to south Wales for use as admixture to improve the quality of finished iron from about the 1830s and, from the 1850s, as a raw material for making Bessemer steel.

This expansion in the market for ores could not have been exploited in the South West had it not been for major breakthroughs in mining technology which enabled mining companies to extract ores underground and at depth. Before the use of gunpowder, breaking rock was performed by simple pick work, lime-setting or fire-setting, all of which were arduously long and slow processes, especially in granite. With the near exhaustion of the best stream deposits and the inconveniently increasing depth of open trenchworks, any expansion in ore production depended on being able to work them underground. This was made a viable proposition by gunpowder. Gunpowder was introduced into British mines probably around 1665, and was brought to Cornwall possibly in the late 1680s.

The cheapest means of gaining underground access to lodes was to drive levels into the hillside at intervals. A drainage level driven just above stream level had the advantage of unwatering all of the ground above, so that in undulating terrain substantial amounts of mineral-bearing ground could be exploited with limited means and simple technology. In flatter terrain, such as central Cornwall, or when deepening a mine below the bottom drainage level, resort had to be made to some form of mechanical pumping and haulage. This produced the second major technological breakthrough in mining.

Until the advent of steam power, the only means of unwatering deep shaft mines were muscle and/or waterwheel-powered pumps. The most common devices used in the South West were large waterwheels, some of over sixty feet in diameter. In spite of important improvements in their design during the eighteenth century, waterwheels were simply inadequate to deal with the problems of ever-deepening mines. The answer lay in the application of steam engines to pumping and it was as much the demand from Cornish mines as that from collieries which prompted Mother Invention to action. The breakthrough came with the invention of the Newcomen engine in 1709 – by the 1770s around seventy of these engines were in use in Cornish mines, being replaced in the late 1770s and early 1780s by the more efficient Watt steam engines. Eventually, and after much experimentation with various forms of steam engine involving high pressures and compounding, undertaken by engineers such as Trevithick, Woolf and Sims, the classic 'Cornish' engine evolved to dominate the industry from the 1820s. These enormous single-cylinder engines were the guts of those gaunt engine houses which nowadays remind everyone of Cornwall's mining past. With steam power to unwater the mines, deposits at much greater depths could be exploited and access gained to the deep tin deposits which it was discovered lay beneath the copper zone.

The speculative nature of metal mining attributable to the unpredictability of the lodes gave rise to the peculiar system of ownership and employment which prevailed in the South West. Since metal mining was, before the Industrial Revolution, one of very few industries which required relatively

Section of a Cornish engine house; the boiler and vertical cylinder in the house operated the great beam which in turn drove the pump shaft.

Botallack Mine, in the Land's End Peninsula, with its engine house perched on the cliff edge, and the workings running out at 350 fathoms for a mile under the sea. From 1815 until 1905 it produced over twenty thousand tons of copper. The picture records a visit by Prince Edward and Princess Alexandra in 1865. (Cornwall Local Studies Library)

large amounts of capital to be invested in a risk venture, provision had to be made to share this risk. The basic form of business organisation was the cost book company which allowed many individuals to own part shares in mines. Although by so doing it enabled large mines to develop, the legal requirement that all profits be divided every three months encouraged short-term interests to dominate. Too often, investors were unwilling to reinvest profits on long-term improvements – shafts were driven following the crooked path of the lodes into the ground in order to produce returns while sinking. This may not appear to be so great a problem since it is the most successful mines which have been most researched, but most mines continued for years making calls on shareholders in the hope of finding payable lodes, if not the bonanza strikes of the few. Indeed, it is probably the case that overall the sale of ores from South West mines did not repay the total investment in the industry. Many incautious speculators invested in mines which had little chance of success, despite the claims made in optimistic prospectuses.

Certainly, some mines were hugely successful. The South Caradon copper mine, for example, paid annual dividends of about £10,000 amounting in total to £316,000 for an initial outlay of only £640. Devon Great Consols was even more successful – formed in 1845 with a paid-up capital of £1,024, in that same year the Company paid a dividend of £72,704 and by closure had yielded a total profit of £1,225,216. Not quite as spectacular but in the long term probably just as profitable were the west Cornwall mines, such as Dolcoath, Cooks Kitchen, Condurrow, East Pool, Levant, Great Wheal Vor, United, Consolidated, St Ives Consols and Botallack. It is worth noting that none of these high dividend paying mines lay on Duchy lands.

To the miner also the working of ores was a speculative employment. Under a system known as tribute, the miners in groups, or 'pares', worked a section of the mine for three months, being paid a proportion of the value of the ores produced according to the appearance of the lode. The working areas were re-auctioned every three months on setting day. A good pitch could yield good earnings for the lode could suddenly widen and the owner could not renegotiate the terms for three months, but the opposite even meant abject poverty and debt.

The heyday of metal mining in the South West ended with the influx of foreign ores into the market in the late nineteenth century. Working virgin lodes, the new mines in such areas as Australia, Malaya and the USA could easily out-price their Cornish rivals which were faced with the increasing costs of mining at greater and greater depths. With the collapse of copper mining in mid and west Cornwall in the 1860s, to be followed by tin in the 1870s, thousands of miners left to find work in the new foreign orefields, in Welsh coal mines or Cumbrian iron mines. In the last forty years the number

Disused engine house at Caradon, near Liskeard, Cornwall, a reminder of the great age of Cornish mining. (Roy Westlake)

of mines working in Cornwall could be counted on one hand and only one, Geevor, contributed to the Duchy through its foreshore mineral rights. The boom in tin prices brought new prospecting licences although just one, Wheal Concord, led to actual mining. It also renewed interest in reworking old spoilheaps. Ten years ago the income from mining only amounted to some two per cent of the western district's revenue; in 1985 it had risen to ten per cent but with the collapse of the tin market in 1986 the percentage looks like falling again to an insignificant figure. Although metal mining has never actually stopped completely in the South West, it has also never looked like regaining its former glory.

MINING AND THE INCOME OF THE DUCHY

How important was mining to the overall finance of the Duchy of Cornwall? This question can be answered fairly easily for the period from the mid-nineteenth century. After 1838 and down to the present day, the annual accounts of the Duchy were published in the Papers of the House of Commons. This practice acknowledged the semi-public status of the Duchy and the accounts often appeared side-by-side with those for the Duchy of Lancaster, another important source of crown revenues. These accounts provide a very detailed record of the principal sources of revenue and directions of expenditure and they can be used to estimate clearly the changing role of mining over time. Table 1 shows the total income of the Duchy at ten yearly intervals from 1840 down to the years just preceding World War I, indicating the total earnings derived from all forms of mining and quarrying and their share of the total. Two very clear trends stand out. Firstly, total income increased rapidly and continuously during this period – more than quadrupling between 1840 and 1910 – the income from mining remained remarkably steady throughout, fluctuating around £20,000 per annum. Whereas mining and quarrying revenues made up nearly a half of the Duchy's total income in 1840, they had shrunk to around a quarter in the 1870s and to just over a tenth by 1910.

The main reason for the rapid growth of total Duchy revenues, and the diminishing status of mining, was the rapid growth of rental income from property and estates scattered throughout southern and eastern England – viz Cornwall, Berkshire, Devon, Scilly Isles, Dorset, Wiltshire, Somerset, Berkshire, Lincolnshire, Norfolk, Hertfordshire and Surrey. Whereas rents brought the Duchy only £5,548.90 in 1840, by 1910 they had grown twenty times to £115,432.80. Most of this growth was derived from property near to London, particularly in Kennington. As early as 1850, property in Surrey was responsible for well over a third of the Duchy's total

The Prince of Wales in the wildflower meadow he has created at his home, Highgrove House.
(Heather Angel, British Wildlife Appeal)

Prince of Wales Mine near Gunnislake, east Cornwall, an old mine which between 1864 and 1914 raised copper, tin and arsenic worth over £126,000. (Cornwall Local Studies Library)

rental income and it produced more than twice the revenue generated by all metal and coal mining royalties in the South West. The latter half of the nineteenth century saw the ignominious spectacle of the ancient heavy metal heartland of Duchy finances being eclipsed and overtaken by the domestic rents of suburban Surrey.

However, it is important not to let the declining trend of mining revenues in Duchy finances in the late nineteenth century disguise and obscure their massive importance in the earlier part of the century. The declining trend becomes a rising trend the further backwards it is traced. In 1840, the contribution of mining revenues to total Duchy income was 48.8 per cent; in 1838 it had been at least 56 per cent and ten years before that it was probably higher again. It is quite likely that mining and quarrying were producing between two-thirds and three-quarters of the Duchy's total income in the end of the eighteenth century and possibly more still in earlier periods.

In calculating these shares and percentages, it is important to note that in the early accounts the apparently non-mining income of the Duchy was often itself inflated by the inclusion of mining items, so apparently under-stating the relative importance of mining activity. For example, in the 1838–42 accounts, the rents section for Devon and Cornwall often included returns for mining property. These were not clearly separated out until 1843. Similarly,

Table 1

The income of the Duchy of Cornwall, showing total receipts from mining and quarrying activity and their contribution to total income, 1840–1910

Date	Total Income	Income from Mining and Quarrying	Income from Mining and Quarrying as % of Total
1840	38,378.8	18,722.0	48.8
1850	60,052.2	19,682.2	32.8
1860	68,547.0	24,885.3	36.3
1870	88,095.1	24,817.7	28.2
1880	92,566.7	20,124.1	21.7
1890	101,747.0	19,777.8	19.4
1900	121,229.7	19,762.1	16.3
1910	164,700.1	20,208.2	12.3

rents continued to include payments which were received as a direct consequence of mining activity, such as the £13 paid for water rights by the Golden Dagger adventurers in 1851 and the much larger £250 paid by the Devon Great Consols Company for the use of water from the Tamar in 1852. It is a reasonable supposition that in many parts of Cornwall and Devon the rental value of agricultural holdings was increased by the enhanced economic opportunities presented by the proximity of thriving mining activity. Until the mid-nineteenth century, the life's blood of Duchy finance and the lion's share of the Duchy's income was derived directly and indirectly from mining activity.

During the mid- and late nineteenth century, the Duchy recorded its direct income under three separate headings: the produce of the Stannary tin duties, post groats and white rents; royalties from coal mines in Somerset; and royalties from mines and quarries on its properties in Devon and Cornwall. Of these, the Stannary duties were consistently the most valuable, notwithstanding the commutation of the actual duty to an annual compensatory sum paid by the national Exchequer out of the Consolidated Fund.

Under the terms of the Act for the Abolition of the Duties Payable on the Coinage of Tin in the Counties of Cornwall and Devon, the Duchy lost the direct source of revenue which it had held for more than five hundred years. The coinage of tin was terminated from October 1838 and no further duty was payable. As compensation, the Act required that the Treasury estimate the average yield of the duties for the last ten years, 'after deducting therefrom all Costs, Charges and Expenses to Officers and others during such period incurred in and incident to the ascertaining, managing and collecting of such Coinage Duties.' This sum was to be paid annually thereafter to the Duchy, less taxes and other charges due to the government. From 1839 through to World War I, this produced an annual income usually fluctuating between £15,741 and £16,216 depending upon the level of taxes and deductions at source. In view of the rapid growth of tin production during the following fifty years, this arrangement almost certainly short-changed the Duchy. It was stuck with a fixed income instead of the variable system which would have reflected the more than quadrupling of tin production during the period. However, the compensation provided a steady and reliable source of income and until the 1840s it was the largest single receipt in the Duchy's accounts.

Compared with the compensation in lieu of the Stannary duties, the Duchy's direct income from its own metal and coal mines, and some stone and clay quarries, was relatively small and unimportant. Table 2 shows the income under the three mining and quarrying sub-headings from their first separate recording in 1843.

Table 2

The mining and quarrying income of the Duchy of Cornwall

Date	Compensation in lieu of Tin Coinage	Royalties from Coal Mines in Somerset	Royalties from Mines and quarries in Cornwall and Devon	Total Income from mining and quarrying
1843	15,741.8	2,690.6	2,842.1	21,274.5
1850	15,741.8	1,759.7	2,180.7	19,682.2
1860	16,216.7	2,531.9	6,136.7	24,885.3
1870	16,216.7	864.0	7,737.0	24,817.7
1880	16,216.7	1,204.3	2,703.1	20,124.1
1890	16,216.7	1,259.7	2,301.4	19,777.8
1900	16,216.7	2,161.3	1,384.1	19,762.1
1910	16,216.7	2,317.8	1,673.7	20,208.2

For much of the period, the income from coal and from metal mines was very similar, notwithstanding the much larger number of the latter, but together they only yielded receipts equal to between a third and a quarter of the tin coinage compensation.

The detail of the royalties from coal and metal mines can be analysed for two brief periods at the mid-century (1838–43 and 1850–54) when the published accounts gave careful mine-by-mine returns. During these years there were nine collieries yielding royalties to the Duchy. They commonly paid 1/10th of the value of the coal that they sold and 1/16th of the value of coke production. The largest producers were Welton, Welton Hill and Clandown collieries in Midsomer Norton, and Farrington at Farrington Gurney. In 1840, these pits were responsible for over ninety per cent of the Duchy's total royalty income from coal, with Welton alone producing over forty per cent of the total. In 1852, Welton still led the field, paying a royalty to the Duchy of 1/8th of the total value of output, equal to £899. It is notable that in 1910 the value of total receipts from coal mining was still very close to its 1843 figure, reflecting a remarkably consistent level of output.

Compared with its Somerset coal interests, the Duchy's metal mining property in Cornwall and Devon was far more extensive and diverse but produced only a slightly higher income. The mine-by-mine returns list over one hundred and fifty separate ventures paying rent and/or royalties to the Duchy, and forty quarries and clay works. However, the great majority of these ventures appear never to have achieved any significant level of production and paid only a minimum rent. Minimum rents were usually only £5 or £10 per annum, though for some ventures, such as East Gunnislake mine, they might be as high as £60. The payment of minimum rents sometimes presented problems to mines – for example, in 1853 East Tywarnhaile had to sell roofing for £20 in order to meet minimum rent arrears. Royalty payments also varied widely, depending on assessments of the cost and profitability of the workings. In the early 1840s, of eleven productive non-ferrous mines, five paid 1/15th, one 1/18th, one 1/20th, three 1/24th and one 1/40th of the total value of output. True to its reputation as a sympathetic landlord, the Duchy halved the royalty payments from Tamar Consols, from 1/24th to 1/48th, when it hit trouble in the latter half of 1841 and was struggling for survival. The Duchy's productive iron ore mines – Wheal Ruby, Garea Moor and Restormel Royal – paid a fixed money sum per ton of ore produced rather than a percentage of the value of output. For the relatively small Wheal Ruby and Garea Moor this was 3d and 6d respectively, but for Restormel Royal, the largest iron mine in Cornwall, it was 9d per ton.

It is noticeable that as the century progressed and metal mining encountered increasing problems from foreign competition and falling prices, the incidence of non-payment of rents and royalties increased sharply. In the prosperous early 1850s only a handful of mines were behind with their rents and none failed to pay royalties on time. By the turn of the century, however, with the industry almost in ruins, arrears had reached alarming proportions. In 1890, two out of five Duchy mines failed to meet their commitments and by 1910 this had increased to nearly half.

During the early 1850s, the Duchy received rents and royalties from metal mines and quarries working in twenty-one different manors scattered throughout Devon and Cornwall. In 1854 over one hundred and fifty workings made returns, though only thirty-five appear to have been in production and paid royalties beyond their minimum rent. The most productive mining districts for the Duchy were in the eastern part of the county, near Callington and the Tamar, and to the west near St Agnes. The leading mines of the eastern district were Phoenix, Hingston Down Consols and South Tamar Consols, each paying royalties of around £1,500 in 1854, usefully supported by Callington and Holmbush, the latter also returning royalties of well over £1,000 a year in the early 1840s. Near St Agnes, United Hills had been in the £1,000 a year bracket in 1842–3 but in the early 1850s the district was dominated by Perran St George, Restormel Royal and the Tywarnhaile mines, all returning royalties of between £500 and £1,000 per year.

The Dartmoor mines, for which there were over twenty returns during the early 1850s, appear to have been at a low level of activity around the mid-century and minimum rent and royalties together rarely amounted to more than £10 per annum. The highest royalty paid by any Dartmoor mine during the early 1850s was £75.8 from Birch Tor & Vitifer in 1854. The Dartmoor manor also contained a few active granite quarries, such as Pew Tor and Harford and Ugborough, the latter paying the substantial minimum rent of £50 a year in 1850, but they were not a major source of income. Granite was also produced to some profit from the Kit Hill works and Cheesewring works but the Duchy's main quarrying income was derived from more than a dozen granite and clay quarries in Treverbyn manor, near St Austell. In 1841 these quarries paid royalties of over £1,300 and ten years later nearly £800. It is important to remember that many other mines and quarries also played an important part in generating income for the Duchy in other periods but individual returns were not given in the published accounts after 1854.

Throughout the first half of the nineteenth century, the income from mining provided a very large proportion of total Duchy revenues and paid several times over for the sums withdrawn for expenditure by the crown. In 1838, the crown received £2,000 from the Duchy and ten years later, Prince Albert (now benefitting from the estates) received £7,376. Even at the end of the century, when the Prince of Wales was receiving a massively increased £50–70,000 per year, mining incomes continued to make a useful contribution. This is what the Duchy took out of mining in the nineteenth century – what did it put back? What did it do to assist an ailing and later desperately sick industry?

Unfortunately, very little. Unlike most other major mineral owners it appears to have taken very little interest in mining enterprise itself. It rarely took a direct financial interest in the companies which leased its properties, and provided no significant flow of capital into mining and quarrying enterprise. Apart from a loan to promote the development of the Tywarnhaile mines in the late 1840s there is little evidence of the Duchy taking an active role to improve and increase the level of earnings and activity on its own or associated properties. Although it employed as agents some of the leading contemporary authorities on mining and metallurgy – such as Richard Taylor, W. W. Smyth, W. J. Henwood – they were given no evangelical role in stimulating the adoption of new technology and improved practice on the lines commonly adopted by the Duke of Devonshire on Grassington Moor or the Greenwich Hospital Commissioners on their Alston Moor estates. The old administrative services provided by the Duchy for south-western mining through the Stannary system were run down from the mid-

Prince Charles underground at South Crofty Mine in 1970, talking to Howard Mankee, the mine captain. (Western Morning News)

century and replaced by no other system to facilitate co-operation and self-regulation in the industry. Even charitable donations were small, largely made outside the region, and directed towards gentlemens' clubs rather than the welfare of the mining community. The Duchy's role was not unlike that of central government in the twentieth century: quick to extract its royalties and taxes but slow to reinvest in infrastructural development; content to take out tens of thousands of pounds each year but laggardly in assisting the wealth-creating activities of entrepreneurs and miners.

tangible monuments of these early farmers also survive, in particular the impressive series of chambered tombs and long barrows which form a varied group with examples throughout the South West. Recent field survey has identified further long cairns on Dartmoor and Bodmin Moor, sometimes with a chamber, as at Bearah Tor on the Rillaton estate.

Most of the sites were intended to be architecturally striking and would have required a considerable investment of labour; the capstone of the Duchy's Pawton Quoit weighs an estimated fourteen tons. More than simply tombs, these monuments are now thought to have stood as territorial markers symbolising ancestral rights to the land. The importance of the long barrows and chambered tombs as ceremonial sites was primarily local; major centres covering a wider area can be identified in a series of enclosed sites: the 'causewayed enclosures' of the early Neolithic, which take their name from their circuit of interrupted banks and ditches; and the henge monuments of the later Neolithic and early Bronze Age, characterised by having their banks outside their ditches.

The Dorchester area was one of a number of centres important throughout the Neolithic. A causewayed enclosure occupied the hilltop that was re-used in the Iron Age for the mighty hillfort of Maiden Castle. Finds from the site suggest a wide range of contacts: they include stone axes from the Lake District and Cornwall, and also pottery from Cornwall. The enclosure was partly overlain by a bank barrow (a 540m (1,772ft) long variant of a long barrow) and was superseded by a striking complex of sites forming a ritual or ceremonial area around Dorchester: to the south of Dorchester, small henges at Maumbury Rings and Lancebarrow (both belonging to the Duchy); to the east, a very large henge at Mount Pleasant where excavation has located the site of a great circle of timber uprights within the enclosure; and in Dorchester itself a new type of monument recently discovered, part of the arc of an enclosure possibly 400m (1,312ft) in diameter and defined by a continuous palisade of massive posts. Monuments of this type demanded the organisation of a workforce on an unprecedented scale.

The ordinary farming settlements of the Neolithic period are more difficult to find, both in moorland and lowlands, perhaps because they were mostly temporary. Like the Mesolithic sites they can be identified as scatters of flints but there has been very little excavation to investigate them. Systematic surface collection of flints over a large area around Maiden Castle is beginning to reveal the otherwise hidden complexity of the changing pattern of land use and settlement in the Neolithic and Bronze Age.

At the end of the third millennium BC settlers from the Land's End peninsula colonised Scilly, then a single main island covered by forest. Their characteristic chambered tombs, the Scillonian Entrance Graves which are derived from types found on the mainland, are monuments on a fairly small scale, typically a roughly circular mound of stone with a stone-lined entrance passage/chamber roofed with massive slabs. Burial may not have been their

Maiden Castle, near Dorchester: erosion of the massive Iron Age rampart under repair by the Prince's Trust in 1985. (Cambridge University)

sole or even their main function. Burial may have been elsewhere, perhaps in the small cairns arranged in dense groups known as cairn fields. The largest of these, at Shipman Head Down, Bryher, contains nearly a hundred cairns within an area 500 by 300m (1,640 × 984ft). Similar cairns are found on Dartmoor and Bodmin Moor but never in such densities. Contemporary settlements and field systems have also been found, some of them below the present high tide mark because of the gradually rising sea level. The first community – no more than a handful of scattered 'founder' households, each with a settlement and an entrance grave within its territory – expanded rapidly to a population of several hundreds, with the remarkable total of eighty or so entrance graves.

On Dartmoor and Bodmin Moor there is abundant evidence for more intensive activity at the end of the Neolithic and in the early Bronze Age. Like Scilly, these areas contain remarkable survivals of prehistoric landscapes, with settlements and fields complemented by the ceremonial and sacred sites – stone circles and rows, standing stones, and cairns. The cairns can range from scarcely three metres (9.8ft) in diameter to over thirty (98ft). The large cairns are often in prominent skyline positions. Some, such as the Rillaton Barrow, were used for the burial of important individuals. A cist (slab-built box) found by miners in 1837 contained an extended skeleton buried with an earthenware pot, a bronze dagger, a metallic rivet, pieces of bone, a few glass beads and the famous gold cup. The find is one of the richest Bronze Age grave deposits in Britain, comparable to finds from Wessex at this date (c.1600–1400BC). Significantly the barrow, 25m (82ft) in diameter and 2.5m (8.2ft) high, is the largest on Bodmin Moor, and is well worth a visit not least to see the fluorescent moss inside the cist.

The stone circles and rows remain enigmatic ritual monuments. Over sixty stone rows are known on Dartmoor, many of them complex multiple rows and some remarkably long; that in the Upper Erme valley runs for over 3km (1.86 miles) between a cairn at one end and a stone circle at the other, crossing three streams that lie in its path. Rows are now also known on Bodmin Moor, half a dozen having recently been discovered, all single rows mostly with small stones. Particular concentrations of circles, rows and cairns seem to form 'sacred areas' as at Merrivale and Shovel Down on Dartmoor or the Craddock Moor – Cheesewring area on Bodmin Moor. At the latter an area containing stone circles, a stone row and numerous cairns is fringed by hut circle settlements. Four of the monuments are linked by a convincing alignment, the key to which is an unusual site formed by two parallel banks of stone 60m (197ft) long and 4m (13ft) apart. If projected to the north-west the line of this 'embanked avenue' cuts through a stone row. Projected to the south-east it runs through the centre of the Craddock Moor stone circle, then through the southernmost of the three circles which form the Hurlers, and on through a barrow cemetery on Caradon Hill (not illustrated). The Rillaton Barrow, visible from the Hurlers as a skyline feature, may have marked the approach to Stowe's Pound, an exceptional enclosed hilltop settlement containing over seventy hut platforms within an elaborate arrangement of stone banks. The site is quite unlike the typical hut circle settlements; it is tempting to interpret it as a major early Bronze Age stronghold, and perhaps place of assembly, contemporary with the network of ritual monuments that includes the Rillaton Barrow, intended as the last resting place of the great chieftain who himself, or whose ancestors, may have organised the whole complex.

Many of the 1,500 or so stone-built hut circles on Bodmin Moor and the 2,500 on Dartmoor are probably later than the ritual monuments. It must be remembered that the settlements cover a long period from before 2000BC to some time after 1000BC during which time the pattern of settlement did not remain static. The term 'hut circle' too disguises a wide range of function. Their internal diameter can vary from scarcely 3m (9.8ft) to 12m (39ft) or more, suggesting very different uses, some as shepherds' shelters or pigsties, others as permanent farmhouses for large families.

Bronze Age landscape, Cheesewring, Cornwall
A Embanked Avenue   E Rillaton Barrow.
B Craddock Moor, stone row   (Source; Royal Commission on Historical
C Craddock Moor, stone circle   Monuments, England)
D Hurlers stone circle

The outstanding achievement on Dartmoor in the last ten years has been
Andrew Fleming's identification and interpretation of major territorial
boundaries, or 'reaves', of the later Bronze Age. The heart of the moor
remained unenclosed but the periphery was divided into ten or more large
territories, mostly by reaves radiating out from the moor along the water-
sheds. The lower part of each territory is generally enclosed as blocks of
rectangular fields, sometimes extending to thousands of acres, throughout
which hut circles (or 'farmhouses') are scattered in ones and twos. Similar
patterns are found on the chalk uplands of Wessex. This major organisation
of the landscape took place around 1500BC and may have been the work of a
regional authority, perhaps at a time when increasing pressure on resources

221

led to a formalisation of existing patterns of use in order to avoid conflict between local groups.

While the fields surrounding the huts were used for both cereal cultivation and as pasture, the moor beyond was probably used mostly as seasonal grazing and perhaps by groups from lowland Devon as well as from the Dartmoor fringe. Strung out along the valley sides of these upland areas, notably along the Plym, Avon and Erme valleys in the south, are the well-known 'pound' sites, typically a cluster of huts associated with one or more pounds or enclosures. A pastoral economy is likely, perhaps predominantly seasonal. Some of the sites with particularly substantial enclosure walls, almost of defensible proportions, may have been of higher status: Grims-pound is the best known example. There are also unenclosed settlements, sometimes with very many huts; that at Watern Oke has a bafflingly large total of seventy-four. Soon after 1000BC this busy landscape was beginning to empty, probably because of climatic deterioration coupled with im-poverishment of the thin acidic soils.

Because of the remarkable remains in the granite uplands it is easy to forget that throughout the Bronze Age the most densely settled areas would have been, as now, on the more low-lying land. The lowland farms are very difficult to trace, having been ploughed out over the centuries, but it is clear from the large number of barrows that still survive – some 1,400 in Cornwall alone – that these areas were well populated.

During the Iron Age, and particularly after c.500BC, the settlements in the south-western lowlands become more visible to the archaeologist, largely because many were surrounded by earthwork defences that have more effec-tively resisted the plough. In Devon and Cornwall two types of defended site can be distinguished, the hillforts – including the coastal promontory forts or 'cliff castles' – and the simple enclosed settlements known in Cornwall as 'rounds'. The hillforts are strongly defended sites, either by virtue of a strategic position such as a hilltop, or by multiple ramparts, or by both as at Castle-an-Dinas, near St Columb Major (Cornwall). This impressive site, one of Cornwall's largest hillforts, was purchased from the Duchy by the Cornwall Heritage Trust in 1986. In minor excavations in the 1960s surpris-ingly little evidence for occupation was found, unlike most hillforts where the density of pits and post-holes suggests intensive use over a long period. Some of the strongly defended sites have complicated defences which include additional enclosed areas or 'multiple enclosures', thought to be for the coralling and protection of livestock. The most striking features of the south-western hillforts are their enormous variety in both size and plan and their sheer numbers, ninety in Cornwall, another eighty in Devon. Classical

Drizzlecombe stone row, Dartmoor, one of a group of three in the Plym Valley the longest of which is 491ft. The menhir, or standing stone, can be seen at the end. (Western Morning News)

Castle-an-Dinas hill fort, St Columb Minor, a multivallate Iron Age fort. (Cornwall Archaeological Unit, Steve Hartgrove)

writers, such as Caesar, describe the proclivity of the Celts towards feasting, drinking, fighting and personal adornment: a warlike but fractious aristocratic society incapable of concerted action. The multiplicity of hillforts in the South West may illustrate precisely this point.

The second type of enclosed site is essentially a mixed farming settlement ranging from a small hamlet to a large village defended by a single rampart and ditch. Excavated Cornish 'rounds' have been found to contain houses belonging to the same tradition as the moorland hut circles. Hundreds of these sites are known in Cornwall, mostly as slight earthworks or merely as cropmarks. Hundreds more have been identified in Devon through systematic air photography carried out in 1984-5 by Frances Griffith. The distribution of settlement enclosures in Bradninch parish (Devon) gives an impression of the well developed character of the farming landscape in the Iron Age and Roman period. The southwestern enclosed settlements are found in broadly the same areas as the medieval settlements. The uplands were avoided for settlement but would surely still have been used for summer grazing. While Devon, Cornwall and probably part of Somerset formed the tribal area of the Dumnonii the areas to the east belonged to the Durotriges and to the north-east the Dobunni. In these areas the Duchy owns hillforts, or parts thereof, at Stantonbury and Widcombe (Avon), White Sheet Hill (Wiltshire), Ham Hill (Somerset) and most famous of all, the classic Maiden Castle (Dorset). Regional differences can be seen. In the Wessex area, the hillforts are generally fewer (though still thick on the ground compared to many parts of the country) but larger. Ham Hill is enormous. Maiden Castle, excavated by Sir Mortimer Wheeler in 1934–37, has been further examined in 1985 and 1986. The towering defences would have sheltered a

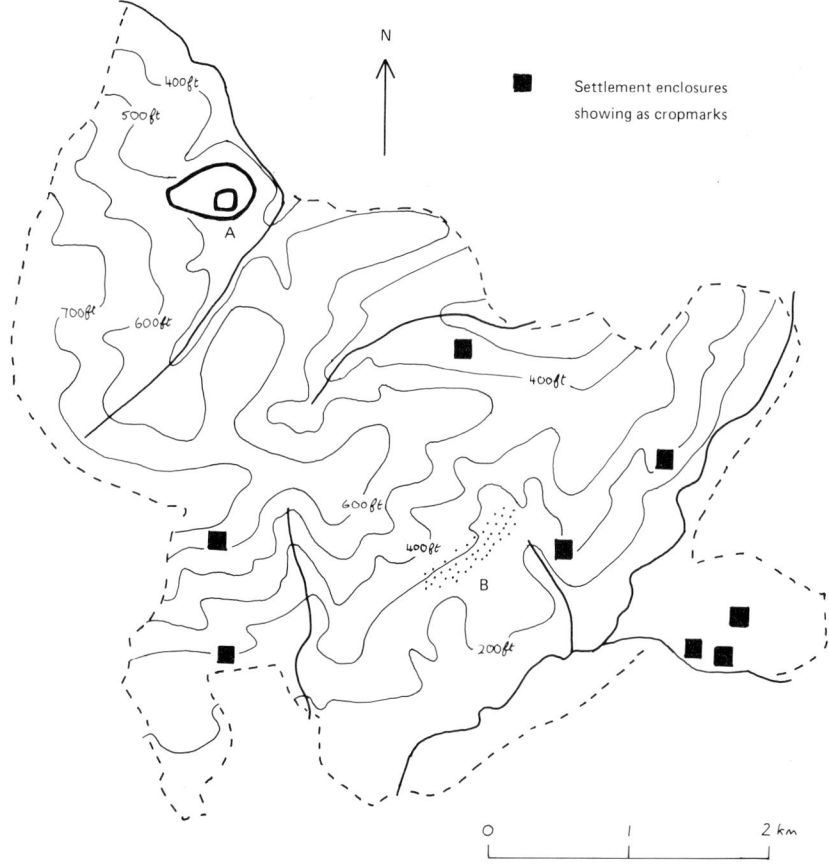

Iron Age and Romano-British settlements, Bradninch, Devon
A *Bury Castle, Hill Fort*
B *Position of medieval borough of Bradninch.*
(Source; Frances Griffith, Devon County Council)

crowded and lively community, perhaps the Iron Age equivalent of a town. The scale and complexity of the tortuous western entrance remains awesome and a walk along the massive ramparts bears eloquent testimony to the prestige of the Iron Age aristocrats and the resources at their command. However, the battle-scarred skeletons of the defeated British defenders found in a war cemetery by the east gate show that even these formidable defences could not withstand the military sledgehammer of Imperial Rome.

During the period of Roman rule a notional line from Bridgwater to Seaton divides a romanised area to the east from the unromanised South West. In Dumnonia the hillforts were mostly abandoned at the time of the conquest but the typical enclosed farming settlements continued throughout the Roman period and beyond. Exeter (Isca Dumnoniorum) was the only town and in most respects the South West remained 'native'. To the east are the Roman roads, the towns such as Durnovaria (Dorchester, planted at the foot of Maiden Castle), Lindinis (Ilchester) and Aquae Sulis (Bath), and the villas, country residences and estate centres of the well-to-do. As Tacitus put it, the sons of the British chiefs adopted the toga and were 'led into the demoralising temptations of arcades, baths and sumptuous banquets'. Typical of many villas in the Bath area is one on Duchy land at Newton St Loe. Excavated in 1837 and exposed again in 1968 it is of the simple corridor type, with interior decor of painted wall plaster and fitted with hypocausts to provide below-floor central heating. A mosaic pavement from the villa depicts Orpheus (now in Bristol Museum).

Settlements of lower status – and these are by far the most common type – also exhibit features of romanisation and, unlike sites in the South West, can be identified in ploughed fields by quantities of building rubble and well-made pottery. In the Duchy manor of Englishcombe (Avon) rural settlements of this type have been identified at a frequency of one every $1.5km^2$ (0.931 miles^2), suggesting a dispersed pattern of settlement actually quite similar to that in the South West. Field patterns sometimes survive to give a more complete picture of the landscape of this period, for example at Newton St Loe and Priston (Avon), widely around Dorchester and on Scilly. Small rectangular fields are typical. Throughout the area most of the Romano-British rural pattern of fields and settlement was already established in the Iron Age.

The political history of the fifth to seventh centuries, following the end of Roman rule in Britain, is characterised by the emergence of numerous small kingdoms, British in the west, Anglo-Saxon in the east, the latter gradually swallowing up the former as well as one another. The Wansdyke, of which the best preserved western stretches are on Duchy land in Avon, probably belongs in this context, but it is not known whether it is a British frontier of the sixth century or a slightly later boundary work dividing rival English kingdoms, the Hwicce and Wessex. By the eighth century the kingdom of Dumnonia had been forced back to the Tamar by the English.

Tintagel Castle, Cornwall: the castle of the medieval Earls and Dukes of Cornwall on the site of a major stronghold of the fifth to the seventh centuries AD. (Western Morning News)

In Cornwall the most immediate threat in the sixth and seventh centuries may have been not from the Saxons but the Irish. Irish influence overseas is recorded both in tradition and archaeologically. Some of the individuals recorded on the early Christian inscribed memorial stones of this date have Irish names and some inscriptions are in Irish ogham script as well as Latin.

The key Cornish site of this period is Tintagel. The most obvious remains on the headland are those of the twelfth or thirteenth-century castle but in 1933–4 C. A. Ralegh Radford identified and excavated six groups of slight rectangular buildings which he interpreted as a Celtic monastery of the fifth to seventh centuries, dated by finds of pottery from the eastern Mediterranean, particularly amphorae for wine and oil. The distribution of this type of pottery throughout the west of the British Isles demonstrates that links with the Mediterranean, perhaps both economic and cultural, continued after the east of the country had fallen to the Saxons. Considerably more post-Roman imported Mediterranean pottery had been found at Tintagel than anywhere else in Britain.

But are the remains on the headland necessarily those of a monastery? Current thought prefers to see Tintagel as a secular site, probably a 'high status defensive settlement'. Accidental fires on the headland in 1983 burnt off the tussocky grass to expose traces of many more rectangular buildings, most of them formed by very slight banks or sometimes no more than rough lines of stone. It is now clear that the whole of the headland was densely packed with buildings – over seventy have been surveyed – and most of these must belong to the fifth to seventh centuries.

Oliver Padel has approached the problem through the literary and linguistic evidence. First, the place-name may be Cornish *tin tagell*, 'fort of the neck', an excellent description of its impregnable setting. Second, in twelfth-century literature Tintagel is not a monastery but the seat of Cornish rulers. Most importantly, as the castle of King Mark it is the setting for the celebrated love story of Tristan and Isolt. In Geoffrey of Monmouth's *History of the Kings of Britain* it is a castle of Gorlois, Duke of Cornwall. While Gorlois was besieged by Uther Pendragon's forces at Dimilioc (perhaps the hillfort in which St Dennis church now sits, in the Domesday manor of 'Dimilioc') Uther himself, disguised by Merlin's magic as Gorlois, gained admittance to the bedchamber of Ygerna, the Duke's wife. And thus, so the story goes, was Arthur conceived. It must be emphasised that Mark, Tristan, Arthur and the rest belong to myth, not history, and that Arthur's links with Tintagel are limited, even in late medieval romances. What is important is the likelihood that the twelfth-century literature derives from an early medieval Cornish folklore tradition which associates Tintagel with the rulers of Cornwall.

When the folklore is combined with archaeological evidence, the large number of buildings, the exceptional quantities of fifth to seventh-century imported pottery, the strong defensive position, it is difficult to escape the conclusion that Tintagel was a royal seat of the post-Roman period. The medieval castle also appears in a new light. The evidence for a twelfth-century date is very limited. It may instead be a thirteenth-century enterprise of the colourful Earl Richard, built on this spectacular but strategically remote headland precisely because it was the most important mythological site in Cornwall, famed in local folklore and international romance as the castle of the Duke or King of Cornwall.

While the Duchy itself is a creation of the later Middle Ages its roots are much older, not just in its descent from the earldom and the fief of Robert of Mortain, but in the probable antiquity of its component estates. Many, perhaps most, were already long established by the time of the Norman conquest. Fordington, for example, surrounds and probably predates the late Saxon town of Dorchester; an origin before the eighth century is likely.

Throughout the medieval period power and wealth depended almost entirely on the holding of land. After the Norman conquest control of this resource was manifested in a proliferation of castles, symbols of the dominion of the Norman lords. Count Robert of Mortain, who held some 277 of the 350 Cornish manors, built strongholds at Launceston and Trematon. The Norman lords and their successors were not usually slow in maximising potential sources of revenue and this can be seen in their encouragement or foundation of towns on their estates, particularly in the twelfth and thirteenth centuries. Almost half the Duchy's fourteenth-century manors in Cornwall had boroughs. Other revenue came from fisheries and ferries, manorial and hundred courts, and most especially the profits of manor and Stannary. The deer parks on the other hand were a luxury that ran at a loss. The seven Duchy deer parks in Cornwall seem an unnecessary extravagance and were but rarely used by the dukes. Some of the park boundaries can still be traced, most particularly at Carrybullock park in Climsland manor where the bank and ditch of the park pale can be followed over Kit Hill. The park was three leagues in circumference and once held 150 deer.

The Duchy's fine collection of castles is a major facet of its archaeology, having been an integral part of its history, but the origins and development of the castles belong mostly to the earldom and before. By the time of the Duchy many were in disrepair and the subsequent history of most, at least in the South West, was as secondary administrative centres at best. Most prominent in the story of the castles is Richard, Earl of Cornwall. He acquired or was granted Tintagel, Restormel, Trematon, Lydford, Berkhamsted and Wallingford, built Mere castle from new and perhaps Tintagel, and instigated major rebuilding in equal measure to his prestige as a figure of international politics. At Berkhamsted he is recorded to have built a tower of three storeys in 1254. At Lydford, the free-standing tower built in 1195 was heightened in the thirteenth century and the basement engulfed in a mound, thus giving the impression of a stone tower built on a motte; this was probably the work of Richard. Archaeologically the castle is particularly important as a rare survival of a purpose-built medieval prison. As well as housing the Stannary prison Lydford was also the administrative centre for Dartmoor Forest.

Extensive excavations in the bailey of Launceston Castle have revealed a major reorganisation by Richard. The thirteenth-century Great Hall continued in use as the Assize Hall until the early seventeenth century. From the eleventh century Launceston was Cornwall's main administrative centre but from the late thirteenth century it lost some of this importance with the transference of many of its administrative functions to Lostwithiel by Earl Edmund.

The Earl's impressive thirteenth-century administrative complex at Lostwithiel (subsequently known locally as the 'Duchy Palace' though never actually a residence) served four main purposes: from here the Cornish estates were managed; it was the venue for the County Court and for the election of the Knights of the Shire; Lostwithiel was a Stannary town, the 'palace' acting as a coinage hall; it also housed the Stannary prison. Although much that is

Berkhamsted Castle, Hertfordshire: the motte and bailey Norman castle which was a major administrative centre for Earls Richard and Edmund. (Cambridge University Air Photo Collection)

shown on the Buck print has disappeared, the shell of the Great Hall survives, incorporated into later buildings and scarcely recognisable as one of Cornwall's most important historic buildings. 34m long (111ft) and 7.3m wide (24ft), the Great Hall was comparable in scale to the grandest of royal halls.

Only occasionally did the earls reside in Cornwall; their principal seats were at Wallingford and Berkhamsted, nearer the political heart of the country, Wallingford apparently being preferred by Richard – and a thirteenth-century strengthening of the castle may be attributable to him – and Berkhamsted the preferred residence of Edmund. Both castles continued to be important residences into the fifteenth century.

The records suggest that on the Cornish manors the typical rural settlement was the hamlet of two to ten houses; villages were rare. This dispersed pattern of settlement, with its roots in the Dark Ages, evidently prevailed throughout Devon and Cornwall and it is precisely settlements of this type

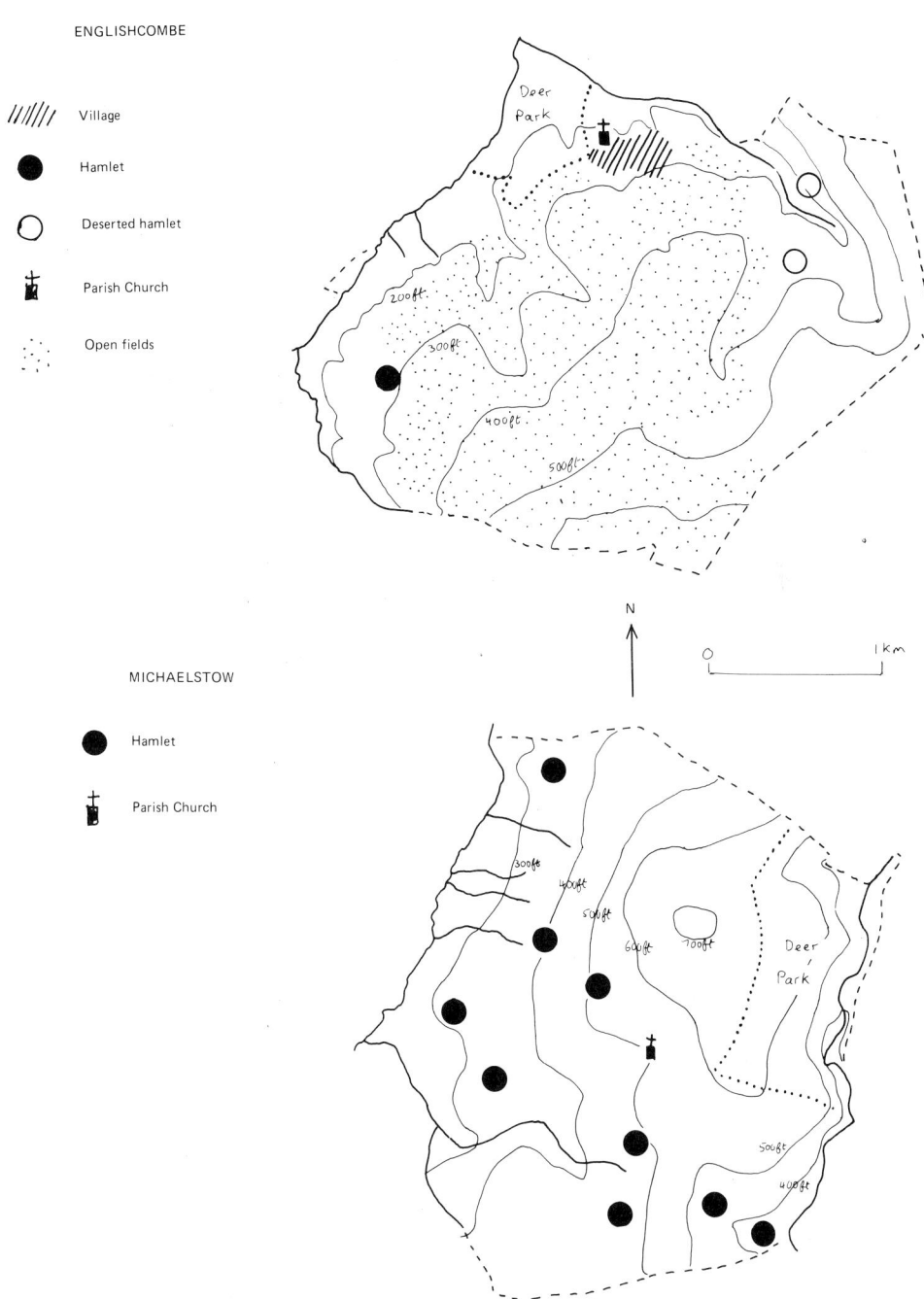

ENGLISHCOMBE

////// Village

● Hamlet

○ Deserted hamlet

✠ Parish Church

∴ Open fields

Deer Park

200ft

300ft

400ft

500ft

N

0   1 Km

MICHAELSTOW

● Hamlet

✠ Parish Church

300ft

400ft

500ft

600ft

700ft

Deer Park

500ft

400ft

Medieval settlement patterns, Englishcombe (Avon) and Michaelstow (Cornwall)
(Source; County of Avon Historic Landscape Survey of the Manor of Englishcombe;
Cornwall Sites and Monuments Record)

231

that one finds abandoned along the valleys of Bodmin Moor and Dartmoor, small settlements of no more than a handful of long-houses with associated garden plots and trackways and in many cases surrounded by the traces of extensive cultivation. The major phase of colonisation of the moors from the eleventh to thirteenth centuries is typical of the contemporary expansion of population and economy. From the late fourteenth century the trend was reversed; climatic deterioration, impoverishment of the acidic soils and the greater availability of better quality lowland holding following the Black Death (1349), all led to a shrinkage or abandoning of the upland settlements. Social and economic change also resulted in desertions in the lowlands, though the remains tend to be more difficult to locate and interpret; some twenty documented settlements in Climsland manor are now lost, and in Bradninch the sites of six deserted settlements are known, though in this case whilst the sites were probably of medieval origin, they were not abandoned until the nineteenth century.

In the east of the area, from Somerset to Gloucestershire, the prevailing settlement pattern is different, probably due in part to the more open topography. The parish of Englishcombe (Avon) is typical, containing a village as the main settlement and two smaller hamlets, Inglesbatch and Barrowmead, both established by the thirteenth century at the latest. Although subsequently deserted the layout of Barrowmead can still be traced as earthworks in permanent pasture. Villages too have been susceptible to change, including shrinkage or movement as well as desertion; earthworks next to St James Church at Curry Mallet (Somerset) preserve evidence of an early focus of settlement in the village. Deserted sites are present throughout the area in surprising numbers. The site of Loxhill hamlet in Milton Falconbridge (Somerset), first recorded in 1268, can now only be identified from large quantities of medieval pot sherds in a ploughed field that has retained the name of the settlement.

In this eastern area there is abundant evidence for the former existence of open field systems surrounding the villages and some hamlets. Some are shown in detail on early estate maps, as at Stoke sub Hamdon (Somerset). Sometimes elements of the strip field layout fossilised by early enclosure of the open fields can still be traced in the modern field pattern, for example at Isle Brewers, Curry Mallet and Shepton Mallet (Somerset). On the steeper slopes the process of cultivation has sculpted the individual strips into the hillside, forming 'strip lynchets'. These have been identified on the Duchy's Avon estates but survive most spectacularly at Mere (Wiltshire), where pressure on land led to the cultivation of the steep chalk downland slopes above the town. Meadows as well as arable land were sub-divided amongst the villagers. In a fascinating late survival of this practice at Milton Mead in Milton Falconbridge the strips were marked by boundary stones which are still in position, carved with the initials of the nineteenth-century tenants.

Although in the past it has been claimed that open fields were not a feature of 'Celtic' Devon and Cornwall it is now clear that many or even most of the thousands of hamlets did in fact have them. However, enclosure of this sub-divided arable seems to have occurred quite early in the medieval period in many areas of the South West. This seems to have been the case in the Cornish Duchy manors, perhaps in part because of the unusual systems of tenure adopted to maximise profits. Abandoned strip field systems can still be seen in the uplands of Bodmin Moor and Dartmoor. The well-known series of strip lynchets at Challacombe on Dartmoor is one of the best examples.

Aerial view of Kit Hill, east Cornwall; a medieval and post-medieval industrial landscape with earlier remains visible. (Cambridge University)

Industrial history has been discussed in detail elsewhere but such an important feature of the man-made landscape cannot be allowed to pass without at least a mention here. The appeal of the industrial sites is very wide. Visually they are more impressive than many of the more subtle elements of the archaeological record. Locally they are important because their history is often enmeshed with the origins of the local communities. But in addition to this, more than any other aspect of the archaeology of the South West, the industrial archaeology can claim to be of international importance because of the world-wide significance of the copper and tin industry and the part played by Devon and particularly Cornwall in the Industrial Revolution.

Other industrial sites should also be noted: many mills, sometimes with their machinery intact, as at Pawton (Cornwall); granite quarries; the Chard canal, running through Duchy land at Curry Mallet, which carried coal, fertilisers, salt, bricks, slate and timber from 1842 to 1867. The Duchy also owns part of the north Somerset coalfield, notably the Clandown Colliery (Midsomer Norton), the deepest in Somerset 438m (1437ft). In the area, eighteenth- and nineteenth-century coalpits still show as black patches when the fields are ploughed.

Although over three thousand 'sites' are at present kown in the Duchy it is more important to see the area as a single continuous site comprising the whole complex and many-layered fabric of the man-made landscape. This is most apparent in the uplands, but applies equally in an estate like Englishcombe where survey has shown how the 'modern' field pattern is an amalgam of prehistoric and Anglo-Saxon boundaries, early medieval roadside hedges and parish boundaries, hedges fossilising the furlongs of the open fields, hedges created when fields were carved from the woodland. Interpreted as a whole they record the history of centuries of changing land use in this typical parish. Each area has its unique history of land use which can be traced back to earliest prehistory, though the evidence is clearer in some areas than in others.

Over the last eighty years the Duchy has helped to secure the future of many of its major monuments by passing them (and the problems of management and conservation that go with them) into the care of the state as 'Guardianship' sites. The Duchy sites, ten castles and six important prehistoric sites, form a major component of the list of Guardianship sites in the South West. A further three hundred or so sites scheduled as Ancient Monuments receive a measure of statutory protection under the 1979 Ancient Monuments and Archaeological Areas Act. Although as a crown agency the Duchy of Cornwall is in theory exempt from the Act, in practice it is applied by consent.

The Duchy has not expressed an overall policy towards archaeology but its stance may be gauged by its report *Future Management of the Dartmoor Estate* (1983) in which one of the main objectives is to ensure 'the conservation of nature, historic landscapes, artefacts and buildings . . . as a key element in all decisions on land use and management.' This can only be achieved if archaeologists and the Duchy work together in seeing first that sites are identified and assessed and second that they are incorporated into the general management plan for each estate or farm. Progress towards this goal is not uniform. At the time of writing most of the county archaeologists (responsible for the Sites and Monuments Records that list the archaeological sites in each county) did not know the extent of the Duchy holdings and conversely the Land Stewards had no record of most archaeological sites in their areas.

The approach has been most systematic on Dartmoor and on the Avon estates. On Dartmoor, in addition to frequent ad hoc consultations, a number of Duchy farms have now been the subject of surveys and reports by the archaeologist of the National Park Authority, identifying the archaeology and making recommendations for its conservation. This is part of a continuing programme. In Avon the County Planning Department has sponsored historic landscape surveys for three Duchy estates in which the archaeological sites have been graded and management recommendations set out.

In the far South West a Sites and Monuments Record for the Isles of Scilly has been collated for the Duchy by the Institute of Cornish Studies. In Cornwall projects arising from Duchy policy have tended to be reactive. An

Cheesewring Quarry with the Cheesewring visible on the skyline: taken c.1910–20.

area of moorland on the south of Kit Hill initially intended for conversion to improved pasture was instead added to the Prince of Wales' gift to the county, after survey by the Cornwall Archaeological Unit identified a range of archaeological remains. Less fortunate was the fate of the Cheesewring Quarry, a well-known landmark of south-east Bodmin Moor of intrinsic interest as a nineteenth/early twentieth-century granite quarry with its various processing areas and sequence of waste heaps intact, but most particularly important as a component of an historic landscape including remains of all periods. In 1984 the quarry was briefly reopened to clear the interior and some of the waste heaps, thereby diminishing the overall quality of the area and at the same time blackening the Duchy's reputation because of the lack of consultation with local residents. One consequence of the episode has been closer liaison with the Cornwall Archaeological Unit, including funding from the Duchy to survey and evaluate specific industrial monuments where proposals were imminent.

In 1983 the Duke of Cornwall decided to set up an Archaeological Advisory Group to provide guidelines for archaeological policy and advise the Duchy on the management of its archaeological remains. The group, chaired by Professor Glyn Daniel, is composed of professional archaeologists from universities, museums and national bodies and meets twice yearly, usually with the Duke of Cornwall in attendance, to discuss precisely the sort of problems outlined above and to look at sites or areas where the Land Stewards have identified a management problem.

One such site was Maiden Castle, where the Prince's visit has led to a programme of conservation work by the Prince's Trust, a new campaign of excavation by English Heritage, and proposals from English Heritage for an elaborate and controversial scheme to interpret the monument and its landscape to a wider public. Indeed it is the surrounding landscape, archaeologically quite as important as the great hillfort itself, which needs the closest attention; although the area is packed with archaeological sites of all periods, not all of these monuments are well-known and well conserved. The archaeological wealth of the area was amply demonstrated in 1985 by the excavations next to Fordington Farm, in advance of building work. A Neolithic long barrow and a Bronze Age round barrow, Iron Age field boundaries, a hundred Roman burials, Roman farm buildings and post Roman timber buildings were all found on this single site, previously an archaeological blank.

Few estates can be as rich in archaeology as the Duchy of Cornwall. It is unrealistic to expect that the archaeology can invariably take precedence in the running of a modern estate but it is crucial that decisions are based on a knowledge of its existence and an awareness of its importance.

CHAPTER TWELVE

WILDLIFE

Robin Page

It is difficult to decide which is the most fortunate, the Duchy of Cornwall for owning land so rich in wildlife and of great natural beauty, or the wildlife itself for being owned by the present Duke of Cornwall, who is very aware of its importance and sympathetic to its conservation.

Since the end of World War II much of the landscape of the British Isles, particularly that of lowland England, has been changed by a new age of intensive agriculture. Grassland has been ploughed up, water-meadows drained, hedgerows bulldozed into oblivion and woodlands felled. Cereal production has inherited the land and large fields have been created to suit the use of modern agricultural machinery. A monoculture of annual wheat production has taken over from mixed farming, once based on a rotation of crops and livestock, and chemicals used for nutrition, weed control, and the eradication of diseases have replaced the traditional methods of crop husbandry. Wildlife has suffered considerably as a direct result; flowers of grassland and arable fields have been sprayed away as 'weeds'; hedgerows, the 'wildlife corridors' of the old countryside, have given way to sterile head-lands, and many once common birds and animals such as the otter, barn owl, and English partridge have found it difficult to survive, and without help would be hastening to join the dodo in extinction.

In total, national parks and nature reserves cover only a tiny fragment of Britain; it is the general countryside on which the bulk of our wildlife depends for its good health and it is only the common sense and understanding of private landowners that will ensure a rich and flourishing wildlife.

Not only does the Duchy take care of its special areas, but it also encourages its tenants to protect wildlife on more general farmland, and plan an attractive landscape for future generations. The Prince understands the need for efficient, well-run farms which allow his tenants to make decent livings, but he believes that farming and conservation can get on well together if encouraged and given support. Because of this a number of 'demonstration' farms have been established throughout the Duchy, where conservation schemes and good farming do not compete, but co-exist quite easily and naturally.

In some areas tenants have also been encouraged to join in tenants' shoots. This is not a contradiction, for pheasants and partridges will only thrive where there is good cover, and a plentiful supply of natural food, and this good habitat provides ideal conditions for many other forms of wildlife – flowers, birds and animals. This is clearly demonstrated on the Bradninch estate in mid-Devon where the tenants on the 3,000 acres, including those who do not actually shoot, have created some extremely valuable and varied wildlife habitats among good farmland, on well-run farms. Trees have been planted – both soft- and hardwoods – ponds dug out, water meadows left undrained, and some hedgerows allowed to grow up without an annual trim. As a result a tour of the farms will not only show pheasants but also buzzards, orchids, frogs and the slot marks (footprints) of deer, as well as many other species of wildlife. To help this process some of the tenancy agreements are even being rewritten so that an overgrown hedge is no longer classified as 'dilapidation'.

In addition to this, at the instigation of Prince Charles, an Advisory Group on Wildlife and Landscape has been set up to keep a watchful eye on both landscape and habitat. The Prince makes time to attend some of the meetings of the Wildlife Advisory Group where he makes helpful and considered contributions.

In addition to the Duchy's general farmland that is gradually being enriched and improved for wildlife, there are areas of special interest and importance throughout the Duchy, from Maiden Castle near its eastern boundary to the Isles of Scilly in the extreme south-west. Indeed, for its small size, Scilly possesses possibly the richest and most varied natural history in Britain.

To most people Maiden Castle, just south of Dorchester, is an important and impressive archaeological site. Yet it is also of great wildlife value, for its spectacular earth ramparts and fortified hilltop represent a relic of Dorset's ancient downland. Elsewhere much of the county's traditional sheep grassland has disappeared beneath the plough, or been 'improved' by the application of weedkillers and artificial fertilisers. Maiden Castle has escaped and its flower and insect life remains the same as it has for many generations. From spring until autumn there is a succession of flowering plants and grasses, including the cowslip, bee orchid, thyme, squinancywort, quaking grass – 'maiden hair' – eyebright, fairy flax, meadow oat, salad burnet, tor grass, bird's-foot trefoil, horseshoe vetch, smooth hawksbeard, sticky mouse ear, knapweed, devil's bit scabious and stemless thistle.

A rich flora seems to be a feature of old landscapes of archaeological importance, for quite nearby, at Mere in Wiltshire, is more rich grassland, together with countless ant-hills, another feature lost throughout much of Britain; they cover the spectacular strip lynchets, dating from post-Roman times, that still dominate the landscape. It can be amusing to listen to archaeologists each with different theories on how the lynchets were created,

Mere, Wiltshire; strip lynchets on the Downs north-east of the town. (Kate Havinden)

but naturalists are united in welcoming the pockets of downland saved by archaeological accident. At Mere a survey is to be carried out to check and record the flora, which in turn will also give an indication of the likely butterflies present.

The butterflies at Maiden Castle have already been recorded and they form an impressive list, including four members of the blue family – the common blue, the small blue, the chalkhill blue and the scarce and dwindling adonis blue. All these butterflies love the rich downland flowers of Maiden Castle's grassy slopes and hollows, and the food plants of the caterpillars, the most vital elements of a healthy butterfly population, also do well in the conditions. The caterpillar of the common blue can feed on most members of the wild pea family, being particularly fond of bird's foot trefoil, whereas the much scarcer adonis blue is very local and depends entirely on horseshoe vetch. Because the right vegetation is so critical to the welfare of butterflies, English Heritage, which manages Maiden Castle, is also responsible for managing the flora to ensure the survival of the butterflies.

The marbled white, another attractive butterfly of grassland, is to be found on the site and whenever there is an invasion of clouded yellows, Maiden Castle often benefits from the influx. The clouded yellow is a most striking Mediterranean migrant and there seems to be a great eruption in its population about once every seven years, when Britain receives many thousands.

One of the country's most important conservation successes in recent years occurred on Duchy land and that too involved butterflies. It took place in a beautiful, secluded Cornish wood, on a bank of the river Tamar. It is surrounded by rolling farmland and wooded coombs and forms a 135 acre haven of sheltered peace and seclusion. It contains plantations of conifers as well as old indigenous trees and can accurately be called a 'butterfly wood', as over thirty species of butterfly have been recorded within its boundaries, including six of the ten British fritillaries and both the purple and the green hairstreaks.

For several years the wood was known to have a colony of the very rare heath fritillary butterfly. But in 1980 it was discovered that another colony existed where the Duchy had just planted conifers as part of its commercial woodland programme. This meant that the second colony faced certain death as the butterfly needs open woodland glades, not the dense, dark conditions of a pine plantation. Prince Charles immediately ordered the young pines to be uprooted and planted elsewhere. Since then the Nature Conservancy Council has been managing the site as a butterfly reserve, and in 1985, despite an appalling summer, an estimated one thousand butterflies flew. The Duchy has two of the eight remaining sites of the heath fritillary, and largely because of the Duchy's attitude the butterfly has been brought back from the edge of extinction and is now considered to be safe for the immediate future. The exercise has been so successful that some butterflies from Duchy land may even be used for re-introduction programmes elsewhere.

At his home, Highgrove House in Gloucestershire, Prince Charles has planted a paddock with the grasses and flowers of old meadowland and he also has a butterfly garden. He is pleased with the progress at the Tamar wood, saying: 'The Duchy is not in the business of encouraging extinction and it was possible to sacrifice an area of commercial forestry for the heath fritillary. There are only a few areas where they survive and it was important to make a contribution to their conservation.' But at the same time Prince Charles plays down the importance of what he has done, saying: 'It is not something we could afford to do every day.'

The butterfly itself is interesting, for one of the main foodplants of the caterpillar is the ribwort plantain, and the flower head of the plantain and the caterpillar itself look remarkably similar – a good example of camouflage or mimicry in nature. In a field adjoining the wood, also owned by the Duchy, there is a colony of the scarce marsh fritillary, where there is a natural abundance of the food plant, devil's bit scabious. Again the marbled white is present; it is a striking black and white colour, yet scientists have excelled themselves by calling the family of butterflies to which it belongs 'the

Moorland landscape at Minions, Bodmin Moor; ponies in the foreground and a ruined engine house beyond. Ray Bishop. (Mulberry Studio, Molesworth St, Wadebridge)

Looking down Tamerton Creek to the Tamar estuary, with the mudflats and salt marshes beloved of waders. (Molly Gill)

browns'. Most butterflies lay their eggs carefully on the caterpillars' food plant, but the female marbled white scatters her eggs at random while flying. The only other British butterfly to rely on such a haphazard method is the ringlet. The wood has ringlets too as well as common garden butterflies, the gatekeeper, orange tip, brimstone, peacock and small tortoiseshell.

Birds, animals and flowers also thrive in the wood, as well as dragonflies and damsel flies, including one of the most attractive in Britain, the 'beautiful demoiselle'. Buzzards, cuckoos, tree pipits, marsh tits, willow tits and a host of woodland birds all find it ideal habitat, as does the fox. It also seems perfect for the dormouse as there are plenty of fruit and nut-bearing plants, such as hazel and blackberry, as well as honeysuckle, strips of which it uses when building its nest; consequently this shy little animal could well be present. Flowers and plants give an interest throughout the spring and summer from wood anemones, lesser celandines, marsh marigolds, ransoms and wild daffodils, to red campion, herb bennet, herb robert, hart's tongue fern and maidenhair spleenwort. In addition a number of unusual plants are also present such as bastard balm, pink purslane, yellow bartsia and the rare, but very ordinary, Cornish bladder seed. Orchids include the early purple, heath spotted, marsh, fragrant and bird's nest.

Dartmoor overlooks the Tamar valley and dominates much Duchy land. It does not possess the concentrated wildlife wealth of the butterfly wood, yet it has much to attract the amateur naturalist. At one time Dartmoor was probably largely wooded with small oaks, stunted by the cold and wet. With their removal for fuel, both domestic and for the smelting of tin, came grazing with livestock, and the moor became an area of grassland and heather. Land improvement and over-grazing have since hit the heather, with cultivated grasses taking over much of the low-lying land and purple moor grass invading the high open moor.

There are just two areas on Duchy land that give an indication of what the moor was once like; Black Tor Copse and Wistman's Wood, both ancient areas of aboriginal oak. They grow on valley sides overlooking moorland streams, with the copse covering a larger area than the wood. The most attractive and easily accessible is Wistman's Wood. It is a remarkable place, that led the Reverend Samuel Ward to write in 1848: 'The whole world cannot boast, probably, a greater curiosity in sylvan archaeology than this solitary grove in the Devonshire wilderness.' Another clergyman, Canon Ellacombe, considered it to be: 'the most weird and curious wood in England if not Europe.'

The reason the wood remains is possibly caused by the trees having grown in an area of clitter, where those wanting firewood, or smelting fuel, would have experienced great difficulties in moving timber over the clefts and holes of frost scattered rock. It is still difficult to walk through the wood because of the irregular jumble of plant-covered granite and it would be easy to slip and suffer injury if trying to carry a load. The trees themselves are gnarled,

Sand dunes at Rock on the Camel estuary, Cornwall. (Western Morning News)

The Heath Fritillary butterfly, a rare species for which the Prince of Wales has set aside a Cornish woodland as its natural habitat. (Nature Conservancy Council, Peter Wakeley)

twisted, stunted and spread-eagled, with their trunks and branches covered with luxuriant life. Even when leafless they retain a covering of different greens and browns from the numerous mosses, lichens, liverworts and ferns that thrive in Dartmoor's dampness. During the course of this century twenty-six types of moss, twenty-one liverworts and about seventy lichens have been recorded in the wood. Lichens develop from an intimate partnership between fungi and algae, and they are very intolerant of air pollution. Their abundance in Devon and Cornwall shows how much of the air in south-west England is still clean.

The shapes, angles and airborne fronds on the branches give the wood a unique and ancient beauty, exaggerated by the damp smell and the trunks themselves, which appear to be growing out of solid rock. In places the trunks of mountain ash and oak grow so tightly together, before splitting away at the top, that one tree appears to have two varieties of leaves and fruit. In this high, harsh land the English name of mountain ash seems far more descriptive and appropriate than the Scottish rowan. The oaks are the native English or pendunculate variety, distinguished from the other indigenous oak, the sessile, by stalks on the acorns. The pendunculate oak is most common in southern England, while the sessile is more numerous in the north and north-west. Children who grow up in areas of sessile oak miss a small pleasure of childhood, for an empty acorn cup, with stalk, makes an imitation miniature pipe.

Simply by walking to the wood it is possible to sense the flavour of the moor – a mixture of moorland, fast-flowing stream and bog – a unity found all over Dartmoor. Buzzards wheel overhead, to be mobbed by crows; skylarks sing and meadow pipits parachute down in display. In summer they are joined by the wheatear. An astonishing 20,000 pairs of meadow pipits nest on the moor, as well as 15,000 pairs of skylarks and 1,000 wheatears. Ring ouzels and ravens are other breeding birds, as well as golden plovers and dunlins. These last two are at the southern edge of their breeding range and need as little disturbance as possible during the breeding season to ensure their continued survival on Dartmoor. Sadly the Ten Tors walk – when hundreds of young people trek from tor to tor – takes place at the most crucial time during the breeding season, in the spring, and the sooner it is changed to September, or even later into the autumn, the better.

Another interesting bird found in the heather, particularly around Warren House Inn, is the red grouse. It is not a native of the moor but was introduced just before World War I by the then Prince of Wales, later the Duke of Windsor. The birds find life difficult because of foxes and human disturbance, but they hang on, with about fifty pairs nesting each year. Black grouse were once indigenous to the moor, but unfortunately they have disappeared probably because of a reduction in the amount of habitat suitable for them.

The streams are also valuable for birds, being ideal for dippers and pied and grey wagtails. They are also perfect for frogs and each spring tadpoles in their thousands can be seen. They make a welcome sight, for in many parts of Britain the once-common common frog is now extremely uncommon. Salmon complete their romantic journey in some Dartmoor streams, returning to the moor to breed, after travelling far out to sea. Their numbers are declining, due to commercial poaching, disease and over-fishing in river mouths and on the open sea, where some of the traditional feeding grounds have been discovered; but there can be no finer wildlife sight than the curving leap of a returning salmon. Eels too inhabit the streams; the life cycle of the eel is just as remarkable as the salmon's, but it lacks the romance. Sliding through mud holds far less appeal than leaping into clouds of drifting spray. The eel begins its life at sea and moves into fresh water, only returning to its ocean of origin to breed. It is thought that the eggs are laid in the Sargasso Sea, between the Caribbean and the bulge of the West African coast. They grow into leaf-like larvae that drift to the Continental Shelf of Europe, there they change into elvers and swim into fresh water. They remain in lakes, rivers and streams for several years, until maturity, when again they head for the sea.

The presence of eels is good, for they form the favourite food of the otter, and otters still breed on Dartmoor, as well as in some Cornish rivers, sections of which are owned by the Duchy. The South West is now one of the last strongholds of the otter in England; elsewhere it has vanished, due to disturbance and pollution. In some parts it has been replaced by mink, and they too have spread on to Dartmoor. Among naturalists there is some disagreement as to whether the mink and the otter can live happily side by side. Some maintain that they can. Others claim that the increase in mink is one of the reasons for the decline in the otter.

The Duchy is aware of its responsibilities to maintain suitable conditions for the otter and this was demonstrated recently when plans were being made to open up a site on the moor to the public. It was an attractive area of archaeological and wildlife interest, with much commercial potential, yet because otters were known to be breeding in the area the scheme was abandoned to avoid disturbing the family.

Foxes abound on the moor and it is said that the rocks of Vixen Tor look like a crouching vixen. Even the most agile fox, however, would find it difficult to cross Foxtor Mire. Numerous plants of wet places can be found there, which are widespread over the entire moor – bog asphodel, marsh thistle, pennywort, sundew, cotton grass, heath spotted orchid and the ubiquitous foxglove. Various types of sphagnum moss also lie in great squelching beds. In days gone by the women of Princetown collected sphagnum; it was washed and dried and used for medical dressings, up to and including World War I.

The moor can be of interest at all seasons of the year. It can even give the odd surprise, with a fleeting glimpse of a merlin, a hobby or a peregrine falcon, while badgers are quite common, and a red deer occasionally wanders over from Exmoor. A few old grass meadows can also still be found, full of wild flowers – a reminder of what Dartmoor was like in an earlier age. The more the visitor wanders, then the more wildlife he or she is likely to see. For the sedentary, 'wild' animals can still be seen, as Dartmoor ponies make a common as well as an attractive sight. For those struggling to acquire a knowledge of wild plants, one pleasant exercise is to study them in liquid form; for both the Dartmoor Inn and the Warren House Inn sell English country wines, including dandelion, birch and blackberry. It gives botany a wonderful new attraction. Parts of Bodmin Moor are also owned by the Duchy and, together with Dartmoor, form some of the most important moorland habitats in southern Britain.

From Dartmoor it is possible to see down the Tamar valley to the coast, where again the Duchy owns much valuable foreshore and fundus, in both north and south Cornwall. The Tamar itself is important, not only for otters, sea trout and salmon, but because of its winter population of wading birds which thrive on the tidal mud flats. The mud is rich in food, with large populations of cockles, rag-worms, lug-worms, sand-hoppers and many more. As a result curlew, dunlin, golden plovers, knot and redshank are plentiful throughout the winter and a flock of avocets is also usually present.

The avocets have wintered on the Tamar for several years; some are conti-nental birds, and it is thought that a few were hatched and ringed at Minsmere, a reserve of the Royal Society for the Protection of Birds, in Suffolk. Although there is a growing tendency for English avocets to remain on the coast throughout the year, most European birds spend their winters well away from the mud of the Tamar, spreading southwards from Brittany to East Africa. The avocet is Britain's most striking and graceful wader and its return was most welcome. In the early nineteenth century it was wiped out as a breeding bird through drainage, egg-collecting and shooting – for taxidermy, and for its feathers, which were popular for making fishing flies. Re-colonisation began in the nineteen-forties. The Tamar has far more than its wintering waders, as during the summer its marshes have many attractive salt-loving plants such as sea-purslane, sea aster, sea-lavender and samphire.

Also along the south coast the Duchy owns two of the widest 'drowned valleys', both extremely valuable to wildlife especially in winter – the Kingsbridge estuary, and that of the Helford river. The Kingsbridge estuary is a most unusual area of shallow water, stretching about four miles from Salcombe to Kingsbridge. Although the estuary runs north-south, long creeks branch off at right angles from it, giving acres of uncovered mud at low tide. In places small cliffs give shelter, and by foot or boat it is possible to get away into a wilderness of water, rocks and mud. It is a large, shallow extension of the sea, for strangely no major river flows into it, simply a few insignificant streams. It is thought that at one time the estuary formed the outlet of the river Avon, but then streams cutting into the softer rocks diverted the river several miles to the west. Because it is sea water and so sheltered, it provides unique conditions and is one of the richest areas for marine biology in the country, with various forms of specialised life, including numerous worms, molluscs and sea-squirts. It has sponges, sea-mats, sea-firs, tube-worms, flat-worms, fan-worms, rag-worms, sea anemones (including the burrowing anemone), starfish, butterfish, brittle stars, sea-cucumbers, corals (including Devonshire cup coral), sea-gherkin, peppery furrow shells, Baltic tellins, laver spire shells, oysters, and many other plants, creatures and algae. The fan-worm is one of the most unusual species; it builds a small mud tube in which to live and, when covered in water, a fan of tentacles extends from the top like a net to obtain minute particles of food.

Because of the estuary's abundant and varied marine life, Colonel George Montagu became extremely interested in its wildlife. He was an army officer who lived between 1751 and 1815 and was the first man to differentiate between the hen harrier and the bird named after him – the Montagu's harrier. After leaving the army and spending some time in Wiltshire, he moved to Kingsbridge. There he studied the worlds of sea, shore and mud, and as a result, in addition to Montagu's harrier, there is a Montagu's sea-snail, a Montagu's blenny – a small fish that lives in rock pools and eats acorn barnacles – and Montagu's plated lobster, a green lobster just one and a half inches long.

The estuary has larger and more easily identifiable species too – shoals of grey mullet, as well as bass, plaice, mackerel, flounders and many more varieties of fish. Herons are always present, stalking small fish in the shallows, but it is winter when birds are attracted in large numbers. Well over eighty species of gulls, terns, water birds and waders have been identified, either stopping off briefly during migration, or wintering to take advantage of the plentiful supply of food. There can be up to 2,000 wigeon, 1,000 golden plovers, 700 dunlin, 350 redshank, 350 shelduck, 300 curlew, and smaller numbers of many other species. Some call in every winter, while others appear infrequently; visitors include grey plovers, spotted redshank, greenshank, goldeneye, red-breasted mergansers, Bewick's swans, long-tailed ducks and both the bar-tailed and the black-tailed godwits.

The coast of north Cornwall where the Duchy owns much foreshore as well as small pockets of land, is much more rugged than that of the south, and although in summer it tends to be over-populated with 'grockles' and 'emmetts' – two local names for tourists – it still has good areas for wildlife and can supply many surprises. Here the Atlantic Ocean meets sheer rock faces, giving some of the most spectacular coastal scenery in England. On a quiet, hot day in summer, with gulls wheeling and a seal breaking the surface of the resting sea, it is a scene of perfect tranquillity, but when onshore gales drive huge waves against the hard, cold cliffs, it gives a view of nature at its wildest.

On the foreshore as the tide goes out there are rock pools, barnacles, sea shells and straggling weed; a world over which scolding oystercatchers stand as sentinels. There are caves too, tunnelled into lines of weaker rock where in the autumn grey seals give birth to their young. High up above, pairs of peregrines and ravens rear their offspring. The coast of north Cornwall has always been a favourite area for peregrines, but during World War II many birds were shot, to prevent them killing carrier pigeons, released during times of radio silence. After the war numbers slowly recovered, until by 1956 there were over six hundred and fifty pairs throughout the country. Then, like the otter and the barn owl, the peregrine was hit by pesticide sprays used in agriculture and numbers plummetted to just sixty-eight known breeding birds. Fortunately restrictions were imposed on the chemicals concerned, with several species of wildlife teetering on the brink of extinction in Britain, and the peregrine was saved. Since then numbers have slowly improved and now many of the old nesting sites are again occupied during the breeding season.

Although many of the cliff tops are not strictly owned by the Duchy, they are extremely interesting botanically, with sea carrot, spring quill, Cornish gentian, hairy greenweed, burnet rose, silvery hairgrass and many others. Some of these can be seen at Tintagel on land definitely owned by the Duchy, but administered by English Heritage. Even in an area of outstanding coast-line it stands out for its towering beauty and superb views. Flowers abound, as do birds and butterflies. Peregrines can sometimes be seen, and fulmars are common, wheeling effortlessly through the ebb and flow of the uncertain air. Jackdaws, in contrast, ride and tumble in the turbulence, a habit that has given them the local name of 'rock choughs'; sadly the chough is no longer to be seen, having become extinct in Cornwall in the late 1960s.

Another contrast is to be found at the inappropriately-named Rock, on the Camel estuary, for there the Duchy owns some magnificent sand dunes. They form another spectacular summer habitat for flowers and butterflies, with kidney vetch, lady's bedstraw, eyebright, dwarf blackthorn, privet, red and white valerian, orchids, evening primrose, thyme, traveller's joy and ox-eye daisies among them. The butterflies include common blues, meadow browns, gatekeepers, small skippers, and again marbled whites.

But despite the appeal of most Duchy land, the Isles of Scilly must stand out as the most important area for wildlife, being unique, beautiful and unspoilt. They are not over-crowded, pollution is small, and so far, man and nature seem to be in reasonable harmony. The islands formed part of the original Duchy in 1337, when the Black Prince could demand a rent of 6/8d (33½p), or 300 puffins per year. That continued without review until 1570, when the puffin gained reprieve. As Prince Charles says: 'Perhaps even by the sixteenth century the Duchy was becoming conservation conscious. Sadly, the Scillies would be hard pushed to count a hundred puffins today.' The appeal of islands is obvious to Prince Charles, as are their problems:

Grey seal and its baby, Isles of Scilly. (Frank Gibson)

The islands are extremely beautiful, although according to the EEC they make up a 'less favoured area'. The people are splendid, and several families go back many generations – they are traditional and conservative. The peace and pace of life in the islands are among its biggest attractions, for there are not too many people. At the moment there is a very precise and delicate balance and we must be sure not to disturb it. That is one of the problems in trying to create more wealth, to ensure that we do not damage what is already there.

It is difficult to manage the wildlife side, but again we want to conserve the islands' richness, without upsetting the islanders. We want to do it together, to set an example and preserve them in the best possible way.

Being islands, the Scillies have several oddities. They form the only area in Britain where the lesser white-toothed shrew, or Scilly shrew, is found. The same is true of the dwarf pansy, which can be found in Brittany. The meadow brown butterfly differs from that of the mainland butterfly, as it

A puffin, Isles of Scilly.
(Frank Gibson)

does from island to island. In addition, evolution and isolation have made the beaks of the blackbirds orange, instead of the mainland's yellow, and many house sparrows have reverted to their 'weaver' origins and build in trees; the wood mouse has a conspicuous light stripe, and house mice live mainly away from houses. But just as some species are peculiar to Scilly, there are many mainland creatures not to be found on the islands such as the fox, badger, hedgehog, hare, squirrel, mole, stoat, weasel, snake, newt, lizard and horse fly.

The maritime climate and virtual lack of frost make the flowers a great attraction to visitors — made even more spectacular by the numerous exotic escapees from Tresco Abbey gardens and from the bulb fields. Consequently an ordinary stone wall can become a wild rock garden, with flowers such as pennywort, the great flowering arrowheads of aeonium from the Canary Islands, red campion, 'whistling Jacks' from North Africa, fennel,

Guillemot, Isles of Scilly.
(Frank Gibson)

alexanders, three-cornered leeks, red valerian, ivy, various lichens and Hottentot figs. The Hottentot fig is a most attractive South African plant that now grows wild. It was given its name when the early European settlers at the Cape saw the Hottentots eating the ripe fruit, or 'figs', after the flowers had faded. It was introduced into this country as long ago as 1690, and once had the botanical name of mesembryanthemum; this was much too difficult for the Cornish, who adapted it to 'Sally-my-handsome', a name still used today.

The small farm fields are full of 'weeds'; pink oxalis, corn marigold, English catchfly, fumitary and Bermuda buttercup. The Bermuda buttercup is not a true buttercup and does not come from Bermuda, but is another escapee from South Africa. The fields are made windproof by evergreen hedges – many of them with shrubs from New Zealand – pittosporum, coprosma and hedge veronica or 'hebes'. Plants of the cliff top and sea shore include thrift, English stonecrop, thyme, lousewort, birdsfoot trefoil, sea radish, sea holly, sea beet and tree mallow.

Sea birds on the Isles of Scilly are not in the huge numbers of some of the Welsh and Scottish islands, as several are at the southern edge of their breeding range. Nevertheless they can often be seen at close quarters and the boatmen run regular trips around the nature reserve of Annet, as well as the Eastern Islands and the Western Rocks. Guillemots, razorbills, puffins, kittiwakes, Manx shearwaters, shags and cormorants are all reasonably common, from early spring until the end of the breeding season in mid-July.

Two of the most interesting breeding birds are the storm petrel and the roseate tern. The storm petrel is a small, dainty bird, about the size of a chaffinch; it spends almost its entire life at sea, returning to land only to breed. The female lays her eggs deep down among the boulders of storm beaches, or in cracks and crevices. One ringed bird has been returning to Annet each year for seventeen years. The rarest breeding bird is the roseate tern, which winters along the coast of West Africa. From 1927 roseate terns were thought to be extinct in the islands, until in 1943 a young serviceman, Humfrey Wakefield, discovered a nest by accident, in a colony of common terns. The birds have bred ever since, and Humfrey Wakefield has also stayed on the islands, establishing a highly successful business as a potter. Almost inevitably it was George Montagu who first recognised the roseate tern as a separate species; it was he too who first realised that the cirl bunting and yellowhammer were different birds. The other tern to breed in the Scillies is the sandwich tern, but that did not arrive as a breeding species until 1978.

Gulls are present in large numbers and one of the boatmen, John Hicks, has a simple way for the layman to distinguish between a great black-backed gull and a lesser black-backed gull: 'The Greater black-back's back is blacker than a Lesser black-back's back, because a Lesser black-back's back isn't as black as a Greater black-back's back – it's lighter.'

Each autumn Scilly receives an influx of rare birds from America, eastern Europe and even Asia – birds that have become lost or blown off course during migration. The rarities include such things as the Radde's warbler, black-throated thrush and lesser yellowlegs. Earnest bird-watchers, 'twitchers', arrive in large numbers to add more species to their life lists of birds. They help to bring business to the islands, but by their behaviour, herd instincts and one-track minds, they can give all bird-watchers a bad name and damage the cause of conservation. Also in the autumn the grey seals have their young on the remoter islands; most twitchers do not notice, as they are too busy tracking down obscure little brown birds – 'lbj's', little brown jobs. In an earlier generation most twitchers would probably have been train spotters.

All in all the Duchy has a wealth of wildlife riches. It is lucky to have an owner who appreciates them and who wishes to protect them, not only for the present, but also for the benefit of future generations.

CHAPTER THIRTEEN

THE WAY AHEAD

Oliver Franks

A yachtsman sailing among the Isles of Scilly or in other difficult waters has to find his marks. He has to look behind him, and identify them, for only then can he move forward with confidence. Any attempt to forecast the way ahead for the Duchy of Cornwall must employ a similar method. It is not good sense to grasp a crystal ball and speculate on the future of the Duchy. Only by identifying characteristic marks of the historical Duchy is it possible to arrive at guidelines which can suggest the way in which it will move into the future.

One mark which has been there from the beginning is the close and intimate connection of the Duchy with the monarchy. Another is its paradoxical character of being a publicly accountable private estate. A third mark is that, while the Duchy has always been primarily a landowner, it has never depended for its revenues solely on agricultural income. Lastly the management of the Duchy has always been able to change and adapt, though at times slowly, to changing circumstances and altered expectations.

In 1337 Edward III made his son Duke of Cornwall and endowed his Duchy with ample lands in a charter presented to the whole council of Parliament. The charter went further: the Duke of Cornwall must succeed to the throne and only the eldest son of the monarch can be Duke of Cornwall. This settled the issue of succession. But yet more the charter laid it down by an extraordinary stroke of imaginative decision not just that, when there is no Duke of Cornwall, the Duchy reverts to the crown but that all monarchs in future must give it up to a son and heir, so soon as he is born.

It is obvious therefore that the Duchy of Cornwall is indissolubly bound up with the monarchy. This has been the case for more than six hundred years: it is so today. It follows that whether there will be a Duke of Cornwall and a Duchy of Cornwall in the future must depend in the first place on whether the monarchy will continue. If the past gives any guide to the future, it will. Over many centuries and through many vicissitudes it has been an institution which has commanded the affection and loyalty of the British people. Of course the character of the monarchy has changed with changing times. In the Tudor period kings and queens held great executive power, though not unchecked: Henry VIII was by far the most powerful man in the state. In more recent times the monarchy has become a constitutional monarchy: it has been described by Sir Lewis Namier as

> a sovereign placed above parties and policies: a Prime Minister and Government taking rise from Parliament and received rather than designated by the Sovereign, yet as 'H M confidential servants' deriving from the Royal Prerogative that essential executive character which an elected legislature could not impart to them.

As such, the monarchy is a functioning part of the British constitution. General elections are held, the complexion of Parliament changes, governments come and go. The monarchy exists, as Bagehot said, as the 'disguiser of change': it represents the element of continuity in the state. And this continuity is something the British people need and like.

Recent reigns, those of George V, George VI and Queen Elizabeth, have worked greatly to strengthen the hold of the monarchy over the British people and its secure place in the state. The manner in which these monarchs and their families have conducted themselves has inspired affection and loyalty. Of course time brings its changes. Perhaps the most important is in the ways by which the monarchy shows itself to the people. This kings and queens have always done: unless monarchs show themselves they cannot be known and, unless they are known, they cannot enjoy full acceptance. This is a part of the meaning of the great ceremonial occasions, such as a coronation, a marriage or a funeral. It is equally one of the reasons for the many visits of members of the royal family to institutions, occasions and to individual people over the length and breadth of the country.

But in recent years there has been a change of emphasis. Now, apart from all the other ways in which the monarchy shows itself, it is seen on television. It is seen not only on the great state occasions and on royal visits to different parts of the country, but the lives of the royal family have been shown and documented on television. In 1986 the Duke of Cornwall was seen and heard for an hour, explaining his responsibilities for his Duchy, expressing his interest in, and concern for it and its improvement, and illustrating his frequent visits to his tenants whether on farms or in Duchy workshops. No doubt this change of emphasis has resulted from a deliberate decision. Watching the television screen is the way in which now most people absorb most of the news, acquire their views and opinions, and generally react to what is happening. The monarchy has decided to keep up with the times.

Yet this carries a certain degree of risk. All action does, but so does taking no action. Here the risk can be that, by being brought close to the people on television, viewers might come to look at the monarchy as a show, not necessarily differentiated in kind from other shows to be seen on the box. But the dignified part of the Constitution, again Bagehot's phrase, cannot become ordinary like other things. It has to remain, however approachable, at a certain distance from the daily scene. Success has attended the enterprise: exposure to television has been a gain, not a loss. For example, on great ceremonial occasions the dignity of the monarchy has not been lessened despite the probing eye of the camera. There is every reason to expect this state of affairs to continue. The monarchy will hold its place in the minds and hearts of the people. Given this, the Duchy of Cornwall, so intimately bound up with the monarchy, can look forward to the future with confidence.

It is a paradox, as Dr Haslam says in the second chapter of this book, that the Duchy is a publicly accountable private estate. It is a great, mainly agricultural, private estate. When there is a Duke of Cornwall, he enjoys its revenues, indeed he has to live off it for he has no other income. But this estate is publicly regulated by special acts of Parliament. What is more, by virtue of an act of Parliament passed in 1828 and still in force, the accounts of the receipts and expenditures of the Duchy must be submitted every year to the Treasury which must then present them to both Houses of Parliament. The Duchy is publicly accountable. In the latter part of the eighteenth and in the early decades of the nineteenth century the Duchy's conduct of its affairs did not enjoy a good reputation. It was medieval in its administration: it was associated with pocket boroughs: it looked stagnant and unhealthy as Britain moved into the brisk and more efficient era of the Industrial Revolution. It also generated very little income and a great part of it was consumed in expenses. This is why, after the accession of Queen Victoria in 1837, it was enacted that the accounts of the Duchy should be open to public examination. The measure was designed to ensure that the affairs of the Duchy were respectably conducted and could be seen to be so.

A paradox may ultimately be either a nonsense or very good sense. If pressed to logical extremes the two sides of a paradox conflict, indeed appear contradictory. How can anything, the Duchy of Cornwall or any other institution, be both private and public? It must be one or the other. But pure logic is one thing, practice and practicality another. A paradox can be a way of stating something sensible and thoroughly practical in its working. The colleges of Oxford and Cambridge came into being by royal charters: the conduct of their affairs is regulated by their statutes which must be approved by the Privy Council, and they are required annually to submit in prescribed form their accounts of receipts and expenditures to their universities which publish them. They too are private institutions publicly accountable. So far it has been held that this practical device is salutary and should continue. The case is the same with the Duchy of Cornwall. Public accountability is at once a discipline and a protection. At the present time the Duchy with an active and concerned Duke, a modern outlook and an efficient administration does not require the discipline. But the protection afforded is advantageous. It prevents suspicions based on ignorance slowly accumulating, or suggestions that the assets or income of the Duchy are being used in ways which are against the public interest. The Duchy can move forward and face the future in the knowledge that it regularly keeps Parliament and the public informed of its activities.

The third mark characterising the Duchy concerns its sources of income. It would be natural to suppose that this great landed estate would draw its income from its farms and other agricultural properties, and indeed it has always had such an income. But it has never been the case that the Duchy depended solely on income from land. It has depended heavily on other sources. For the first five hundred years of its existence royalties and taxes on minerals had great importance. Royalties were paid on metals extracted from Duchy property in the South West, tin and copper, and to a lesser extent, silver and lead. Later on, there were also royalties on coal from coalfields on Duchy land in Somerset. But it was the tax on tin which mattered most. Until 1838, when this tax was abolished and the Duchy received in compensation a fixed annual sum from the Treasury, all tin produced in the South West, whether from Duchy property or not, had to be brought to the officers of the Duchy to be assayed before it was sold. The Duchy levied a tax on this operation and the income was large. In the Middle Ages the revenue from this tax often equalled or exceeded that from agriculture. The Duchy derived financial strength from possessing this diversity of sources of income.

Even after the end of the Middle Ages, when the modern era began, the Duchy continued to benefit from having more than one major source of revenue. In 1840, after the abolition of the tax on tin, the compensation payment from the Treasury and royalties from minerals and stone quarries amounted together to nearly one half of the Duchy's receipts. Thereafter there was a change: agricultural rents rose while the second source of income remained broadly static. Proportionally its importance diminished until by 1910 it amounted to only twelve per cent of total income. This trend continued and in the decades immediately after World War II the Duchy was nearer to total dependence on its land holdings than ever before.

When in 1969 Prince Charles on attaining his majority assumed his full responsibilities as Duke of Cornwall, it became evident that the situation was approaching a crisis. The net profits of the Duchy were insufficient adequately to maintain the Duke of Cornwall. Action was quickly taken. A revolution in farming techniques had been happening and the advent of large-scale machinery had greatly diminished the number of workers needed on farms. As a result there were many vacant cottages. The Duchy decided to sell them: it also decided gradually to sell residential property in Kennington. In a comparatively short space of time the proceeds of sales produced a substantial fund which was invested in government stocks and equities. This portfolio investment provides an important source of the Duke's income. The crisis was averted as the Duchy's total revenues rose strongly.

Chagford, one of the Devon Stannary towns through which the Duchy obtained so much of its early wealth. (Western Morning News)

Learning from its own history the Duchy in 1984 constructed a strategic plan for the deployment of its assets. For historical reasons and also because it was the firm view of the Duke of Cornwall, the Duchy would remain what it has always been, a great landed estate. But it would deliberately seek to build up alternative sources of income to buttress the receipts from agriculture. One already existed: the investment portfolio. But it was further decided, as money came in from sales, to invest a modest proportion of the Duchy's total wealth in commercial property and shops, a new departure. The first investments of this kind have already been made. Additionally it was decided to diversify the land holdings, to become a little less concentrated in the South West and acquire good-quality arable land elsewhere. Farms have been bought in Lincolnshire. The wheel has come full circle. Once the Duchy had had land in Lincolnshire but it had been taken by Henry VIII who gave in exchange a number of manors in Cornwall. Now after 400 years the Duchy properties once more extend eastwards.

These changes have put the Duchy back on course. It has returned to its historical position and does not depend too much on any one source of revenue. This gives it financial viability and ensures that it will not suffer too much if some of its assets meet with misfortune. It is now well equipped to move into the future with diversified investments. Financially it can see the way ahead.

The final historical mark relates to the administration of the Duchy. It has always been able, though at times slowly and sometimes only in the very nick of time, to adapt to changing circumstance. Throughout the Middle Ages and indeed far beyond, the landed estate was administered on the broad lines laid down by the first Duke of Cornwall, the Black Prince. There is a splendid quotation from Dr A. L. Rowse in the chapter of this book on Cornwall. He refers specifically to Cornwall but his words have a general application to the lands of the Duchy.

> One derives the impression of an institution tenacious and conservative, one that neither relaxed its right nor vexed its tenantry with new and unexpected impositions . . . At bottom, it was the age-long reverence for custom and tradition, the bed-rock of human history, that prevailed and ruled in and through the Duchy.

Indeed this was bound to be the case. Distances, especially to the West Country, the slowness and badness of communications, militated against change. The only exception, and an important one, was the collection of the dues on tin. Here an effective organisation under the Lord Warden of the Stannaries reacted to changing circumstance. The main mining areas changed over time, and with them the main towns for assaying tin. As is pointed out in the chapter of this book on mining, in the fourteenth century the main Stannary towns were Bodmin and Lostwithiel: then in the sixteenth century they were Helston and Truro and in the seventeenth century it was Penzance which dealt with the tin produced in the Penwith peninsula. The revenues from tin were so important that the Duchy in its administration had to be alert to follow the movements of the tin miners.

The Duchy remained essentially medieval in its administration for many centuries. It remained so into the early decades of the nineteenth century. Under the Duchy Council it was run by office holders, men not on salary or

The Secretary's office at the Duchy headquarters, 10 Buckingham Gate, after the 1950 reconstruction. (Planet News)

professionally equipped but deriving their income from fees and charges. Inevitably a complex system of charging for every duty they undertook grew up. The whole system was inimical to change. It is true that from time to time the Duchy had employed men with skills to investigate and report on its condition. John Norden had been so employed in the seventeenth century and William Simpson in the eighteenth. But in general there was nothing resembling a modern system of management. This state of affairs became intolerable as the nineteenth century advanced. At the time of the accession of Queen Victoria, England was alive with change: the cotton industry was booming, railways were being laid down and restraints on trade were being lifted. It was obvious that the Duchy could not go on as it was, particularly as its income, after expenses, had become quite inadequate to sustain a Duke of Cornwall. In 1838 a special commission was appointed to investigate, report and recommend. Its recommendations were far reaching. Among the changes the management proposed were the appointment of local agents, the abolition of copyhold estates (which had meant that tenants of the Duchy were often absentee tenants letting their properties to sub-tenants whom the Duchy did not know), and the granting of leases for a fixed term of years.

In 1840 Queen Victoria appointed the Prince Consort to the Council and in 1842 he became Lord Warden of the Stannaries. For nineteen years he presided over a revolution in management. Salaried officers began to be appointed. The first Land Steward, to be followed by others, a professional land agent, was sent to Lostwithiel. A lawyer was made Secretary to the Lord Warden with the duty of organising the flow of paper work at head office. The Prince Consort acquired powers to buy and sell land and he was able to buy out the copyholders, and negotiate annual leases direct with the tenants of the Duchy. The income of the Duchy rose rapidly. In 1838 the surplus after expenses was approximately £11,500. In 1861, the last year of the Prince Consort as Lord Warden, it was £46,600. The growing income made it possible to improve the estates of the Duchy; farm buildings and cottages were repaired or built, and the land itself was put into better condition by such measures as drainage and fencing. The revolution in management was crowned shortly after the death of the Prince Consort when in 1863 a Duchy of Cornwall Management Act was passed by Parliament, giving legal effect to the reforms which had been made. The verdict of Dr Haslam on this great period of reform is that 'The Prince Consort had brought the Duchy back from the precipice, reinvigorating it by a new management structure, and providing it with a sense of purpose.' The management of the Duchy had been brought up to date.

For more than a hundred years the momentum imparted by the drive and reforming energy of the Prince Consort kept the administration of the Duchy going. Ultimately there were five Land Stewards responsible for the districts into which the Duchy was divided. The Land Stewards were professional men of competence and gradually the role of the Duchy Council diminished and the role of the Land Stewards was enhanced. Effective decision tended to be located where the expertise was. More and more the recommendations of the Land Steward were accepted by the Council without major discussion. The Council itself met much less often than in the Prince Consort's time; instead of meeting nine or ten times a year it met on three or four occasions. The administration of the Duchy became insensibly more and more decentralised with each Land Steward largely looking after his own district. The outcome was a state of affairs in which rents were low, there was not much expenditure on repairs or capital improvement on the Duchy farms and management costs were not high. In addition one effect of so much decentralisation was that there was no general plan or strategy for the Duchy as a whole. In the latter part of this period, in the years after World War II, when British agriculture was prospering, other major landlords had embarked on major policies of securing higher rental income through higher expenditure on repairs and capital improvement: but the Duchy did not change. The great mineral source of revenue had fallen away, so that agricultural income was all important. More and more the Duchy had become concentrated in the South West. There was very little liquid capital.

Then in 1969 Prince Charles took over his responsibilities as Duke of Cornwall. He took his place as Chairman of the Council and immediately showed active interest and concern for his inheritance. But the immediate question was that the net surplus of the Duchy threatened, as once before, to be quite inadequate to maintain the Duke of Cornwall. The methods adopted to secure a rapid rise in income have already been described. Here it is enough to say that in 1970 most of his income had to come from the portfolio investment in government stocks and equities that had been built up from the sale of surplus assets in the districts of the Duchy.

From the early 1970s the Duchy entered on a second period of large-scale reform. At its heart was active management from the head office in 10 Buckingham Gate. It was realised that if the income of the Duchy was to grow with sufficient rapidity and be secure it was necessary to take a strategic view of the whole Duchy and view its parts in relation to the whole and not as more or less independent units. One important step was taken in 1974 when the Council called for two reports, on Cornwall, the western district, and on the Duchy property in the counties east of Dartmoor, the eastern district. These reports specified assets which might be sold, and made recommendations on the level of rents. This information came to headquarters and formed a basis for action. Rents were raised, a large programme of repairs and capital improvement initiated on the farms. The policy was successful: gross income rose from about one million in 1974 to about three million in 1980. The capital fund invested on the Stock Exchange in the same period was increased from £0.6 million to £3.66 million despite the spending of £2.65 million on improvements. This led to the general plan for an investment strategy in 1984. There was a decision to reduce acreage in Cornwall. Another to sell, if appropriate, farms which became vacant. Thirdly, it was decided gradually to sell property in Kennington. The investment portfolio in government stocks and shares should be brought up to a prudent level and, as has been noted earlier, further funds were to be invested in commercial property and shops.

This policy of the active management of the assets of the Duchy was a great change in substance and also in attitudes of mind. The policy must operate under proper constraints. One lies in the historical character of the Duchy. There is in some degree a special relationship between the Duchy and its tenants and this is the more evident when, as now, there is an active Duke of Cornwall, keenly interested in his estate, spending a great deal of time and effort to get to know his farms and his tenants, familiarising himself with working conditions on different types of farm, working for a week with his own hands on a hill farm on Dartmoor or on a mixed farm down on more level ground. The pace of change has to be graduated so as not to impair the historic relationship. A second constraint lies in the fact that so much of the Duchy's capital is tied up in land. But apart from the easy sale of surplus cottages, change is slow. The first farm with vacant possession was sold in 1975. The investment strategy is for the longer term, not tomorrow. Nonetheless the change to active management produces its uncertainties and

The Prince of Wales on a cold winter's day working on Yardworthy Farm, Dartmoor.
(Westen Morning News)

its tensions. It is not easy for all concerned, tenants, Land Stewards and their staffs, and the officers at headquarters to accustom themselves to seeing local problems as well as the problems of the whole Duchy and its management. One of the particular responsibilities of the new style of management is to cope with understanding and successfully with the human factors.

These problems of adaptation to new policies have been complicated both for the Duchy management and for its tenant farmers by a general change in the outlook for farming. For many years farming in Britain was prosperous and the more that could be provided the better. Recently burdensome surpluses of wheat have occurred in the world: grain, butter, milk and beef are in surplus in the EEC countries. These surpluses exert a downward pressure on prices. There are already quotas for milk production in Britain. This is not a situation which is likely to disappear rapidly and the pressures on price and quantity are likely to grow. The Duchy, like any other landowner, is affected: some of its tenants face difficulties, particularly perhaps in Cornwall where dairy farming is predominant. On this score too there has been a need for management to show sensitivity and understanding on the problems that arise.

But in addition there is a new factor: rising concern for the environment, and particularly the rural environment. In a paper written by Sir John Higgs, the late Secretary of the Duchy, the following passage occurs.

The major problem facing all landowners at the moment is that of reconciling competing demands on land, namely the need to make an economic return against social and other demands. The need for integrated rural development is a modern phenomenon not yet well understood which could lead to much greater changes in rural management than anything we have had to face up to in the post-war period. None of us can be complacent about the future of the agricultural industry which has been the bread and butter of land management but at the same time there is a growing awareness that agricultural management alone is insufficient if those who own the land are to give an adequate account of their stewardship. There are many able experienced land managers who at the present time find themselves perplexed, needing to rethink their attitude to the whole problem and to work in a much wider spectrum than has been demanded of them in the past. After years in which increasing agricultural output and maximising rents were paramount, we are entering a period in which subjects like low-input agriculture, conservation, employment creation in rural areas, tourism and recreation, to mention but a few aspects, all form part of the equation which an estate owner must consider.

There is a special reason as well as more general reasons why this new dimension of management matters to the Duchy. The Duke of Cornwall knows that his estate must be efficiently managed and produce a proper income now and in the future for himself and his family but, and in this he is very much a man of his own generation, he is deeply interested and concerned about the environment, conservation and rural employment. He has given an active lead: he is anxious that the Duchy should be in the forefront and not a laggard in this dimension of policy. Under his inspiration two important but difficult areas have been taken in hand. In 1983 after much consultation with all interested parties a Dartmoor National Park Plan was produced which set out the guidelines for the management of this vast area, balancing the interests of the farms and their tenants with the ambitions of the National Park, so that Dartmoor could be both productive and accessible. In the same year another report was published entitled *The Isles of Scilly comprehensive land use and community development project*. As a result there have been discussions with the Island Council on their taking over some of the public responsibilities undertaken by the Duchy, and the assistance of outside agencies such as the EEC Commission and the Nature Conservancy Council has been invoked. An Isles of Scilly Environmental Trust has been set up with the Duke of Cornwall as its patron and interested islanders as trustees.

The Duchy itself has been active in the planting of trees and in choosing appropriate materials for the repair of old and the construction of new buildings. It has enlisted the help of the tenants. Most farmers are conservationists by instinct and are willing to see how they can improve the landscape and encourage wildlife, provided that the cost in terms of the living they have to earn from the farms is not unreasonable. Advice is given by the Farming and Wildlife Advisory Groups on the different parts of the Duchy and the Nature Conservancy Council has conducted surveys. With the cooperation of tenants, model farms are worked which take full account of the new environmental objectives of policy. The Duke of Cornwall has set up advisory groups to advise the Duchy on archaeology, and on wildlife and the landscape.

As regards unemployment in the countryside the active leadership of the Duke of Cornwall has encouraged the provision of rural workshops, created by the remodelling of existing buildings. They make for immigration into rural areas so that people can practise their trades and skills there and earn a living. They are now scattered on Duchy lands from Gloucestershire to the Isles of Scilly.

In recent years, therefore, the management of the Duchy has had to modify and adapt its attitudes in at least three ways. First, there has been the need to think of the Duchy as a whole, with a strategic plan for the use of its assets and their consequent redeployment. Then there has been the necessity to review the arts of farming in the light of the distinctly less favourable

The Duke of Cornwall milking cows during his week's work in February 1983 at Yardworthy Farm, Chagford, on Dartmoor. (Western Morning News)

264

prospects for farming that the pressure of burdensome surpluses has imposed. And lastly there has been the application of a new dimension of policy, bringing active concern for the environment within the objectives of land management. It would be untrue to say that the implementation of all these changes has been completely smooth. In the nature of things this could not be: old habits of mind do not change readily or at once. There have at times been tensions and disagreements. That is not surprising. What has been surprising is the volume of cooperation that has been evident on all sides in the Duchy. Most people are anxious that the new policies should work and wish to find ways of carrying them out. The Duchy is embarked on a long-term programme of which the first fruits have already been gathered, but there is a great deal yet to be done in future years. What is important is that a new pattern for the management of the Duchy has been set and is in operation.

This survey of the marks which characterise the history of the Duchy of Cornwall has been necessary and relevant to any judgment of the future. It is strong in its intimate relationship with the monarchy. It is protected by its public accountability from misunderstandings and suspicion. Its finances are sound because it now draws its income from several different sources. Its management has shown the ability to adapt to altered circumstances and changed policies.

With the knowledge of the administrative reforms in recent years it is possible to dispense with guesswork and the crystal ball. The forecast can be made that, with the keen, active and informed interest of the present Duke of Cornwall, supported by a sound administration, the Duchy will go forward with confidence. It has shown, more than many human institutions, that it can live with the shifting situations that history will always bring to this country. Prophecy may be rash, but who would be surprised, could he revisit the scene in the year 2087, if he found there was a Duke of Cornwall with estates and other assets providing him with his living and that the Duchy conformed to high standards in management and humanity. The Duchy with its many strengths can face the way ahead, sure that it can rely on its capacity to survive and prosper.

FURTHER READING

Andrews, Canon Martin, *Canon's Folly* (Michael Joseph, 1974)

Arlott, John *et al, Island Camera* (David & Charles, 1973)

Ashbee, P., *Ancient Scilly* (David & Charles, 1974)

Ashton, M. & Burrow, I. (eds), *Archaeology of Somerset* (Taunton, 1982)

Atthill, Robin (ed), *Mendip: A New Study* (David & Charles, 1976)

Axford, E. G., *Bodmin Moor* (David & Charles, 1975)

Barton, D. B., *History of Tin-mining . . . in Cornwall* (Bradford Barton, 1961); *History of Copper-mining in Devon & Cornwall* (Bradford Barton, 1961)

Berry, Claude, *Portrait of Cornwall* (Robert Hale, 1963)

Bettey, J. H., *Rural Life in Wessex 1500–1900* (Moonraker Press, 1977)

Branigan, K. & Fowler, P. J., *The Roman West Country* (David & Charles, 1976)

Canon, P. J., *Parliamentary Reform 1640–1832* (Cambridge, 1973)

Coate, Mary, *Cornwall in the Great Civil War & Great Interregnum* (Oxford UP, 1933)

Cornwall Archaeological Unit, *Bodmin Moor: A Survey* Vol I (Forthcoming)

Courtney, W. P., *Parliamentary Representation of Cornwall to 1832* (London, 1889)

Crossing, William, *Hundred Years on Dartmoor* (1901, reprinted David & Charles, 1967); *Guide to Dartmoor* (1912, reprinted David & Charles, 1965)

Devon County Council, *Archaeology of the Devon Landscape* (Exeter, 1980)

Down, C. G., & Warrington, A. J., *History of the Somerset Coalfield* (David & Charles, 1970)

Edwards, Roy, 'Survey of . . . Kennington 1785–8', Chap VIII *London Topographical Record* Vol XXV (London Topographical Society, 1985)

Elliott-Binns, L. E., *Medieval Cornwall* (Methuen, 1955)

Freeman, Ray, *Dartmouth* (Harbour Books, Dartmouth, 1983)

Gill, Crispin (ed), *Dartmoor; A New Study* (David & Charles, 1970); *Isles of Scilly* (Island Series, David & Charles, 1975); *Sutton Harbour* (Sutton Harbour Improvement Co, 1970)

Grigson, Geoffrey, *The Scilly Isles* (Paul Elek, 1948)

Grinsell, L. V., *Archaeology of Wessex* (Methuen, 1958)

Halliday, F. E., *Richard Carew of Antony* (Melrose, 1953)

Harris, Helen, *Industrial Archaeology of Dartmoor* (David & Charles, 1986)

Haslam, Graham, 'John Norden's Survey of . . . Kennington 1616', *London Topographical Record* Vol XXV (London Topographical Society, 1985)

Haslam, J., *Anglo-Saxon Towns of South England* (1984)

Hatcher, J., *Rural Economy and Society in the Duchy of Cornwall 1300–1500* (Cambridge, 1970)

Havinden, Michael, *The Somerset Landscape*: The Making of the English Landscape (Hodder & Stoughton, 1970)

Henderson, Charles, *Essays in Cornish History* (Oxford UP, 1935)

Hook, D. (ed), *Medieval Villages* (Oxford, 1985)

Hoskins, W. G., *A New Survey of England* (Collins, 1954)

Inglis-Jones, E., *Augustus Smith of Scilly* (Faber, 1969)

Jenkin, A. K. Hamilton, *Cornwall and its People* (David & Charles reprints, 1970)

Matthews, G. Forrester, *The Isles of Scilly* (George Ronald, 1960)

Miles, D. (ed), *The Romano-British Countryside* (BAR British Series, Oxford, 1982)

Mumford, Clive, *Portrait of the Isles of Scilly* (Robert Hale, 1967)

Page, Robin, *Wildlife of the Royal Estates* (Hodder & Stoughton, 1984)

Pearce, Richard, *Ports & Harbours of Cornwall* (H. E. Warne, 1963)

Pearce, S. M., *The Kingdom of Dumnonia* (Padstow, 1978)

Pennington, P. R., *Stannary Law* (David & Charles, 1973)

Rowse, A. L., 'The Duchy of Cornwall', *West Country Stories* (Macmillan, 1944); *Tudor Cornwall* (Cape, 1941)

Taylor, Christopher, *Dorset*: The Making of the English Landscape (Hodder & Stoughton, 1970)

Thomas, Charles, *Exploration of a Drowned Landscape* (Batsford, 1985)

Toy, H. Spencer, *The Cornish Pocket Borough* (Penzance, 1968)

Wheeler, Mortimer, *Maiden Castle* (London, 1943)

Whetter, James, *Cornwall in the 17th Century* (Padstow, 1974)

Whitlock, Ralph, *Somerset* (Batsford, 1975)

Woolf, Charles, *Introduction to the Archaeology of Cornwall* (Bradford Barton, 1970)

INDEX

Figures in italics refer to illustrations